ALEISTER CROWLEY AND THE CULT OF PAN

Paul Newman

GREENWICH EXCHANGE
LONDON

Greenwich Exchange, London

First published in Great Britain in 2004
All rights reserved

Aleister Crowley and the Cult of Pan © Paul Newman, 2004

This book is sold subject to the conditions that it shall not, by way of
trade or otherwise, be lent, resold, hired out or otherwise circulated
without the publisher's prior consent in any form of binding
or cover other than that in which it is published and without
a similar condition including this condition being imposed
on the subsequent purchaser.

Printed and bound by imprintdigital.com
Cover design: December Publications
Tel: 07951511275

Greenwich Exchange Website: www.greenex.co.uk

Cataloguing in Publication Data
is available from the British Library

Cover Credit: Mary Evans Picture Library/Harry Price

ISBN: 978-1-871551-66-2

Acknowledgements

Aside from the writings of Aleister Crowley, I have been indebted to various biographies and apologias, from Major General Fuller and P.R. Stephensen down through to John Symonds, Charles Cammel, Martin Booth, Lawrence Sutin and Richard Kaczynski. Writers on G.K. Chesteron – from Maisie Ward to Joseph Pearce – have extended my grasp of the cultural scene and, of particular assistance in compiling the second chapter, was Patricia Merivale's scholarly survey, *Pan, the Goat God* along with a more recent monograph by Sir John Boardman. For permission to use extracts from Crowley's extensive writing, I am indebted to Marcus Jungkurth of the OTO (Ordo Templi Orientis) and also Bill Heidrick for his illuminating notes and commentaries.

Introduction

Kept at the top of my father's wardrobe was a paperback book, priced half a crown, that it was thought unwise to let fall into the hands of children. The cover showed a bald man with a forceful face and horn-brown, malevolent eyes, glaring at a world that had not found his talents or antics socially acceptable. The book came out in 1952 and was called *The Great Beast*. Its author, John Symonds, was a journalist and story-writer who had written for *Lilliput* and *Picture Post*, aside from producing novels like *William Waste*. During a friendly conversation Clifford Bax had recommended that he should write a biography of the occultist, poet and mountaineer, Aleister Crowley, who was born in 1875 and died in 1947, a chronic asthmatic and heroine addict.

After contacting Crowley, befriending him and subsequently being appointed his literary executor, Symonds produced the biography *The Great Beast* which quickly went through several editions, although certain libraries banned the book, for it contained descriptions of practices considered to be shocking, odd and disgusting. Not only, apparently, was Crowley sexually liberated, he was also gastronomically liberated, eating for ritual purposes substances from his own body and taking nearly every drug under the sun.

In those days, before the Lady Chatterley trial and the wide acceptance of authors like Henry Valentine Miller, the book held a hypnotic fascination for any teenager or developing adolescent, containing as it did a full-length portrait of a man who spurned conventional morality, travelled widely and experimented with drugs, sex and magical rites. From the standpoint of the 1950s, it left the reader unhealthily charged, in that it contained statements that made the imagination reel, about such unusual customs as hanging women upside down in cupboards, and squandering money with cheerful profligacy.

Its humour was daubed with pitch, showing Crowley making barbaric jokes about the death of loved ones, treating prostitution and venereal disease as comic accidents and invoking exotic and demonic deities in the same way one might say good morning to the milkman. It was a book that turned values upside down and, although

Symond's tone was ironically distanced, the personality of the Beast somehow burned through the pages, creating a packed, pregnant narrative, half-horrific, half-pantomimic, yet in its way unforgettable. Thus the Beast and his strange antics became part of my youthful mythology, counterbalancing the effect of more apparently salubrious figures like Richmal Crompton's William Brown or Sapper's Bulldog Drummond.

Now my father had met – and spoken to – Crowley on several occasions. As I remember it, the meetings took place in the 1930s when he would regularly visit a cafe in Soho, often in the company of an out-of-work actor called Alec Waters. The latter was a drinker, a jocular ginger-haired man. He often attempted to bait Crowley who, my father said, was frequently to be seen encircled by what he termed "nubile women" – although, at that stage in his career, his skin had been burned parchment-dry and his looks had greatly deteriorated. Apparently Waters would shout within hearing distance of Crowley: "If that man was a proper magician, he'd be able to pull a rabbit out of his hat." My father would laugh as Crowley stared back at them, and that was the extent of their contact, save for sundry occasions when Crowley had asked him whether a certain chessplayer had called at the café.

This information was extracted from my father by my brother, Caspar, who had undergone a 'character change' in his teens. As if taken over, he became obsessed with the Nazis and right-wing pagan cults revolving around the worship of Thor and Odin – subjects that hardly guaranteed a flow of vivacious topical chatter. And Crowley was another of his icons. The fact that one of the Beast's German disciples, Martha Küntzel, had sent Hitler a copy of *The Book of the Law* did not go unremarked. Caspar would stampede around town dressed entirely in black, pockets bulging with pernicious pamphlets, haranguing various upright and uptight citizens and attempting to impregnate them with his peculiar views. The whole tone of his approach was too choppy and charmless for him to make any converts, though he startled and vexed many people, including Father, who was then working for the Conservative party and was highly embarrassed at spawning a son whose enthusiasm embraced such bizarre extremes.

To my father, Crowley was a man of "odious reputation" who had squandered a fortune, been dubbed a traitor to his country and engendered scandal, despair and suicide among his followers. My father had also heard about Crowley from his brother, my Uncle Bertram, a scholar and biographer of Edmund Burke, Jonathan Swift and Lord Melbourne. Uncle Bertram had met the writer Mary Butts; she had told him about the motley activities that took place in the Abbey of Thelema at Cefalu, Sicily, but he did not think it fit to confide what he had heard to Caspar.

Caspar read *The Great Beast* with absorption and excitement. His appetite was whetted when he learned that Father had actually met the Beast and was offered a seat in the famous *Crowley versus Constable* trial which, however, he did not bother to attend. Caspar was amazed that he had turned down the opportunity to observe such a famous libel action, but Father simply was not interested in hocus pocus or weird sexual rites – his tastes erred towards writers like Boswell, Dickens or the poetry of Alexander Pope. Listening to Crowley trying to defend his beslimed reputation was simply not his idea of a pleasant afternoon.

Such lack of interest Caspar almost found offensive. He did not have Father's urbane and distant outlook. He was drawn towards the shocking, the blasphemous and the obscene – not, I should add, because these designations offered any lasting reward or satisfaction. No, it was rather because they generated a frisson of shock and unease and it is possible to derive a morbid pleasure from alarming conventional or merely respectable people.

As both of us, as young boys, had been stopped and preached at by fervent middle-aged Christians, the implications of Crowley's revolt ran deep. It shattered the pane of reverence that protected and sanitised the Christian religion and opened an almost terrifying vista of freedom, for Crowley seemed to have done every forbidden act that was thinkable and many others that would fall entirely beyond the scope of the imagination. And when Caspar began to demand from my parents implements like crystal balls and magic wands, arguments would ensue in which my mother berated my father, saying. "You laughed at old Crowley, but he's getting his own back on you. Look at the way Caspar's going, the Nazis, black magic – where's it going to end!"

In the matter of the execution of a magical operation, Caspar started off enthusiastically, but after a while one sensed an element of weariness setting in. First he had to bathe himself thoroughly and cut his nails, and then he had to gather his implements together, chalk out a pentagram, work out north from south and remember to do the banishing ritual, if he was not to be later besieged by bad dreams.

There was always a preparatory rumpus; the necessary appurtenances could never be quickly located.

"Where's my sacred salt?" he would snarl. "What's happened to it?"

On one occasion, I confessed that I had been inadvertently adding it to my boiled egg, and he bristled.

"What! How dare you, you swine, use my salt for that! That's special salt – it's been ritually prepared!"

A regular magical operation was a "quick'n easy rite" designed to make a ten pound note appear. Caspar would often perform this when low on cash. If nothing resulted, after a few days he'd assume a peevish tone: "Christ, Paul, I've done this operation which took over an hour – no money has appeared yet! What should I do about it?"

This complaint would be repeated daily until I, eroded and defeated, angrily handed him a ten pound note; and thus, in a sense, the efficacy of 'The Most High and Sacred Art of Magic' was vindicated.

Being of a reflective and reasonably enquiring disposition, I felt duty bound to examine as dispassionately as I could the life of someone who had proven so disturbing and unusual a presence in my early life and, curiously enough, the date of my birth, 12th October, is the same as his. While disputing Kimberley Cornish's (1998) incredible statement – "Reading Crowley is like dipping one's hand into a bag full of lice and leeches" – I would concede he is not the easiest writer to appraise. His mode of expression often tends towards the extreme, a habit that encourages recourse to ironic quote marks or euphemism, but the body of work he left behind is nothing if not varied.

Culture may be accessed through any number of gateways, some of which resemble cottage doors (Richard Jefferies), others rather splendid drawbridges (Sir Walter Scott) and others Gothic archways that lead into fantastic, elaborate palaces (William Beckford). Having now looked at Crowley's œuvre, I would say it presents a slippery threshold for an adolescent reader or university graduate to step over and find himself inside a kind of ramshackle crazy house that switches between a pagan temple, an Alice-in-Wonderland madhouse, a sweaty orgiastic banquet and a philosophy seminar.

It was often Crowley's aim to spiritually 'detonate' a personality and then allow it to come together in a different way. Similarly, his writings dislodge normal perceptions; there is an implicit arrogance in a stance that loftily revokes the assurances of family, morality and society. Were there nothing behind the gesture save callousness and wastrel rage, Crowley might easily be abandoned as any sort of guide or authority, but a mass of intellectual furniture belies the façade.

Apart from his own writings, there is the further challenge of the authors he recommends: *Essays* of David Hume, *Three Dialogues* of Bishop Berkeley, the *Prolegomena* of Kant and William James' *Varieties of Religious Experience* – to name but a few. Hence those initially attracted by a malign image may end up immersing themselves in Buddhism, yoga, philosophy and poetry. For all his unconformity, Crowley is an educator and a mind-opener. Not in the sense that one finds oneself agreeing with what he says, so much as that he expresses himself forcefully enough – indeed aggressively at times – to provoke reflection or dissent, thus setting in motion an active thought process and, curiously enough, a way of looking at and translating the world. In his wake there comes a view of life and history that is mystic, obsessional and lopsided – but not lacking in a grandiose *raison d'etre*.

1

Indescribably Ecstatic
The life and ideas of Aleister Crowley

Crowley was a poet, and a poet of lyric genius so prodigious in range and volume, so splendid in its sweep of eloquence, imagery and witching music, as to command admiration. Were Crowley not a great poet, not all his adventures, his scandals, his learning, his imperious knocking at the gates of Celebrity, would have made him the wonder to posterity, which he already is and which he shall be increasingly. It is his poetry which makes all the rest interesting, and it is the combination of his poetry, his personality and his life which makes him the most extraordinary figure of his age, and one of the most extraordinary figures of any age
(Charles Richard Cammell)

On Saturday 28th November 1998, the *Daily Telegraph* reported the death, at the age of 91, of Greta Sequeira. As a young woman, she had been racy and beautiful, a cultured bohemian who had charmed many with her vitality and wit. Born June 1907 to an English doctor of Portuguese descent, Greta grew up to be an intensely social young woman who threw herself into the London high life of the 1930s. Her tastes ran to fast cars – she drove a white Packard convertible – partygoing, philanthropy and spirituality. While holidaying with her family in Cornwall, she met and developed a platonic relationship with the landscape painter Lamorna Birch who symbolised his love for her by placing images of swans in his paintings. Along with her opulent lifestyle went several brave, generous acts. Before the outbreak of the Second World War, she went over to Germany and helped a number of Jewish doctors escape the unfolding holocaust. Eventually she married Ranald Valentine (d.1956) who owned a company in Dundee that made greeting-cards and calendars.

What was unusual about Greta, and what also died with her, was a unique fund of images linking the 1990s with our now-shadowy Edwardian past. For she and her husband, owning mansions in London and Tayside, lived an elegant, fashionable existence, throwing parties that included guests like Alexander Fleming, Enid Blyton and Sir Robert Watson-Watt, the inventor of radar. After a long, full life, composing poetry and painting, cooperating with Austin Wormleighton in a biography of Lamorna Birch, she retired to a studio on a Sussex farm where, blind and almost helpless, she slept in the same room as the plywood coffin she had commissioned for her dead body.

More curious and less well-known is the fact that Greta was one of the last people to retain a living memory of Aleister Crowley (1875-1947). For she had been an active member of the Café Royal set of bohemians among whom Crowley held the title of Magus. After their first meeting in 1936, when she was studying the anthroposophy of Rudolf Steiner, Crowley was smitten. "What is life without you but dust and ashes?" he wrote to her. Greta cultivated Crowley as an unusual guest and piquant conversationalist, but he seemed to have desired better things. In August 1938 he pursued her to Cornwall, to the fishing-village of Mousehole, where they had a bottle of chablis together at the Lobster Pot Inn. Aged 31, dressed in a loose cotton frock, with shoulder-length golden hair hanging at her shoulders, she was an enticing dryad, while Crowley, aged 62, looked sinister, flabby and florid. Perpetually optimistic, he made an entry in his diary: "Wooed Greta on the cliffs. She is a comedian. Will one day come and snatch."

Greta Sequeira had too many delightful options in her life to take on a bald, strange-smelling magician as a partner, but he continued to root her out, writing letters even after she was married: "Dear child, I knew you would be up to some mischief the minute my eye was off you ... You might have told me. I shouldn't have taken actual measures to stop you. And you would certainly have got a No.1 epithalmium. All the same, give me a week or so notice and you shall have an ode for your divorce." Crowley did not acquire Greta as a lover, but he succeeded in fathering a child on another young woman in her circle and in establishing a bond with Lady Frieda Harris, one of Greta's many friends, who produced the paintings for *The Book of Thoth*, a unique and powerful interpretation of the Tarot.

It appears that, while Crowley was allowed entry into certain enclaves of polite society, others held him determinedly at bay. Notably his sulphuric charms failed to melt the steely heart of Dame Edith Sitwell who avowed that, if ever they should meet, she would rebuke him thus: "Mr Crowley, you are to go straight to hell, where you will meet no one but yourself over and over again and you can take Lady —––– with you!"

Upbringing and education

The Greta episode is one of the many shadowy alcoves in the life of Edward Alexander or 'Aleister' Crowley, as he re-christened himself after reading Shelley's *Alastor, The Spirit of Solitude*. A socially ubiquitous, alternately maligned and admired figure, who achieved the distinction of being called "The Wickedest Man in the World" and "A Monster of Depravity" by the time he had attained his mid-forties, Crowley was born (12th October 1875) in Leamington Spa, to parents who were Plymouth Brothers, a fundamentalist Christian sect who accepted the literal truth of the Bible. Like Philip Henry Gosse – although less severe – Crowley's father, Edward, saw Christmas as a pagan festival and frowned upon any frivolity or debauchery. Aleister or 'Alec' respected and loved his father, but during his teens reacted against the strict religious teaching. He found himself responding as excitedly to the demons and evil geniuses in the Bible as to the saints and angels. When his mother, in a fit of rage, called him the Beast, he enthusiastically embraced the designation.

Inheriting a fortune after the death of his father, he attended Trinity College at Cambridge University, where he wrote Swinburnian poetry, acquired a homosexual lover and travelled to places like Russia, Holland and Scandinavia during the holidays. Although he did not study hard, he read many books, published poetry and played chess, a game at which he had excelled since a schoolboy, contributing a regular column to the Eastbourne Gazette between January and July 1884. But the significant event of his early youth took place while he was staying in Stockholm in December 1896. At midnight he had been shaken by a disturbing yet exalting spiritual encounter that imbued him with the knowledge that he possessed magical powers. "It was an experience," he recalled, "of horror and pain, combined with a certain ghostly terror, yet at the same time it was the key to the purest and holiest spiritual ecstasy that exists." The Holy Ghost entered him and "loosened the girder of his soul", opening him up to possibilities and visions he felt compelled to explore.

Meanwhile he continued to dash off poems, spiritual and decadent, and distinguish himself in university chess tournaments. However, all thoughts of becoming a chess master left him during a long vacation in 1897, when he visited the international tournament in Berlin and had a glimpse of some of the world masters – "one, shabby, snuffy and blear-eyed; another, in badly fitting would-be respectable shoddy; a third, mere parody of humanity ..." Concluding that it was not worth struggling to gain admission to their ranks, he vowed never to play another serious game.

Not long after the Berlin episode, in October 1897, a second revelation followed during a mild bout of illness. He had an intimation of the futility of all endeavour in the face of death. It led him to question what he saw as the mechanic, trivial occupations open to a young man of his class and talent. If he became a famous politician or diplomat, his name would ultimately fade out of the time zone, but if he sought instead to penetrate the veil – to become a magician and make an imprint upon the spiritual construction of the cosmos – therein lay an immortality beyond ordinary dreams.

The Golden Dawn

Crowley left Cambridge before completing his degree. From thence the study of magic began to obsess him. It was close to his heart because it was both mysterious and preposterous – an attempt to attune with and command the fleeting possibilities that life presented. But his fervour was checked by a cautionary scepticism. If half of him was ensnared by the witcheries and rhapsodies of Eliphas Levi, the other half was captivated by the keen scepticism of David Hume and Thomas Henry Huxley, and he strove to reconcile the opposing outlooks.

Intrigued by hints of there existing a body of "hidden masters" or a Secret Sanctuary of the Saints, he spoke of the matter to an analytical chemist while on a mountaineering holiday in Switzerland. This led to his being introduced to George Cecil Jones, a member of the Hermetic Order of the Golden Dawn, an occult society led by Samuel

Liddell Mathers, offering an attractive brew of Hebrew magic, the cabala, astrology and divination by cards and other oracles.

Officially founded in 1888 by Dr William Wynn Westcott (1848-1925), earlier writers tended to see the Golden Dawn as a shadowy anomaly, but it has gradually come to the fore as a powerful cultural influence. Strands of it can be traced back to the Celtic Revival which had a 'psychic' as well as literary lineage. Furthermore the second half of the 19th century had shown an unprecedented interest in the 'otherworld'. Starting with the Fox daughters in 1848, spirits once confined to ruined abbeys and Gothic novels entered the living rooms of polite society. Reports of séances, table rapping, trance and luminous phenomena filled the daily newspapers. Experiments were made in hypnotism, healing and telepathy. Allied to this was the foundation of mystic orders like the Theosophical Society in Dublin (1886) of which Yeats' friend 'AE' or George Russell was a founding member.

What Westcott did was to lay down grades of spiritual ascent based on the ten degrees of the Sephiroth or 'rays' branching out from the body of God. Members went up through these cabalistic levels by sitting exams and partaking of rituals in temples named after the Egyptian gods. Within the Outer Order, they could rise from Neophyte to the pinnacle of Philosophus. Allegedly Westcott based his system on an ancient magical manuscript written in cipher whose authenticity became a matter of heated dispute when rebellion arose within the order.

In the face of an all-powerful capitalistic materialism and the decline of organised religion, organisations like the Golden Dawn launched their own mystical counter-cultures. They drew those who desired to work within a creed that was personally emancipating rather than constrained by an excess of dogma and doctrine. Hence the Golden Dawn was very much of its age with forward-looking members, some vegetarians with an ecological turn of mind. Arthur Machen, Algernon Blackwood and W.B. Yeats were accredited authors, who believed in an inspirational muse, while Florence Farr was a dancer (and sometime lover of Max Beerbohn), Maud Gonne an Irish nationalist and Constance Wilde (whose membership prefigured Crowley's) the socially active wife of Oscar. The scientifically inclined included Peck, Astronomer Royal for Scotland

and Imperator of the Edinburgh Temple – for branches quickly established themselves over the country – and George Cecil Jones, a chemist who, Crowley claimed, bore an uncanny resemblance to Jesus Christ. What they all had in common was that they sought to enrich their lives by contact with the spiritual hierarchies. They were taught to translate the cabala, scry, interpret symbols, induce visions, invoke angels and entities. Emphasis was laid on self-development: hence whom you loved, what you felt, what you ate, what colours you wore – all were significant, magically speaking.

Apart from taking into account an individual's personality, magic was also prepared to absorb advances in science and technology. This appealed to the intellectual element in the order. Traditionally the occult had alchemical beginnings, springing from the study of things like crystals, plants and metals, and cabalistic studies in particular had tended to draw on subjects like anatomy, biology, geology and astronomy. Hence magic had an easier relationship with science than formal religion. Whereas Darwinism, astronomy and the structural analysis of myth had delivered hard knocks to Christianity, the mystical fraternity took these things in their stride. Their basic tenets had always been an accommodating jumble and men like Crowley delighted in science, chemistry, mathematics and medical knowledge. Things like breakthroughs in particle physics confirmed rather than contradicted his views. 'Yes, this is how the immutable laws of nature manifest themselves on this plane,' he might have said.

Schism

After initiation in 1898, entailing entering a darkened chamber, being consecrated by fire and water and ritually challenged and interrogated by brightly gowned figures, who blocked his path and held up swords, knives, bells and banners, Crowley was admitted and rapidly ascended the grades of the Golden Dawn – too rapidly in the view of W.B. Yeats, whose dislike of Crowley's homosexuality and wilful temperament led him to believe that he was more suited to a reformatory than a mystical society. More seriously, he found nothing to praise in Crowley's poetry either, save "six lines" that have never been identified.

But Mathers took a liking to earnest, energetic young Crowley. He allowed him into the Inner Order and divulged to him many Gnostic secrets, one of which was to have a disturbing effect: namely that the androgynous Sammael or 'Satan' was lord of this world and not Jehovah – in other words, *Daemon est Deus inversus*. Sammael had a female counterpart, Lilith, and the union of these two produced the Antichrist or Anti-Logos known as Hay-yah or 'The Beast': hence the young magician was handed a mythos that he was to adapt and personalise throughout his career to sensational effect. The various 'scarlet women' he subsequently appointed were his Liliths whose destiny was to produce a magical child.

In 1900 Florence Farr was left in charge of the London branch while Mathers directed the order in Paris. When Yeats denied Crowley the rank of Adeptus Minor, the latter confided in Mathers who overruled Yeats by initiating Crowley in the Temple of Horus in Paris. The Golden Dawn was by now rife with dissension. Mathers had accused Farr of trying to create a schism in the order and charged another member with forging documents. When Crowley went back to London to claim the papers to which his new grade entitled him, Yeats turned him down. Once again Crowley consulted Mathers who was enraged by what he saw as the mutinous behaviour of the London branch and appointed Crowley as his envoy plenipotentiary. Having secured the older man's approval, Crowley returned in a kilt and black mask to take possession of the premises and properties relating to the society – but was rejected a second time by Yeats. The fracas, half-serious, half-ludicrous, petered out in a haze of lawsuits and acrimony, cracking apart the mystical order, but not Crowley himself who set off on a long journey around Ceylon, Mexico and the United States.

Appeal of Buddhism

While he was in Mexico, climbing mountains with his friend, Oscar Eckenstein, a grave-faced official entered their hotel in January 1901 and told them of the death of Queen Victoria at Osborne House, the Isle of Wight. When the two men broke into shouts of joy and an impromptu war-dance, he was mildly shocked, for he did not know that, to some English men and women, Victoria had come to stand for suffocation and stagnation. "She was a huge and heavy fog,"

Crowley commented. "We could not see; we could not breathe."

Curiously, he did not attack Victoria for her ability to crush or strangulate but rather for her tendency to absorb and stabilise. Under her reign, radical scientific breakthroughs and startling innovations had not split the social structure but had become assimilated and transformed into sober institutions. Darwinism was now respectable. James Thomson had been placed in the library alongside the sermons and standard classics. Swinburne had been dusted down and restyled as a penitent elderly gentleman. The Church of England "persisted placidly" despite the volleys of rationalist critics. "It was impossible to dynamite the morass of mediocrity," he complained, "progress was impossible."

But Crowley had not been held back by Victoria or anyone else. Since becoming an adult he had enjoyed unusual freedom. What's more, travel was stimulating him – he had a desire to distil practical insights from the religious and mystical practices he had come across. To this task he applied himself, casting them in prose that was often more effective than his poetry. 'The Soldier and the Hunchback' (1903) attempts to reconcile scepticism and mysticism. As such elementary philosophical maxims as, "I think – therefore I am", rely ultimately on blind faith, opposing viewpoints should be grasped as mere swings of a pendulum, subjective dugouts into which minds retreat, but united in that they hang from the same point of suspension, the pivot of a mighty universe in which they are mere rhythms of its being.

Equally forcefully, *Science and Buddhism* (1903) argues that Buddhism is a rational religion offering a unique methodology of phenomenal investigation from which science should learn to benefit. For well over a century, Buddhism has exerted a strong pull over Western intellectuals because it so lucidly evaluates the human situation and is far more restrained in what it offers than, say, Christianity. "If I may so put it," wrote Bryan Magee (1997), "Buddhism came across to me as an agnostic religion, one that often did justice to the difficulty and complexity of the fundamental questions facing human beings (which commonsense realism failed to do) without attempting to impose dogmatic answers."

Not only was Crowley in accord with this, he was also preoccupied by the ecstatic states, attainable by yoga and meditation, that seemed indescribably intenser – more 'real' – than everyday experiences.

Thereby they challenged a wide range of ordinary responses and evaluations. At the basis of many of his ideas are the writings of David Hume who had demonstrated that the laws of science are not empirically verifiable and therefore, by implication, not provably more 'authentic' than so-called magical phenomena. In similar vein *The Psychology of Hashish* (1903) analyses Buddhist philosophy, time consciousness, halluconogenic sociology and science in an evocative treatise arguing that hashish provides root insights into how the mind works; the perceptual distortions caused by the drug enable one to grasp the manner in which thoughts organise themselves, enabling them to be apprehended both as separate entities and harmonious continuums. It examines time as a sensation rather than a measurement and space as an interpenetrating factor, throwing in comments that invite a reassessment of the most basic activities: 'So that if I cross a room, and think a million thoughts on the way, the room seems immense. It is by the tedium of the journey, not by any hallucination of the physical eye, that this illusion is produced.'

Marriage

Returning to Britain in 1903, he took a holiday at his lodge, Boleskine, in Scotland, where he entertained his friend Gerald Kelly, later President of the Royal Academy, and his sister, Rose, a young and voluptuous, auburn-haired widow. She confided to Crowley that she did not know how to extricate herself from the coils of an engagement she had foolishly contrived. In a fit of bizarre chivalry, Crowley proposed to her, and they married in secret and went on an extended honeymoon.

Staying in a house in Cairo in early 1904, Rose entered a trance state and told her husband the god Horus was trying to contact him. This surprised Crowley, for Rose had shown no previous interest in mythology or magic. As a test, Crowley took her to the Boulak Museum and asked her to point out Horus to him. After passing several well-known images of the god, she led him to a painted wooden funerary stele from the 26th dynasty, depicting Horus receiving a sacrifice from the deceased, a priest named Ankh-f-n-khonsu. Crowley was especially impressed by the fact that this piece was numbered 666 by the museum, a number with which he had identified since childhood.

Believing something important was happening, he began to attend to his wife closely. In a series of trance visions, Rose indicated a number of symbols relating to the god. At her direction, on three successive days beginning 8th April 1904, he entered his chamber at noon and wrote down what he heard dictated from over his left shoulder by a dark man with the face of a "savage king", later identified as Aiwass, the minister of Horus. The result was a strident medley of entreaties, rhapsodies and blasphemies called *The Book of the Law*, inaugurating the new aeon of Horus, governed by the Law of Thelema, the latter being a Greek word meaning "will".

Chesterton Declines a Challenge

Back in London, Crowley abandoned trying to decipher *The Book of the Law* and released further volumes of poetry, one of which caught the eye of G.K. Chesterton. Three years earlier he had given an approving notice to *The Soul of Osiris* and, being presented with *The Sword of Song*, Chesterton reviewed it (*Daily News*, 24th September 1904). His appraisal of "this Browningesque rhapsody in Buddhist mood", as he called it, was calm and fair, for Crowley's writings would have seemed far less exotic to him than they might to a contemporary reader.

Queen Victoria had died but these were still the palmy days of Empire and, of course, the British conquest of India was not a one-sided affair. Through the stories of Kipling, through scholars, missionaries, army officers and anthropologists, a great deal of Eastern culture had flowed back into Britain. Hence Crowley's immersion in Buddhism took place within a social framework that had been well-established, and in this sense, at least, he could be called a man of his age. Many of the strange deities and esoteric allusions in Crowley's texts would have been not unfamiliar to those well-versed in Anglo-Indian matters. Furthermore there was a whole branch of fiction (now classified as 'Empire Gothic') that exploited the supernatural and sensual aspects of palm and pine.

For his part, Chesterton puzzled over the poet's "hatred of Christianity" and promised he would "make a fuller study of Mr Crowley's interpretation of Buddhism." However, in the next issue, he backed out of further debate, opting for an article on Ireland rather than intellectual engagement with a young man of religious inclinations so sharply at odds with his own. Crowley wrote to him, suggesting the discussion should be transferred to another journal: "I am anxious to meet you in a fair fight ..." But Chesterton must have been less anxious, for nothing came of it.

This was a disappointment to Crowley who would have enjoyed a sparring match with an emerging man of letters. Who knows, maybe some accordant notes would have been struck, for they both, theoretically, were seeking a religious ray of light to show them the way ahead. However, comparing Crowley's self-published reply to Chesterton's original review, it seems likely that the latter would have come off best, not because of any intellectual superiority, so much as the fact that Chesterton wrote plainer, more supple prose. Crowley's problem was that he was anxious to appear hilariously witty and stupendously learned at the same time. This sometimes clogged his early style while Chesterton had the expertise of a man who had filled more newspaper columns than anyone else of his age.

It is possible that Chesterton withdrew from debate with Crowley because he sensed danger. With commissions flowing in from all quarters, he was riding high on the crest of a brilliant reputation and feared guilt by association – by a smudge of Crowley's lechery or diabolism touching his shining Christian breastplate. Crowley, only a year younger, had not yet acquired the dark, alarming reputation that was to become his hallmark, yet there were rumours about his character and practices that may well have reached Chesterton's ears.

For Chesterton was far from an innocent in the matters that Crowley stood for. He, too, had thought about and struggled with dark forces. As a student, he had dabbled with the planchette board and inhaled the fumes of decadence. "I had reached that condition of moral anarchy within," he recalled of the period, "in which a man says, in the words of Wilde, that 'Atys with the blood-stained knife were better than the thing I am.' I have never indeed felt the slightest temptation to the particular madness of Wilde; but I could at this time imagine the worst and wildest disproportions and distortions of more normal passion ... As Bunyan, in his morbid period, described himself as prompted to utter blasphemies, I had an overpowering impulse to record or draw horrible ideas and images; plunging deeper and deeper as in a blind spiritual suicide."

This outlook was compounded by one of his close associates. While at the Slade School of Art, he had befriended a young student with "a horrible fairness of intellect" whose "dirty, drunken society" he enjoyed. Together they would talk for hours about Milton, God and Gothic architecture and seemingly gain much satisfaction from each other. But the young man "with a long, ironical face, and close red hair" had no moral values. Chesterton called him a 'Diabolist', but whether in outlook or ritual practice he does not make clear. When he told Chesterton that what he called 'evil' had its own inner logic and vitality, the latter pointed to a bonfire and said that, in an earlier age, he would have been burned as a heretic. "Perhaps," the young man replied, "Only what you call evil I call good."

The young sinner left Chesterton, who went to pick up his hat, and then he overheard him in conversation with one of his associates. The other was saying, "Nobody can possibly know," while the Diabolist responded, "I tell you I have done everything else. If I do that, I shan't know the difference between right and wrong."

Chesterton never forgot those words and concluded:

> I have since heard that he died; it may be said, I think, that he committed suicide; though he did it with the tools of pleasure, not with tools of pain. God help him. I know the road he went; but I have never known or dared to think what was that place at which he stopped and refrained.

From that point, Chesterton shunned such contacts as that which the young student and Crowley represented. Not only did they scare him, there may have loomed a vague possibility of temptation. What were those terrible images and "disproportions of passion" that haunted his youth? Most commentators, drawing on the exuberant, blood-soaked imagery of *Lepanto*, assume a latent streak of sadism in Chesterton's persona, but there was probably a powerful sexual curiosity at large as well as a fascination with evil in its grosser aspect. Usually he was a man forever throwing out the arm of comradeship, yet he had a canny side, an instinctive intelligence, that told him to draw back from those who could stoke up fires in him that he preferred to think of as under control.

However, Chesterton was one of the few of Crowley's literary contemporaries who had thought deeply about the philosophical differences between the East and the West. While turning from open debate, he was able to provide a coherent criticism of Crowley's outlook in stories like *The Wrong Shape* in which, with considerable skill, he contrives the murder of a dilettante to dramatise his objection to the cultivation of foreign gods on English soil.

The Star in the West

Crowley quickly recovered from Chesterton's rebuff. During the summer of 1905, he did more travelling and mountaineering, including a failed assault on Kanchenjunga, leading to further allegations about his callous and stubborn character. In the meantime, someone had responded to the prize he had offered of £100 for the best essay on his writings. The challenge was taken up by a talented young army officer, Captain J.F.C. Fuller (1878-1966), who was stationed in Lucknow, when he saw a review of 'Why Jesus Wept' in *The Literary Guide*. Ordering a copy, he found a leaflet in it advertising the competition. In the summer of the following year, he was invalided back to England and received a letter from Crowley in reply to one of his own saying, "I am sorry to hear of your enteric fever, but fate has treated me even worse; for after a most successful trip through China without a day's illness for any of us, our baby girl died of that very disease on the way home."

Fuller met Crowley and his wife at the Hotel Cecil in the Strand and, shortly after, finished his essay *The Star in the West*, published in 1907. It is a curious work that surges along on a rousing swell of purple foam. "He loved a sentence so much," Crowley wrote, "that he could not persuade himself to finish it." By contemporary standards, its 300 pages of rodomontade and scholastic swagger are excessive. Yet it does offer a detailed commentary on the themes and ideas behind Crowley's poems and dramas. With their stilted casts of mythological figures, titled nobodies and preposterous walk-ons, the latter can hardly give rise to elevated structural criticism. Instead Fuller has recourse to fulmination and caricature:

> The affluent marry out of sensuality, or to engender sons to inherit their selfishness, the middle orders trot their daughters round the London ballrooms just as strumpets fall in to the cry of, descendez mesdemoiselles! Women marry for title,

> clothing, shelter, and food; men because they think it is cheaper to keep a cow, and once and for all to have done with it, than to be constantly running round the corner for a penny-worth of milk; and the lower stratum – the blessed poor – spend most of their lives in the act of engendering the elite of heaven and the scum of the earth, 'mere shells, husks of the golden wheat that might grow even here, if it were not for our prudery, our religion, and our laws.'

Ostensibly this is paraphrase, but Fuller does seem to be in sympathy with Crowley's frenzied scythes of the pen. That such a view of matrimony should be taken seriously is curious, for Fuller himself had recently married an attractive, firm-minded woman and, one presumes, had been tactful enough to suppress his bovine analogies while popping the question.

Initially Fuller was not drawn to Crowley's religious side – disliking all faiths – but to the lyrical raptures and scorching blasts against Christianity and morality. He was persuaded to add a final chapter 'The New Wine' covering magic and mysticism. Here he makes good account of himself, in that he does not just *make* a point but *demonstrates* it. He has not just heard of Kant, Hume, Berkeley, Spencer, Thomas Henry Huxley and Plato, but has *read* them and is also acquainted with Buddhism, Zoroastrianism, Hinduism and many another belief and heresy. His case for Crowley is less brilliant than the language in which he frames it, but it is quite a clever, considered one. According to Fuller, Crowley has evolved the most capacious religious system of all time. As if to offer diagrammatic proof, he draws a series of concentric circles, in which we find at the centre Mysticism, moving through to Idealism, Agnosticism and Crowleianity that unites or happily wraps up all three.

How does he reach such a conclusion? After a whistlestop tour of Western philosophy and Eastern mysticism, Fuller slips in Crowley as its logical culmination – a startling claim as Crowley had only then published a handful of papers on religion and ontology – and attempts to show how his ideas dissolve the distinction between Idealism and Empiricism. While Berkeley and Hume showed admirable rigour, they were simply processing aspects of 'maya', or the appearances taken on by truth in the phenomenal realm. Both Hume's scepticism and Berkeley's affirmation were opposite sides of the same coin, stopping short of the 'mystery' at which reasoning ceased. Hume saw a world comprising of sense impressions. Berkeley saw very much the same, except he held God responsible for the illusion. But neither had experimented with their perceptions. They had no knowledge of how ecstatic or exalted states, such as Samâdhi or Dhyâna, could take them out of themselves. A yogi, for instance, could meditate through their respective modes of perceiving. He could start in the realm of Hume, where objects are solidly, separately, anchored in experience, moving through to Berkeley's realm where they seem more like 'ideas' and, still further, to where they blend in mystic union, and what's more, each appearance would be equally *true*. Behind all such objects or hallucinations is an Almighty Nothing, from Whom forms proceed, and to Whom Being and Non-Being are much alike.

In other words, Crowley played the noumenal card, finding God in a phenomenon that would appear to most as either neutral or agnostic, with no elaborate mythology attached to it, only the inner certainty of transcendence. This outlook Fuller called Pyrronhic Zoroastrianism or Sceptical Transcendentalism or Scientific Illuminism. The East had been embracing such ideas for centuries but Crowley, being a Westerner, was able to philosophically argue his way through to such a stance and, in so doing, radically clarify the problem. Being a magician, such ideas were naturally of central importance – he needed to define what sort of reality he was working on when he performed his spells and incantations. The interaction of spirit and matter – training mind to induce change – was pivotal to his occult beliefs: thus philosophy provided a cornerstone for his new religion.

'Rites of Eleusis'

In 1906, distressed by the death of his daughter, Nuit, of typhoid in a hospital in Rangoon, he rejoined his wife in England, and enlisting his friend, George Cecil Jones, formed the Silver Star, an order combining Golden Dawn ritual with Crowley's own brand of 'energised enthusiasm' or sexual magic.

A restless experimental period followed, rife with domestic disharmony, during which he divorced Rose, published volumes of poetry and 'Magick' and devised rituals and ceremonies. Never did he contemplate anything resembling menial work, for unlike Tolstoy he held "any mechanical labour degrades" and favoured a "leisured class" free to pursue their higher destiny.

To this period belongs the famous 'Rites of Eleusis', a theatrical invocation of the planetary forces, assisted by the violinist Leida Waddell and the poet Victor Neuberg – an aesthetically stimulating spectacle devised by Crowley and performed at the Caxton Hall in 1910. Briefly it featured Man, trying to solve the riddle of the universe, asking questions of the old gods, Saturn, Jupiter, Mars, Sol, Venus, Mercury and Luna, all of whom are found wanting. Finally the Virgin Moon takes the floor, but she is barren of hope, till the Great God Pan springs into action and tears aside the veil revealing the hope of humanity in the Crowned and Conquering Child of Horus. This 'entertainment' was saluted politely by some and reviled by others.

In John Bull, under the headline IS A NEW SMYTH PIGGOT AMONG US?, a biased but not unamusing account of these ceremonies appeared. The reporter described entering the "chamber of mysteries" that was in semi-darkness and sitting down on a large cushion. When the Master of the Temple was at last aroused, "he came forward, crouched behind the cauldron, and recited a most blood-curdling composition, filled with horrible allusions to the "stony stare of dead men's eyes," etc, etc. After all, one couldn't blame him for getting angry at being disturbed, I suppose. However, suddenly he lifted what looked like a tin of Nestle's Milk, and pouring the contents on the flame, extinguished the fire, declared that "there is no God," that everybody was free to do just as he or she liked, and left the audience in utter darkness!"

Although the rites were proper enough for Fuller to take his mother along to see, their veiled sexual implications were apparent to initiates, and it was in this area that Crowley's activities came to the notice of the distinguished occultist, Theodor Reuss, Grand Master of Germany and of other Masonic orders. On learning that Crowley had 'intuited' rather than 'stolen' their sex secrets, he made him their British and Irish head. The tenets of this body, as Reuss set them out, are that God presides over a limitless cosmos, visible and invisible, activated by two forces, positive and negative, the first being male, or the power of creation, and the second being female, or the cosmic egg, concerned with the duplication and spontaneous generation of new worlds and life forms. These forces, not dissimilar to matter and antimatter, give rise to chaos as well as harmony. Later (1914) Crowley produced his gloss in which the positive force became "one secret and ineffable LORD" or "one Star in the company of Stars of whose fire we are created", called Father of Life, also Chaos, who found material expression in "one Earth, the Mother of us all, and in one womb wherein all men are begotten, and wherein they shall rest," the latter being called Babalon.

American Interlude

The 'Rites of Eleusis' attracted notice in the papers, but they did not effectively 'spread the word' or obtain additional funds. Crowley wanted to head something larger than a small, obscure mystical body that would inevitably backslide into anonymity. Although he styled himself "the spirit of solitude", he craved public recognition and applause, but was overshadowed to a large extent by the war in Europe. During that troubled period, he moved to America, where he effectively edited the pro-German *Fatherland* and the more literary *The International*, taking his 'Magick' with him, mingling with every strata of society, always convinced of his singularity, and that he had a mission to fulfil that would perhaps, in the end, secure his immortality.

In *The Old Absinthe House*, he evokes the rundown and morbidly appealing French-Spanish quarter of New Orleans in which he is sipping absinthe, "the green goddess", reflecting on the bracing mixture of peoples and types, the opalescence of the drink which could be compared to the rainbow (whose symbiology he also explores) and the stark obsessiveness of the prohibitionist who does not realise that, once a man has paid his dues to toil and effort, there is a surplus of will left over that naturally gravitates to wine, women and song, for in such pleasures are the stirrings of true religion and artistic appreciation. That is why men of genius, like Shakespeare, Fitzgerald, Verlaine, Rimbaud and Marlowe[1] , have always embraced low life, as both an anchorage and restorative, but made poor husbands, the latter point leading to some reflections on contemporary marriage ("Only the hero is capable of marriage as the church understands it; for the marriage oath is a compact of appalling solemnity, an alliance of two souls against the world and against fate, with invocation of the great blessing of the Most High.") and modern woman's inevitably disappointed expectations. Equally estranged from everyone, in the fervour of their elevation, it hardly matters to the genius whether a man is judged gross or fine:

> There is beauty in every incident of life; the true and the false, the wise and the foolish, are all one in the eye that beholds all without passion or prejudice: and the secret appears to lie not in the retirement from the world, but in keeping a part of oneself Vestal, sacred, intact, aloof from that self which makes contact with the external universe. In other words, in a separation of that which is and perceives from that which acts and suffers. And the art of doing this is really the art of being an artist. As a rule, it is a birthright; it may perhaps be attained by prayer and fasting; most surely, it can never be bought.

Many would identify Crowley's implicit elitism in *The Old Absinthe House* – that harping on about genius – but there is a largesse there, too, a broad umbrella of principles and ideas, a willingness to say exactly what he feels with grace, erudition and humour and also – an inescapable part of his character – more than a little plumage display. It is not so much that what he says is testably true but that, in order to authoritatively state such things, he must have thought about them long and hard. Notable as well is the fact that the prose, with its persistent play of imagery and allusion, is devoid of the 'popular touch'. In *Margin Released*, J.B. Priestley recalled dipping into articles he had written as a young man, one of which bore the statement: "To the average man one can say nothing." No wonder, he reflected, no newspaper editor had taken up that one. And no wonder Crowley encountered literary difficulties – he had none of Priestley's reach-me-down accessibility!

If Crowley drank wine and absinthe and recklessly experimented with any narcotic that might vary or enrich his perception, he was no blithe hedonist. When he tried things out, he observed his state of mind and accompanying sensations with astonishing vigilance and transcribed lengthy accounts afterwards. While in New York in 1916, for instance, he held parties, which included guests like Theodore Dreiser, wherein he passed around anhelonium and ethyl oxide. Later he set down his ideas about the latter and the insights it supplied:

> The first experiments should, in my opinion, be directed to straightening out any kinks in the consciousness of the experimenter; (i.e. he should seek to discover who he really is, his true relation with the Universe as opposed to the conscious idea of himself which he has created, or has been imposed on him by his early training & experience. i.e. analyze away Wish-phantasms, Fear-spectres, False idiosyncrasies, & prejudices). He should thus get rid of fear, desire, false idealism, & in particular of the doubt which exists (as I suppose) in practically all men as to their own ultimate validity. I mean that we all have moments when we wonder whether we really exist, or merely persuade ourselves that we do.
>
> (*Ethyl Oxide*)

What Crowley is referring to (this becomes clearer when one reads the whole essay along with complementary reflections) is not dissimilar to Edmund Husserl's notion of there being, in Kant's phrase, a 'transcendental ego' that can be awakened by the methodical elimination of the blocks or obstructions to self-knowledge acquired through childhood damage and years of habit and indoctrination. Thus, all past prejudice, clutter and bias must be excluded by rational analysis, a stripping of false layers (Husserl used the term 'bracketing'). What is left after all of this is, presumably, pure trustworthy perception.

In more Baudelaireian mode is his essay on cocaine, a potent literary fix, marred by a deficiency of urbanity. Opening in the manner of Charles Lamb or De Quincey, with a polite flounce of classical drapery, it signals cosy, agreeable musings, but quickly plunges into hard-hitting argument, tracing the *raison d'etre* behind the consumption of the drug: the pursuit of happiness.

> Of all the Graces that cluster about the throne of Venus the most timid and elusive is that maiden whom mortals call Happiness. None is so eagerly pursued; none is so hard to win. Indeed, only the saints and martyrs, unknown usually to their fellow-men, have made her theirs; and they have attained her by burning out the Ego-sense in themselves with the white-hot steel of meditation, by dissolving themselves in that divine ocean of Consciousness whose foam is passionless and perfect bliss.
>
> (*Cocaine*)

Significantly, instead of selecting a noble savage as an exemplar for happiness, Crowley opts for the heroes of religion who eradicate the 'I' by blissful contemplation. Happiness, therefore, in his view, is an unselfconscious state, an observation followed by a superb paragraph of prose imagism:

> Look at this shining heap of crystals! They are Hydrochloride of Cocaine. The geologist will think of mica; to me, the mountaineer, they are like those gleaming feathery flakes of snow, flowering mostly where rocks jut from the ice of crevassed glaciers that wind and sun have kissed to ghostliness. To those who know not the great hills, they may suggest the snow that spangles trees with blossoms glittering and lucid. The kingdom of faery has such jewels. To him who tastes them in his nostrils – to their acolyte and slave – they must seem as if the dew of the breath of some great demon of Immensity were frozen by the cold of space upon his beard.

Superficially such a presentation may seem irresponsible, but it holds the right hint of baneful enticement. The pile of cocaine has a elfin quality: quick, sparkling and fatal. Anything so irresistible must hold a hint of warning, of bewitching disaster, for white has always hoarded the pallor of death as well as the dogma of virginity. Hence, at both symbolic and dialectical levels, *Cocaine* is provocative and interesting. Yet an essay should be a flotation, a play of reflection, a consideration of possibilities; too definite or muscular a viewpoint disrupts the essential geniality of the form. Parts of *Cocaine* read as if a domineering but superbly eloquent preacher is laying down the law. This becomes all too clear when Crowley avers a 'man of the world' – whoever he is! – can master the drug as opposed to the 'clod' who is rendered a slave to it. However, he does emphasise that cocaine is dangerous because it *confers instant happiness at market price*: "It tells man what he is, and what he might be; it offers him the semblance of divinity, only that he may know himself a worm. It awakes discontent so acutely that never shall it sleep again."

Naturally Crowley fulminated against prohibition, using the familiar argument that it would drive drugs and alcohol underground, increasing vice and trading on the black market – an attitude that contrasted with G.K. Chesterton who half-jokingly argued (*A Plea for Prohibition*) that the prohibition of alcohol in America had revived home-brewing which was one of the traditional creative crafts. "Let the Government forbid bread, beef, boots, hats and coats," he exhorted, "let there be a law against anybody indulging in chalk, cheese, leather, linen, toys, tales, pictures or newspapers. Then it would seem by serious sociological analogy, all human families will begin vigorously to produce all of these things for themselves, and the youth of the world will really return."

Chesterton was energised by two visits to America, setting down his impressions of things like skyscrapers, mechanisation and native hospitality. Crowley also benefited from his long stay. Although in the *Confessions*, he does fitfully direct vituperation against the United States and the various characters who tried to swindle or undermine him, from his writing it becomes clear that the mix of tongues and racial types, the energising swirl of cultures and classes, the willingness of Americans to go along with new ideas and initiatives, together with the editorial power he briefly flourished, did much to inspire his literary enterprise. Being compelled to write to order, his prose acquired a new breadth and flexibility, apparent in novels like *Moonchild* and the stories that make up *Golden Twigs* and the *Simon Iff* sequence, and his travel and essay writing prospered, too.

Abbey of Thelema

After the First World War, society emerged disillusioned and spiritually depressed. Before it had emerged from its infancy, the new century had got itself buried up to its neck in mud, wounds and arid slogans. Europe had lost some of its youngest, most gifted men and, despite the patriotic poetry, the experience proved disabling rather than ennobling:

> There died a myriad,
> And of the best among them,
> For an old bitch gone in the teeth,
> For a botched civilisation.
>
> (*Hugh Selwyn Mauberley* – Ezra Pound)

But parts of this society were in a ferment. This showed itself in artistic movements like the surrealists, promoting the articulation of 'desire' and startling juxtapositions of images and objects, a feather boa draped around the neck of a rhinoceros or a naked man with the legs of an ostrich. Structures were breaking apart in the musical world, too, where atonality was the rage and symphonies were written around chords that seemed to oppose and clash. A deeper harmony, it was claimed, emerged from the dissonance – for it exposed the long-buried tensions of the soul. A restlessness was abroad that demanded free expression and the right to be eccentric or different. Underlying all this was the message of Sigmund Freud, hinting each personality was a powder-keg of sexual desires that seethed and sputtered rather than healthily exploded.

This was an aspect of the social world to which Crowley returned with the intention of implanting his magical philosophy. He hoped to heal what he saw as the madness and disarray by a new religion that would enable each man and woman to know himself of herself at such depth that all friction and conflict would vanish. After leaving America in 1919, he began to revisit old haunts and renew former contacts, re-establishing himself first in London. He decided that it was time he demonstrated how 'magick' might function as a practical proposition and, with this in mind, along with a few disciples and mistresses, he founded a religious community, the Abbey of Thelema, in Sicily, whose activities he publicised in his novel *Diary of a Drug Fiend* (1922).

The 'abbey' was a rundown Sicilian farmhouse near Cefalu, the interior walls of which Crowley had decorated with a series of startling murals. He styled the place as a paradisial restorative to those corrupted by drugs, alcohol and city living. But Crowley was playing his hand too boldly. Soon the thelemic conclave was attracting a string of sensational sex-and-sacrifice articles in *John Bull* and *The Sunday Express*, especially after the death of a brilliant young pupil called Raoul Loveday. It seems likely that Loveday died from enteritis – probably acquired by drinking infected water – but the real culprit, so far as the reporters were concerned, was the Beast 666 and the abominable rituals he made his pupils endure. "The facts," said the *Sunday Express*, "are too utterly filthy to be detailed in a newspaper, for they have to do with sexual orgies that touch the lowest depths of depravity."

Because of the notoriety of this "College of the Holy Ghost", the ambisexual Hollywood director Kenneth Anger visited the Abbey in the 1950s along with the sexologist, Dr Kinsey, and uncovered the murals Crowley had painted in the *Chambre des Cauchemars* or the

'Chamber of Nightmares'. They made up a weird pictorial sermon, the purpose of which was to assail the soul and immunise it against evil. With the assistance of a little hashish, disciples would spend the night in Crowley's equivalent to the Sistine Chapel where they would see, "cheek by jowl with poetic raptures, the most grotesque, terrible and revolting phantasmagoria ..." The compositions would seem to come alive and invite them into their world. By stark immersion in such a swirling medley of purity and corruption, it was hoped they would confront and overcome the worst of their hidden desires and neuroses – a necessary shake-up prior to the long search for their own true wills.

Whatever their shortcomings of draughtsmanship or colour sense, the paintings were entertainingly miscellaneous and included a Chinese demon, Egyptian Aztecs arriving from Norway on the seacoast of Tibet, dancing girls, four monks carrying a black goat across the snows to nowhere, the Great Gooby Glacier, a Tahitian girl and her Eurasian lover, a monastery in the Caucasus, an acrobatic blonde on a high bar, the scarlet woman, flowers, fruit, heaven and hell and the equinox of the gods. Each had a little text or instructive homily to explain it; for instance the Egyptian Aztecs told one, "You never know in how strange a world you live and what strange things may come to you", while the red monks carrying the goat signified, "Holy Power, walking in the ways of Purity, can safely dispose of the Evil Brute personality which man is compelled to carry." The Great Gooby Glacier indicated, "The summits of the soul, purity (of ice) and environment (of rock) send forth a slow irresistible river which, melting as it reaches the outer world, fertilises the valleys of life."

Obviously Crowley took his gospel and accompanying visual memorandum seriously. He was obsessed with 'significances' and 'correspondences'. Magic centred on the relationship between the individual and the world. It was a science of the emotions, enabling a man or woman to shape and control unseen forces, but it naturally depended on the relatedness of phenomena. You made nature "do one's will" by understanding and redirecting the subtle influences that worked upon it. Crowley, confident in the presence of disciples, was jarred by arguments hinting at non-causality – that, for instance, each instant was a separate entity and did not connect with what followed or came before. He did attempt to answer such problems, for he was intensely serious about his magical philosophy and could not paint a picture or play a practical joke without yoking it to some lofty concept. Even his lurid representation of hell – showing a variety of familiar objects in unfamiliar colours, shapes and attitudes – spelt out how nature had "gone sick" and that the messages of the senses deceive. Nothing can be known for certain – not even the axioms of mathematics. That the world functions at all is largely a tribute to human complicity and trustingness. It was Crowley's jarring combination of Humean scepticism with an open-eyed, vigorous optimism that impressed and befuddled his most earnest students.

In this matter, he has something in common with Aldous Huxley, who also combined elements of the sceptical and credulous in his mental make-up, but the latter, despite his eventual espousal of mysticism, tended to be witheringly sarcastic about magic. "Man is so intelligent," he wrote in *Texts and Pretexts* (1932), "that he feels impelled to invent theories for what happens in the world. Unfortunately he is not quite intelligent enough, in most cases, to find correct explanations. So when he acts on his theories, he behaves very often like a lunatic. Thus, no animal is clever enough, when there is a drought, to imagine that the rain is being withheld by evil spirits, or as a punishment for transgressions. Therefore you never see an animal going through the absurd and often horrible fooleries of magic and religion. No horse, for example, would kill one of its foals in order to make the wind change its direction ... asses do not bray a liturgy to cloudless skies."

This amounts to a formidable criticism to which Crowley would (conceivably) reply that magic does not seek to alter the causal patterns or mechanical laws of the universe but to demonstrate how these forces interact with human psychology. In this complex aim, drugs, chanting and ritual can be used as facilitators: the type of insight, in fact, that Huxley enshrined in works like *The Doors of Perception* and *The Perennial Philosophy*. Although magic undoubtedly *inspires* men and women, as it did Crowley, Yeats and Huysmans, and awakens in them exalted or ecstatic states, the idea that it can alter things on the material plane tends to make scientists scoff. You cannot manipulate outcomes by spells or correspondences, they say, any more than 'Open Sesame!' will unlock your front door.

The Soul of the Desert
The core tenets of his mystical philosophy can be found in essays like *The Soul of the Desert* written in March 1914. As a great deal has been written about Crowley's turgid style or inflated, sub-Nietzschean rant, it is perhaps fair to point out that he could write tersely and effectively when he wanted, but he also wrote within a tradition inherited from figures like Macaulay, Carlyle and Sir Richard Burton where a degree of alliteration and bombast was admired rather than despised. Turning to *The Soul of the Desert,* we find a prose that is eloquent and euphonious, like a deep-pile carpet embroidered with dragons, stars, hieroglyphs and temples. Firstly it states the desert strikes the refugee from civilisation as an awful, forbidding, rocky place, making him long to flee back to the bustle and vitality of Paris or London. It is made up of hard edges and 'genii' which assume eight manifestations; these Crowley identifies as male and female, the lingam or 'life', the yoni or space and stars, the sun and moon, fire and water, air, wood and earth. "In the desert," he states, "all these are single; all these are naked. They are pure and untroubled; not breaking up and dissolving by any commingling or communion; each remains itself and apart, harmonizing indeed with its fellows, but in no wise interfering. The lines of demarcation are crude and harsh; but softness is incomprehensibly the result."

Because of its unerring vitality and implacable regimen, the mind is shocked awake by the desert. It is an autocratic place that forces the refugee to conform to its harsh tenets. Unable to escape into novelty, his thought processes clarify; he attunes himself to its stark rhythm. The vehemence of sand and blue air soothes him. As he opens out, the old discontent seeps away; he starts to enjoy things like dawn and night, walking, eating and sleeping under a silent sky. All such phenomena become rich, satisfying, utterly absorbing. From such a standpoint, he is able to divine the nature of love which is "the bodily ecstasy of dissolution, the pang of bodily death, wherein the Ego for a moment that is an aeon loses the fatal consciousness of itself; and becoming one with that of another, foreshadows to itself that greater sacrament of death ... " In other words, in touching the soul of the desert, the stubborn ego endures first the anguish of its isolation and then learns to surrender itself and partake of the peace of the 'Father of Life'.[2] Not only does it plumb the mystery of love

– epitomised by the word union – it also gains an insight into the nature of death, the ultimate ego-less state, or the abandonment of any physical manifestation. This type of discipline, in theory, enabled a magical pupil to establish the nature of his 'true will' or the unique and definite life-path designed for him alone.

Parenthetically, it should be noted that many people misunderstand Crowley's constant reiteration of the word "love" as the solution and fulfilment of being. Sometimes they read his more sensual poetry and think he is hinting at a higher type of orgy. But he uses the word in a yogic sense, signifying a mingling of object and perceiver, so that a new element emerges like oxygen and hydrogen making water. Love, then, is an ecstatic state of wholeness, not a 'relationship' in the conventional sense, but a state of self-sufficient joy in which pain of separation has ended, for the 'One' has become the 'All'. Crowley's American disciple, Bill Heidrick, provided a gloss on this doctrine: "Love is an ultimate act of daring. Love cannot effectively act within a person. Unless you love yourself, you cannot love another in any way. Once the inner love is established, it may be projected outward. This active form is a giving of energy without fear of loss or abuse."

The *Book of the Law*

Such mystical insights were dispensed to the Thelemites on a daily basis and the disciples of the Abbey were also instructed in the *Book of the Law*, the contents of which, as we have seen, were dictated to Crowley through his wife Rose during their stay in Egypt. The phrase 'Book of the Law' derives from Freemasonry and the book has three chapters, one for each of the ruling deities. Full of rage, rant and rhapsody, the Book of the Law lends itself to different interpretations – indeed, several commentaries were written by Crowley himself.

The trinity of the *Book of the Law* is composed of three Egyptian deities: Nuit, the goddess of the night sky, also known as the Egyptian Venus. Her message is of freedom, love and the mystical bliss of union. She is the eternal dark womb out of which all points of possibility shine, a reservoir of unformed potential. Second is Hadit, the winged solar globe, standing for the individual within each of us, the star that each person is, an aggregate of urges and unresolved desires.

Third in the trinity is the child Horus, produced by the union of Nuit and Hadit. He has two contrasting incarnations, the first a warrior and conqueror, the second an innocent or restless child. Crowley, who had a reactionary component, hinted that many fads and fashions of the time – nudism, vegetarianism, wireless, cinema, football pools – were manifestations of babyish enthusiasm or the "abortive births" of Horus the Child. The population of the planet had been increasing rapidly. Where did all these new souls come from? Crowley replied that the earth was passing through a period when "human units were being built up with increasing frequency" – hence these naive young souls were akin to first-born, living human life for the first time. And it was naturally up to the Thelemites to take matters in hand and make sure the Child of the Aeon grew up to be a mature adult. Thus he will be able to make the gods *incarnate in him* rather than set up images of them for external worship – in other words, in the Aeon of Horus, man will realise his divinity.

Two other sinister figures rise out of the *Book of the Law*: the Great Beast, and Scarlet Woman named Babalon. The former is usually associated with rapacity and destruction and the latter with lasciviousness. Crowley incorporated the two into his system as agents of the Aeon of Horus, avatars of solar power and sexuality. When a lawyer cross-examined him – asking him if the title 'Beast 666' reflected his outlook – he replied mildly that the Beast 666 only meant sunlight. "You can call me little sunlight," he riposted.

Interpretations of the *Book of the Law* may be divine, psychological or oracular. In the first reading, we have a holy text, therefore unimpeachable, containing predictions and prescriptions for the future of humanity. In the second reading, we analyse the emotions expressed and make a comparative judgement about the author. We contemplate a series of chaotic, prophetic utterances, comparable to those produced by the Anabaptist Thomas Munzer and other aspirant messiahs who elected themselves as spiritual channels. And thirdly there is the oracular reading, wherein one evaluates the Book of the Law from a personal standpoint, finally achieving self-appraisal. You read it and register a reaction, and it therefore becomes a sliderule against which to measure and test your opinions. If one utterly rejects it, that would be as valid as becoming a convert.

The main problem with the work is Aiwass' dramatically fluctuating temperament. Individual verses are often ambiguous or disjointed. Erotic entreaties jostle against commands to lay waste and destroy. Some verses are so plangently autocratic, so untainted by contemporary preoccupation, that to extrapolate a future from them would seem an act of reckless faith. If one wanted to indulge in special pleading, one could agree that each age finds some personification of a ranting war-god, counterbalanced by a gentler principle. Hence, with hindsight, an acolyte may find the passages about the 'warrior lord' and the 'Queen of Space' prophetic. But the acid test would be a definitive reading of the *Book of the Law*, complete with dates and details, so that the unconvinced and unconverted could test its accuracy against events as they unfolded.

Needless to add, few took up the *Book of the Law* (although nowadays popular editions of the work abound). When it first appeared, hardly anyone, including Crowley, knew what it was trying to say and, even if they did, could hardly carry out all the precepts it endorsed without getting hanged or banged up in a madhouse. But though odd, the *Book of the Law* was hardly without contemporary parallel. It can be loosely equated with prophetic works like D.H. Lawrence's *Apocalypse,* Yeats' *A Vision* – also peddling a distinctive view of history – and C.G. Jung's ominous "night-sea journeys" and dream fantasias, in which the psychologist sees a civilisation-drowning flood, a tree in a frozen landscape, a devouring sea-monster and a spirit-guide, Philomel, an old man with bull's horns and kingfisher's wings, holding a bunch of four keys. If Crowley's world was rent by apocalypse, ecstasy and angst, he was by no means the only one who went to heaven and hell and back.

In 1929 the Magus published a less inscrutable occult text, his masterwork *Magick in Theory and Pratice*, a manual that seems destined to be read whether one is a magician or not; for it so firmly and clearly sets out the magical theory of the universe, the meaning and significance of ritual, the relationship of the microcosm to the macrocosm, the nature of the astral plane, silence, secrecy, invocation and other 'sacred' matters. What is presented is a complex, spacious philosophical outlook which incorporates what many might see as the views of sceptics – "Gods are but names for the forces of Nature themselves" – within its formation. There are insights which make one feel uneasy: "Any symbol which has once definitely entered your environment with your own consent is extremely dangerous;

unless under absolute control. A man's friends are more capable of working him harm than are strangers; and his greatest danger lies in his own habits." Allied to this is a backward logic that awakens a radical way of perceiving things: "The mind is a great enemy; so, by invoking enthusiastically a person whom we know not to exist, we are rebuking that mind." Thirdly, an ability to use language to paradoxical effect that is faintly comical, yet yields a deeper sense after contemplation: "A man who is doing his True Will has the inertia of the Universe to assist him." And an emphasis that the manner in which we function as living beings involves processes that are inherently mysterious: "Every man must do Magick each time that he acts or even thinks, since a thought is an internal act whose influence ultimately effects action, though it may not do so at the time."

That sex was central to his 'magick' is a highly publicised fact, and the details of his operations in this arena have been handled elsewhere. But chroniclers tend to get so caught up with the specifics that they ignore the overall philosophy which informed such operations, and had, ideologically speaking, been brewing since the early Middle Ages. Oscar Wilde perfectly and precisely hinted at the gospel of Crowleianity when he observed in *Dorian Gray* that "the worship of the senses has often, and with much justice, been decried, men feeling a natural instinct of terror about passions and sensations that seem stronger than themselves, and which they are conscious of sharing with the less highly organised forms of existence. But it is probable the true nature of the senses has never been understood, and that they have remained savage and animal because the world has sought to starve them into submission or to kill them by pain instead of aiming at making them elements of a new spirituality for which beauty will be the dominant characteristic."

In this brief paragraph, we find an excellent compression of the philosophy of Aleister Crowley, D.H. Lawrence, William Blake and a great deal of Jung, Freud and Nietzsche too.

Although *Magick* was the high water mark of his middle period, Crowley developed his strain of mystical wisdom. He was a persistent explorer of reality which, he maintained, focuses in this world upon the distinctions and differences between things. In such a frame of mind, the best of his later publications was *Little Essays Towards*

Truth (1938) which treats gracefully and limpidly subjects like Memory, Indifference, Truth, Silence and Sorrow. Admirably concise, loftily abstract, replete with picturesque analogies, the essays are like tiny meditation cells in the centre of life's hurricane. Of 'Truth', for instance, he begins by demolishing the linguistic confusion, saying that it is "absurd to attempt to define it, for when we say that S is P, rather than S is Q or S is R, we assume that we already know the meaning of Truth. This is really why all the discussions as to whether Truth depends on external correspondence, internal coherence, or what not, neither produce conviction, nor withstand analysis."

Equally revealing are his observations on 'Sorrow', showing he had retained the Buddhist doctrines of his youth:

> What man 'sees' is in fact just that which obstructs the rays of light. This is the justification for the Buddha saying: "Everything is Sorrow": in that word "Everything" he is most careful to include specifically all those things which men count joyous. And this is not really a paradox; for to him all reactions which produce consciousness are ultimately sorrowful, as being disturbances of the Perfection of Peace, or (if you prefer it) as obstructions to the free flow of Energy.

And on silence:

> He is the All-Wandering Spirit; the Pure and Perfect Knight-Errant, who answers all Enigmas, and opens the Closed Portal of the King's Daughter. But Silence in the vulgar sense is not the answer to the Riddle of the Sphinx; it is that which is created by that answer.

On 'Laughter', however, his views are a bit flip, with a hint of that callousness that flaws a great deal of his prose. Like Yeats, he believes wise men should be essentially gay – that life springs up with a smile on its face after being knocked down like Mr Punch with his cry, "Roo-too-too-tit! Here we are again!" He omits to state laughter is liable to erupt when purpose collapses into absurdism – when the man with the hammer strikes his own thumb instead of the nail. Neither does he point out that, faced with grim situations, people 'select' laughter as a more durable alternative to tears. Instead, in rather puerlile, Greyfriars fashion, he is fervent about its cathartic value:

> Oh the huge wholesome contempt for the limiting self which springs from the sense of Gargantuan disproportion perceived by this Laughter! Truly it slays, with jolliest cannibal revels, that sour black-coated missionary the serious Ego, and plumps him into the pot. Tee-hee! – the Voice of Civilisation – the Messenger of the White Man's God – bubble, bubble, bubble! Throw in another handful of sage, brother! And the sweet-smelling smoke rises and veils with exquisite shy seduction the shameless bodies of the Stars!

Reservations aside, such observations as are to be found in *Little Essays* sweep away any lasting confusions people may harbour with regard to the paradoxes implicit in the eastern religions. To quote Wittgenstein, they do not solve a problem so much as "dissolve" it, recast it so that it takes on a new dimension. They make one see that most definitions are tautologies, and that ideas themselves are thought-swarms that attach themselves to language, but their real meaning begins where language ends. In short, *Little Essays* are replete with clarifications and patient, spacious overviews of rather nebulous topics, showing that Crowley retained a remarkably clear head until the end.

Fernando Pessoa

Having accomplished his magnum opus, Crowley went on to spend a large part of the 1930s restlessly moving from place to place and having affairs with women and men. His urge to be constantly on the move, to immerse himself in warmer climes, may have been connected not only with his asthma, but with his eminently prosecutable sexuality – homosexual acts between adults were then adjudged criminal – that did not feel free to indulge its full range while in England.

During a significant interval, he visited Lisbon and made contact with Fernando Pessoa (1888 – 1935), a poet associated with the avant-garde magazine *Orpheu* (1915). Virtually unknown in his lifetime, Pessoa is now regarded as key figure in European Modernism. He lived a quiet life in a furnished room in Lisbon until his sad and lonely death of alcoholic poisoning in 1935. Yet both he and Crowley had a side preoccupied with orgy and ecstasy. Although his life was sexually restrained, a submerged homo-eroticism is evident in *Antinous*[3], and he promoted Crowley's work, conducted magical experiments with him and visited him in London. They played chess at the Gambit Chess Rooms where a photograph shows them together. Pessoa is soberly and neatly dressed in hat, overcoat and spectacles. With small moustache and patient manner, he looks mild and appealing. Crowley's profile is blurred and flabby, his bald head eerily round, like a cherry or plum. As he smokes a cigar and studies his pieces, one gets the impression of a wily, debauched financier.

Interested in cabalism, occultism, Buddhism, freemasonry, theosophy and astral visions, Pessoa believed in reincarnation and at one point thought of becoming an astrologer. He foretold the year of his own death and translated Theosophical writers such as Madame Blavatsky and C.W. Leadbetter as well as Crowley's 'Hymn to Pan' into Portuguese. It seems a pity that Crowley did not reciprocate the influence, for Pessoa's light, incisive way of probing existential matters might have proven an exemplar to his more hectoring mode.

A poet of wit and subtlety, Pessoa generated a lonely, secretive euphoria, out of which he spun numerous poetic identities, a waxworks of projections that externalised his inner struggle rather than reconciled it, creating personae with accents and attributes who could differ and communicate within a shared personal space. He actively hymned the faces we put on and the confusions they engender:

> How many masks wear we, and undermasks,
> Upon our countenance, and when,
> If for self-sport the soul itself unmasks,
> Knows it the last mask off and the face plain.
> The true mask feels no inside to the mask
> But looks out of the mask by co-masked eyes.
> (38 Sonnets)

Like Crowley, who used exotic titles to express aspects of himself that would otherwise be censored or derided, Pessoa devised "heteronyms" or literary alter egos who had precise birth dates, careers and attitudes and interacted with each other. Pessoa even went so far as casting their horoscopes. They included Albert Caeiro, a pastoral existentialist, Ricardo Reis, a doctor who wrote classical odes and Álvaro de Campos, a marine engineer who wrote free, rhapsodic verse.

In an article in *Presenca* (1928) Pessoa wrote: "A pseudonymic work is, except for the name with which it is signed, the work of an author, writing as himself; a heteronymic work is by an author writing outside his own personality: it is the work of a complete individuality made up by him, just as the utterances of some character in a drama would be." Pessoa claimed such a technique to be integrally self-effacing, that his voices were autonomous, separate beings. Nevertheless he must have understood that the more heteronymns he devised, the more pervasive became the godlike shadow of the author. Inevitably the names take their place in a unique literary constituency for which there is only one candidate.

Crowley also viewed himself as a poetic channel though which various voices flowed. "The only things I complete," he wrote in the *Confessions*, "are those of which I am not the real author but an instrument impelled by a mysterious power which sweeps me away in an effortless enthusiasm which leaves no room for laziness, cynicism and similarly inhibiting qualities to interfere." Under such compulsion, he composed works like 'Clouds Without Water', 'The Scented Garden' and 'Amphora' – the last being a collection of hymns to the Virgin Mary, first issued anonymously by Burns & Oates, and later under Crowley's name as *Hail Mary* (1912) to the mild consternation of the Catholic press.

The transcendent impulse in his poetry being strong, Pessoa was fond of adopting the appurtenances of the magician. It was as if he sought a fusion of the parts of him in disarray, those mesmeric inner voices that both released and enchained him. In *The Final Incantation*, a magician laments the waning of his power, his inability to summon elves, fairies and the Great Goddess. He pleads that he cast off his temporal self and blend with "the nameless presence born perpetually" – hinting at faith in a transcendent consciousness in which living forms incarnate.

But Pessoa was a complex character, who did not rigidly adhere to the doctrines he expressed. For the other side of his open-eyed mysticism was the sceptical poet who saw closed systems of beliefs as conceptual blinkers:

> A God's born. Others die. Reality
> Has neither come nor gone: a change of Error.
> Now we have another Eternity,
> And always the one passed away was better.
>
> Blind, Science is working the useless ground.
> Mad, faith is living the dream of its cult.
> A new God is a word – or the mere sound.
> Don't seek and don't believe: all is occult.
> <div align="right">(<i>Christmas</i>, tr. J. Griffin)</div>

However, it was the part of Pessoa drawn to the world of shadows, doubles, blinds and guises that led him to collude with Crowley over the latter's faked suicide in 1930. In early September, Crowley arrived at Lisbon with his girlfriend Hanni Jaeger and was greeted by Pessoa. But soon he and Hanni fell into their habitual mode of rowing, and after having a fit of hysterics in a hotel she walked out on him. Against this background there was found pinned to a rock at the entrance to a cave, known as Hell's Mouth, twenty miles from Lisbon, a message that said: "Year 14. Sun in the Scales. L.G.P. I cannot live without thee. The other Mouth of Hell will catch me. It will not be as hot as thine. Hjsos! Tu Li Yu."

Newspapers picked up the story, asking whether the celebrated English magician, Aleister Crowley, had committed suicide or merely left Portugal to continue his travels. Pessoa made a statement to the effect that he had some correspondence with the real Crowley on literary matters, and that on 2nd September he met a man "representing himself as Aleister Crowley" who arrived at Lisbon on the steamship Alcantara, with the object of spending some time on the Portuguese coast. Shortly after this furore of scandal and gossip, Crowley turned up in Berlin to host an exhibition of his paintings at the Porza Galleries.

Posthumous Celebrity

Seventeen years after the Portuguese rehearsal of his extinction, Aleister Crowley died in Hastings, England, on 1st December 1947, and his character continues to perplex and fascinate. Much has been written about his life and magical system, drawing together salient features of the Eastern and Western traditions, but less about the fact that he bequeathed to the world not only a scandalous reputation and an estate valued at 18/6d (92.5p), but also a prolix literary legacy, including the novels *Moonchild* and *Diary of a Drug Fiend*, the autobiographical *Confessions*, religious essays, drama, poetry and what could be loosely termed 'visionary' works.

Few critics have bothered to evaluate the verse, prose and drama, apart from Major General Fuller's eloquent but uncritical *The Star in the West* (1907) and Charles Richard Cammell's fervent appraisal: *Aleister Crowley: The Man, Mage and Poet* (1951). In fact, this is the first serious modern analysis of a turbulent and disturbing body of work. It is necessarily selective, in that the bulk of the work is considerable and of dramatically varying quality, but it does attempt to identify what is worthwhile, taking into account Crowley's iconic significance as an idol of revolt. Furthermore, it frames his ideas in a specific context, integrating them with currents of thought active during the Edwardian period. The second part, for instance, places Crowley alongside his contemporaries, as a *literal* exponent of the cult of Pan, the far-reaching philosophical implications of which are traced in the works of major writers like Thomas Mann, Joseph Conrad, D.H. Lawrence and Rudyard Kipling. The third part tackles the poetry and the fourth Crowley's shorter fiction and his portrayal as a fictional character in the books of others. Finally there is a conclusion, dealing with his achievement and contemporary status.

Footnotes

[1] Crowley does not say that their homosexuality often prompted them to embrace 'low life' and might have hindered them as 'husbands', too.

[2] The 'positive' spiritual (male) force as opposed to the 'negative' material (female) current, the latter being the earthly manifestation of the former.

[3] The poem shows the Emperor Hadrian weeping over the drowned body of Antinous, the slave boy he loved and vowed to make into a god, so that his memory will linger on and inspire future generations.

2

The Cult of Pan

> We know what happened to those who chanced to meet the Great God Pan, and those that are wise know all symbols are symbols of something and not nothing. It was, indeed, an exquisite symbol beneath which men long ago veiled their knowledge of the most awful, secret forces which lie at the heart of all things; forces before which the souls of men must wither and die and blacken, as their bodies blacken under the electric current.
> (Arthur Machen – *The Great God Pan*)

In 1908 we find Aleister Crowley – by now a suspect if not wholly 'notorious' character – returning to Cambridge University to present poems and papers before the Pan Society, founded by his magical apprentice and fellow poet, Victor Neuburg. Crowley was not a popular visitor with the religious fraternity; they disapproved of both his 'magick' and sexual inclinations. The Senior Dean sought to ban him but not without difficulty, for Crowley, a former student, was a lifelong member of Cambridge. No single person had the right to throw him out and the Dean's resistance made the incident famous. But Crowley's Luciferian arrogance proved too challenging, and he was eventually prohibited from entering the university. While Neuburg did not seek to make the Pan Society historically significant, as Crowley commented, "he found people idiotic enough to make it invulnerable against the arrows of oblivion by dipping it into the Styx of persecution".

Why call a discussion group the Pan Society? Why resurrect a bestial hybrid declared dead during the reign of Tiberius in the first century AD? Students of classics were probably familiar with Plutarch's account of a group of travellers sailing to Italy and drifting by the island of Paxi. A voice was heard calling Thamus, who was the Egyptian pilot, not known to many on board. Twice his name was called but he did not reply. The voice grew loud and impatient, adding "When you come opposite to Palodes, announce that Great Pan is dead." Deciding to obey, Thamus drew towards the island and cried, "Great Pan is dead!" Before he could finish, a great cry of lamentation arose mingled with exclamations of dismay and amazement.

Pan is famous as the goatfoot god of 'panic' or the sudden fear that seizes one alone in the forest. He is the horned face peering between the leaves and the god of vegetation. His name has been translated as 'All' for he stands for every manifestation of nature. He is raw, undirected energy, the dance of blood along the arteries, the rising sap. He is sexual desire running amok, the god of unfettered bodily instinct. No social force constrains him. He is the lord of death, of corruption, bodily decay and dissolution. Pan also is the mindless mob instinct, the beast who takes control of man, the frenzy of the flesh-ripping orgy. Wine, women and song quicken his pleasure. He plays his pipe (the syrinx) and the forest resounds with laughter and celebration. In the esoteric tradition of the West, he often borrows the attributes of Dionysus, lord of the vine, who presides over intoxication and its after-effects. Like the moon-goddess, Pan-equivalents are found in many cultures: Cernunnos, the horned Celtic god, the Roman Sylvanus, the Norse Odin and the horned god of the witches.

Christian legend has it that Pan died on the very day Christ was nailed to the cross. The cry came across the water when the Saviour's agony was over. Christ had left his mortal body to rise and take over as the ascendant deity. Symbolically speaking, the passing of the goatfoot god marked the shift of power from the woodland to the urban centres. The Roman Empire had introduced centralised networks, mastery of communication, bureaucracy and law and order, as a means of containing uprising and dissent. Tribal justice had given way to courts of arbitration; methodology was valued above intuition. The distinction between man and beast was clear-cut. With the spread of Christianity came a more rigid order and during the Middle Ages the stone spire of the cathedral became the focus of a settlement. Forests were cut back further and, although the spirits of nature held out in pockets amid moor and mountain, their primal identities – held so long intact by worship in temple and sanctuary – had been splintered into shards of superstition and half-remembered lore.

Orgy Versus Order

If the formal worship died, the principle Pan stood for was bound to survive: the natural way of life and enjoyment of the senses. In England, during the Georgian and Regency periods, the Romantic movement in literature inaugurated a revival of Hellenism: Lord Byron's death at Missolonghi, Keats' reverence for Chapman's 'Homer' and the acquisition of the Elgin Marbles had a lasting cultural impact. Ancient Greece was honoured as the birthplace of art and philosophy, but there were stronger forces at work than cultural ones – forces that would shake the social pattern of Europe.

With the advent of the Industrial Revolution, a new materialism arose, gaining force and momentum during Victoria's reign when factories spread and railways webbed the landscape. The lineaments of the classical world lingered in civic architecture and painters such as Frederick Leighton held fast to mythological subjects, although showing a demure rigidity of technique. Poetry exhibited a range of mood, from the domestic to the neurotic, but with the exception of Swinburne there was no overt treatment of erotic themes. The age of machines and scientific enquiry made Elizabeth Barrett Browning feel secure enough to draw the curtain on the mythology of the past:

> Gods of Hellas, gods of Hellas,
> Can ye listen in your silence?
> Can your mystic voices tell us
> Where ye hide in floating islands,
> With a wind that evermore
> Keeps you out of sight of shore?
>   Pan, Pan is dead.

The concluding stanza is suitably pious:

> Oh brave poets, keep back nothing,
> Nor mix falsehood with the whole!
> Look up Godward, speak the truth in
> Worthy song from earnest soul;

> Hold in high poetic duty,
> Truest Truth the fairest Beauty!
> > Pan, Pan is dead.

Not everybody shared Browning's attitude to the pagan gods. Her poem was a rebuke to Schiller, the German dramatist who, earlier, had mourned the passing of the ancient pantheon:

> Yes, they did go home, and everything beautiful,
> Everything high they took away with them,
> All colours, all sounds of life,
> And for us remained only the de-souled Word.
> Torn out of time-flood, they float
> Saved on the heights of Pindus;
> What undying in song shall live
> Must in life go under.

Elizabeth Barrett Browning was only partially correct. The communal worship of Pan died but the instinct still lurked in the ancient power-centres of the body. Frederick Nietzsche in *The Birth of Tragedy* (1872) rhapsodised over the orgiastic and volatile aspect of man – contrasting it with rational, individuated behaviour. With the collapse of the Victorian ethic, many writers of the twentieth century were to rediscover and analyse this force. In fact, a major conflict running through 20th-century literature is that of Pan or Dionysus versus Apollo, or orgy versus order, desire versus discipline. Writers like D.H. Lawrence and Henry Miller have openly celebrated the energy of Pan, seeing nature as the fount of goodness. Others have taken the opposing view. To them Pan stands for man's ability to debase himself in depths of mindless horror:

> With hoofs of steel I race on the rocks
> Through solstice stubborn to equinox.
> And I rave; and I rape and I rip and I rend
> Everlasting, world without end,
> Mannikin, maiden, maenad, man
> In the might of Pan.
> Io Pan! Io Pan! Pan! Io Pan!
> > ('Hymn to Pan')

Aleister Crowley wrote these lines as a direct invocation. Far from restricting his admiration to language, he also sought to conjure Pan in specially devised magical ceremonies. On one level his life was a fantastic attempt to reinstate those pagan deities whose passing was mourned by Schiller. Hence that Neuberg[1] called his spiritual debating group the Pan Society was apposite, for both he and Crowley sought in Pan what they could not find in Christ – although they located the god on the astral plane rather than among the rocks and glades of his native land.

Values stand defined at the moment of their passing, and the world of Pan was being engulfed. "Every Russian forest is cracking under the axe," Voynitsky complains in *The Wood Demon* (1888), "millions of trees are perishing, the abodes of birds and beasts are being ravaged, rivers are becoming shallow and drying up, wonderful landscapes are disappearing without leaving a trace; and all this because lazy man has not got the sense to pick up fuel from the ground."

The lament was a traditional one. Even during the Neolithic age, nature had been subject to caging and taming, and the writers of Classical Greece had regretted the passing of rural crafts and customs as much as English pastoral writers like Crabbe and Cobbett. Naturally the practices which replaced them in turn became 'traditional' and embowered in nostalgia. Hence the 'old ways' had been writhing in their death throes long before Rousseau found virtue in the noble savage, but during the 18th and 19th centuries, change in Western Europe had gathered a massive impulsion, with the Industrial Revolution re-sculpting the land so violently, so poisonously, that only the deafest, aesthetically speaking, could fail to hear the death-knell.

The Withering of Arcady

With his humble origins, Pan was the plain-spoken deity of natural living, who would stoutly oppose the destruction of his woodland habitat, the growth of synthetic fabrics, use of face paints and various other fashionable affectations. He was the symbol of a withering once-green world, an Arcadia that was dying, yet might be revived were people to abandon their false ways. Equally importantly, Pan hinted at a nimble, jubilant sexuality that had not been crippled by self-consciousness or body shame. Literary ripples of his following can be traced in Harold Monro's *Overheard in a Saltmarsh,* E.M. Forster's *The Story of a Panic*, James Stephens' *The Crock of Gold* and stories by Saki, Algernon Blackwood and others.

At a more practical level, an offshoot of the Pan cult was the formation of such upstanding groups as the Kindred of the Kibbo Kift, founded by John Hargrave in 1920, whose aims were open education for children, health of body, mind and spirit, craft training, local folk moots and the disarmament of nations. With its relaxed attitude to sexuality and belief in the brotherhood of man, D.H. Lawrence thought of joining the offensive, but was put off by Hargrave's coldness. Yet still the Kibbo Kift were able to enlist on its council Havelock Ellis, Rabindranath Tagore and H.G. Wells. A similar current was evident in Germany where the philosopher, Martin Heidegger (1889-1976), developed a basis for a profound pantheism by celebrating the tactilities of 'dwelling' and 'being here' with rigour and thoroughness. Seeking 'presence' as opposed to 'representation', radical astonishment rather than bland acceptance of one's existence, the natural course of river and lake as opposed to the 'standing-reserve' of dam and reservoir, he finally retired to a hut in the Black Forest where the Jewish poet, Paul Celan, visited him in 1967 and tried to make him explain his affiliation with Hitler and the Nazis.

Heidegger saw Pan as a principle that went deeper than racial memory, the primordial breath of the earth, but English writers portrayed the hoofed, hairy god as mischievous rather than portentous. If people were damaged through contact with him, it was not because of his inherent evil so much as their misunderstanding of the natural world. This was apt, for despite the supercharged revulsion of writers like Arthur Machen, Pan had a companionable aspect as the goat-god of the Arcadian shepherds. However, his shadowy ancestry and attractive attributes enabled him to spectacularly outgrow his limited pastoral status, until he was transformed into a massive intellectual abstraction – a principle so large and sprawling that one could discuss it interminably without reaching a conclusion.

In terms of artistic representation, Pan is very ancient. There is an Athenian vase of 490 BC on which a ghostly reindeer-like figure is standing upright playing pipes. Later there are phallic bronzes showing the god with the proportions of a classical athlete and then there are charming curiosities like a chalcedony gem of a 'girl Pan' and a marble group from Delos showing Pan, Aphrodite and Eros.

Accompanied by his satyr troupe, the hairy prankster skips through the sunlit glades of the Italian Renaissance down through stifling Victorian decors and the pastoral landscapes of Edwardian illustrators. We find Aubrey Beardsley equipping him with female breasts as he attends upon a lady in a parkland setting and, half a century on, the cartoonist Anton showing his hoof breaking through the ceiling of a surprised middle-class couple watching television: "Perhaps that will convince you there's an orgy going on up there," the wife remarks to her husband. With the advent of Margaret Murray's theories, Pan's stature darkened in some quarters. He blended with the horned god of the witches, emblematic of chaos, mystery and magic.

In this diabolic guise, Pan forfeited his bumbling, rustic innocence. For there was, originally, a pathos about him. The nobler, more pompous gods mocked him for his ugliness and, like most of us, he endured the pangs of thwarted love. As a rapist, he was less than triumphantly successful. His seductive technique showed little finesse and the nymph he pursued so energetically, Syrinx, was changed into a reed from which his own unique instrument – the Pan-pipes or syrinx – was forged. Another nymph who slipped through his net was Echo and the phrase 'chasing one's echo' came to stand for elusive quests and delusive desires.

Originally Pan was a god of down-to-earth, modest yearnings. It was comparatively late in the Roman period that etymology lent him the character of the 'God of All'. Such a designation was in keeping with Pan's association with Dionysus, god of wine and orgy. Getting drunk is an effective way of benumbing the brain and allowing cosmic space – 'All' – to seep between the cracks. Furthermore, although Hermes is usually cited as his father, it was alleged that he had no single father, and it was the combined efforts of *all* the suitors of his mother, the nymph Penelope, that resulted in the progeny. However, 'Pan' appears not to derive not from the Greek 'all' but from the root pa-on meaning 'herdsman', a variant of which is found in the English *pasture*.

No Lack of Fauns

As we have seen, Pan's pipes resounded distinctly amid the undergrowth of Edwardian writing. With dry amusement, Max Beerbohm (1917) observed that "current literature did not suffer from any lack of fauns ... We had not yet tired of them and their hoofs and slanting eyes and their way of coming suddenly out of woods to wean quiet English villages from respectability." E.M. Forster, a writer not especially associated with the supernatural, produced *The Story of a Panic*, in which an unhappy, much put-upon English boy on holiday in Italy starts to behave erratically and ecstatically as he immerses himself in the freedom and spaciousness of nature. In J.K. Stephens' *The Crock of Gold* (1912), Pan features as a wayside philosopher, fluently conversing on issues like clothing, morals and personal enjoyment – naturally, his outlook is whimsical and unconstrained: "Virtue is the performance of pleasant actions," he opines. "Life is very simple; it is to be born and die, and in the interval to eat and drink, to marry and beget children."

Similarly Kenneth Grahame's *Wind in the Willows* features Pan in the episode in which Rat and Mole, seeking a lost baby otter, are overcome when they saw "the backward sweep of the curved horns, gleaming in the growing daylight; saw the stern, hooked nose between the kindly eyes looking down on them humorously, while the bearded mouth broke into a half-smile at the corners; saw the rippling muscles on the arm that lay across the broad chest, the long supple hand still holding the pan-pipes only just fallen away from the parted lips; saw the splendid curves of the shaggy limbs disposed in majestic ease on the sward; saw, last of all, nestling between his very hooves, sleeping soundly in entire peace and contentment, the little round, podgy childish form of the baby otter ..."

Less innocently, Algernon Blackwood's *The Touch of Pan* takes place against the brittle chatter of a house-party. An intuitive young woman escapes into the grounds of the mansion with her young man and, as darkness falls, they are transposed into an Arcadian dream, drawn into a romp with nymphs and satyrs that is as sensual as it is mystic. They act out their feelings towards each other and, at the climax, Pan manifests in all his power and glory and then departs:

> Again a footfall sounded far away upon an unruined world
> ... and He was gone – back into the wind and water whence
> He came. The thousand faces lifted; all stood up; the hush of
> worship still among them. There was a quiet as of the dawn.
> The piping floated over wood and field, fading into silence.
> All looked at one another ... And then once more the laughter
> and the play broke loose.

And so, almost sentimentally, Blackwood stoops and touches his forelock to the god who has so generously ennobled his prose. One appreciates Pan had possibilities the virginal Christ was not able to offer. His shaggy dignity could preside over the lovemaking activities of men and women – a role, incidentally, of centrality and significance. Analysis of the libido was, after the repression of Victorian society, relatively new territory.

Death in Venice

Algernon Blackwood, J.K. Stephens, Kenneth Grahame and Saki produced amusing fictions showing Pan in a friendly or vaguely disconcerting guise. But in the broader world of literature, Pan appeared not in name, but as literally 'All', the chaotic spirit or essence lurking behind the phenomenal world who throws open the trapdoor of the Id letting out wild, disorderly demons – an invisible force, neither God nor the Devil, but a catalyst that urges people to break their social shells and openly express whatever is being held in check.

For instance, on the continent, Pan – in his Dionysiac guise – exploded disruptively in the psyche of Gustave Aschenbach, the self-absorbed writer of Thomas Mann's *Death in Venice*. Acknowledged as a combination of Mahler and the homosexual poet Platen, to some degree he reflects Mann's ability to cast an ironic eye upon his own achievements. Mann has often been admired for his intellectual rigour; similarly Aschenbach's novels were renowned for their attitude of "virginal manliness" and ability to endure suffering with refined stoicism.

Aschenbach takes a holiday in Venice to convalesce. He registers at a hotel where a Polish family are staying. One of their children – a boy called Tadzio – has a godlike beauty. Aschenbach is smitten, and as the holiday progresses, the boy becomes his obsession. His spare time becomes a series of strategies in order that he may study the object of his love. His infatuation makes a mockery of his pose of steely resolve and he consoles himself by recalling how Socrates told his pupil that "the lover was nearer the divine than the beloved; for the god was in one but not in the other ..."

Inherent in the worship of beauty is the possibility of downfall and exposure. Back at the hotel, he has a dream which begins on a mountainside. There is a distant sound of clamour and confusion. Flute notes pierce the mist and a group of hairy men and women dressed in pelts and loincloths swarm over a hill. Uttering loud cries and rattling tambourines, the females shriek and hold their breasts in their hands. Troops of beardless youths follow the throng, chasing goats and prodding them with garlanded staves – "His senses reeled in the steam of panting bodies, the acrid stench from the goats, the odour as of stagnant waters – and another, too familiar smell – of wounds, uncleanness and disease. His heart throbbed to the drums, his brain reeled, a blind rage seized him, a whirling lust, he craved with all his soul to join the ring that formed about the obscene symbol of the godhead ..."

One may object that such muscular rhetoric, evoking the orgiastic rites of the past, is hardly an adequate equation for Aschenbach's secret lust. As Socrates remarked, art can lead to "intoxication and excess" – and Mann acknowledges that Aschenbach's statuesque pomposity, his concern with purity of form, actually nourishes and emboldens the vanquished forces of orgy and abandon. Blake wrote belligerently, "Sooner murder an infant in its cradle than nurse unacted desire." Oscar Wilde elaborated upon this, stating: "Every impulse that we strive to strangle broods in the mind, and poisons us." He viewed the expression of latent desire as cathartic and healing: "The only way to get rid of a temptation is to yield to it. Resist it, and your soul grows sick with longing for the thing it has forbidden to itself, for what its monstrous laws have made monstrous and unlawful."

Aschenbach, who denies the body in deference to reason, is akin to a man who has consciously recast himself in bronze, believing the gesture to be manly, pure and moral. But it turns out to be entirely forced. Pan, or Dionysus, the god of primal instinct, rises up and overwhelms him. After the dream, his Spartanism crumbles and he openly pursues the beautiful boy who has shattered his self-possession. Aschenbach rouges his cheeks, dyes his hair to make himself more attractive, but still no word passes between them. The collapse of his principles is followed by the collapse of his body. After digesting infected strawberries, he spends a bad night in the hotel. Next morning, feeling sick and giddy, he goes down to the beach and watches Tadzio playing beside the sand-bar. In his final moment of consciousness, "the pale and lovely Summoner out there smiled at him and beckoned ..."

The Heart of Darkness

Death in Venice came out in 1912. A still earlier work expressing forebodings about man's dual nature was Joseph Conrad's *Heart of Darkness* (1902). Of the Polish author Bertrand Russell wrote, "I felt ... that he thought of a civilised and morally tolerable life as a dangerous walk on a thin crust of barely cool lava which at any moment might break and let the unwary sink into fiery depths."

The novella describes a journey up the Congo into dark, morally polluted waters. The narrator, Marlow, has undertaken the journey to find Mr Kurtz, the eloquent, heroic agent of an ivory trading company. Sent by Kurtz's adoring fiancé, he travels in the company of callous traders who are motivated by personal profit and take pot shots at the natives on the banks. The party arrives at the trading station and Marlow finds his way to the deserted company offices. There he meets Mr Kurtz, an emaciated parody of his former self, utterly burnt out. His recently drafted report for the Society of the Suppression of Savage Customs begins with measured fluency but ends with blood-lust and paranoia – "Exterminate all the brutes." Marlow compares his physical appearance to "an animated image of death carved out of old ivory," for he has become hard and licentious. He dies ravaged by drink and fever; his last words are, "The horror! The horror!"

Aside from a boundless self-esteem, Kurtz has little in common with Aschenbach. But the contrast is illuminating. Aschenbach is an artist. Whatever power he wields will be restricted to his circle of admirers. The expression of his submerged instincts can only lead to personal downfall. But Kurtz is a man of action who holds sway over the lives of natives. European civilisation has shaped his sensibilities. Therefore his folly – his corrupted instincts – are expressed in terms of human victims. Where Aschenbach merely plunges into a dream of bloodlust, Kurtz physically presides over "unspeakable rites", savouring the darkness of the soul, yet retaining the old flamboyant rhetoric.

Marlow asks of these traders and empire-builders: What do these men bow down to? What ideal sustains their activities? The answer is none. They have regressed to the beast, yet, because they are ostensibly superior, cannot abandon themselves to orgy like the Africans they persecute. They cannot even acknowledge that they are barbaric. The primal energy is strained through filters of greed and self-righteousness and emerges in calculated, mechanised slaughter and exploitation. Kurtz's soul struggles against the conquering darkness:

> The shade of the original Kurtz frequented the bedside of the hollow sham, whose fate it was to be buried presently in the mould of primeval earth. But both the diabolic love and the unearthly hate of the mysteries it had penetrated fought for the possession of that soul satiated with primitive emotions, avid of lying fame, of sham distinction, of all the appearances of success and power.

It is likely Conrad himself encountered a prototype Kurtz during his Congo journey in the figure of Léon Rom, a trader who became chief of the Stanley Falls Station. In 1895, according to a British traveller, Rom had a flowerbed decorated with the skulls of men, women and children who had aroused his ire in some way. But it should be borne in mind that *Heart of Darkness* is not a novel about the oppression of the Congolese, but more a demonstration of how far a civilised person will sink if stripped of the trappings of civilisation. Pan, in Conrad's eyes, is a manifestation of a wholly evil, outer-directed energy and, although the god is never alluded to by name, essentially "the horror" to which he descends is that which afflicted and haunted Aschenbach: the knowledge that, in pursuit of some occult gratification, men are prepared to do anything.

In the view of Crowley, the 'heart of darkness' would be no more than the libido of the Unconscious or the suppressed "true will of the inmost self". Disagreeing with Freud's strictures on the 'errors' of the Unconscious, he accused the world-renowned psychologist of re-working the myth of 'original sin'. Abnormalities only indicated the subject was at war with himself. If this duality was resolved, the morbid or violent symptoms would disappear and the personality develop naturally. The other side of Kurtz is epitomised by his docile feminine adorer, the girl he left behind, or the sexuality he fled from and avenged in acts of brutality and torture. Kurtz's cruelties are inspired by a godlike, unnatural pride. In putting up resistance, he finds himself a slave to the 'heart of darkness' or the perverted 'will' that works upon his dreadful egotism and finds expression in acts of mindless atrocity.

Conrad wrote other tales dealing with nervous breakdown, descent into barking madness inspired by a glimpse behind the veil, or the revelation that behind the world of appearance there lurks a force which is menacing and baneful. An effective late example is *Karain*, the story of a proud Malay chieftain who accidentally shoots his best friend, Matara, while trying to retrieve Matara's sister – a village beauty – from her relationship with a Dutch planter. After the murder, Karain is haunted by the shade of his companion. He is unable to rest – each step he takes is dogged. The only man able to lay the ghost is a holy man who accompanies him everywhere. When the old man passes away, Karain visits the crew of an English ship. He pleads that they should provide him with a piece of magic to protect him from the spectre. Initially the crew are dumbfounded. But then they respond by offering him a small Jubilee sixpence engraved with Victoria Regina, the "Great Queen" of Britain. Karain accepts the charm. The ghost is laid and the sailors return to England.

Later two of them meet up in the Strand and discuss Karain and the war in Malaya which has recently broken out. They speculate about the nature of the terror experienced by the chieftain. Then one of the seamen points across the street – "Our ears were filled with a headlong shuffle and beat of rapid footsteps and an underlying rumour – a rumour vast, faint, pulsating, as of panting breaths, beating hearts, of gasping voices ..." A version of what haunted Karain haunts those streets, a kind of unfocussed dread – "It is there, it pants, it runs, it rolls; it is strong; it would smash you if you didn't look out ..."

So a sensational tale of love and brotherhood, betrayal and revenge, broadens into a vision of an inimical something at the pulse of life. London may seem solid, but hiding behind its crowds and clanging trams, its veils of soot and oppressive facades, is the formless 'all', the melting-pot of chaos from which order, symmetry and civilisation are wrested.

The Disturber of Traffic

Conrad's contemporary, Rudyard Kipling, also wrote 'Pan' stories hinting at a nameless horror lurking beneath the surface of things, capable of driving people to insanity. This is seen in *The Disturber of Traffic*, a story of a lighthouse keeper on the Flores Strait. Studying the sea, he detected "long streaks of white running inside it; like wallpaper that hadn't been properly pasted up ..." Soon these streaks begin whipping around inside his head – dislodging his perceptions – and he starts to identify them with ships. He believes there are far too many ships/streaks passing the straits and puts up a huge wrecker buoy to stop them. This works until the ruse is exposed and a ship is sent to investigate. When the crew find him, he is stark naked and gibbering nonsense. Eventually he returns to England, gets cured and spends his time praying at the Salvation Army, still frightened lest the running streaks return.

One cannot pin too precise a meaning here, but Kipling appears to be suggesting that the streaks or flashes are a projection of something more disturbing. Their hynotic monotony *possesses* the lighthouse keeper. He is overwhelmed – *panicked* – by a dizzying procession that transfixes him. At the end he is driven mad – reduced to a naked savage! – after being confronted with 'Pan' or a pattern that is fertile, chaotic, inescapable, yet of which he is unaccountably part. The flashes and streaks make brief, frantic signals and then vanish, just as an individual life goes out and is instantly replaced. The keeper realises that it is only the rhythm, the pattern, that matters and not the elements that compose it, and that knowledge wounds and stupefies his thoughts.

Since *Death in Venice, Heart of Darkness, Karain* and *The Disturber of Traffic,* countless other texts have traced a similar graph of initiative and decline. In a sense, they hint at the cul de sac into which the celebration of Pan leads. If one is prepared to smash through every restraint, one's personality will become formless, fleeting, meaningless, like the running streaks that disorientated the lighthouse keeper.

And, of course, democratic cultures require a curbing of the instinctual drives in order to function efficiently. This point is repeated in William Golding's *Lord of the Flies* (1954), a story of a group of schoolboys cast ashore on a desert island. Step by step, the artifices of a prep-school upbringing dissolve; their behaviour degenerates into squabbles and power struggles. Finally they shrug off Christian values and sacrifice Piggy, the only boy who attempts to invoke their better selves, and fall prey to horror and superstition, ending up as acolytes of the *Lord of the Flies* who presides over the corruption of the flesh. Golding conceived this dystopian fable during the dark months of the last war. "Anyone who moved through those years," he wrote in *The Hot Gates*, "without understanding that man produces evil as a bee produces honey, must have been blind or wrong in the head."

Arthur Machen

The horror! the horror! The dying cry of Kurtz who had peered into the heart of darkness, the rancid crypts of the human soul, finds an echo in Conrad's contemporary, Arthur Machen, a former member of the Golden Dawn who saw Crowley as "a fiend in human form". Machen lacked Conrad's penetrating irony but shared his obsession with human evil which he identified with the submerged spirit of Pan. His first novel *The Great God Pan* had a cover designed by Aubrey Beardsley. It begins with an experiment in brain surgery during which the patient's features become "hideously convulsed" – she has seen "ineffable, impalpable evil" or a vision of Pan. The goat-god enters her body and mysteriously impregnates her. After giving birth to the girl, who is christened Helen, she dies in a state of idiocy. Helen is brought up by a family in Wales who live near some Roman ruins. Frequently she visits the woods, along with two other children, both of whom become disturbed. At one point Helen is seen in the woods playing with "a strange naked man". In time she moves to London, becoming involved with a string of men, whose lives are ruined by her influence. Helen makes herself deeply acquainted with the distractions of Soho "where even the natives, hardened as they were, shuddered and grew sick in telling ... the nameless infamies which were laid to her charge." Finally Villiers, a man whose friend had committed suicide by association with Helen, learns of her true nature and takes her a rope. Helen kills herself and her form changes many times, from sex to sex, animal to animal, until she is reduced to primal slime – a reversal of the evolutionary process.

The fact that Helen Vaugham reverts to a kind of loathsome slime is significant, for a horror of jelly-like secretions may have its origin in sexual loathing. As a motif, it reaches its climax in the *Novel of the White Powder* which is part of a longer work called *The Three Impostors*. It concerns an upright young man of a respectable military family called Francis Leicester who became ill owing to his over-studious disposition. He consults a doctor who prescribes a nerve tonic. The chemist mixes up a harmless-looking white powder which Francis takes with initially agreeable results. The young man begins to socialise and enjoy himself until he is transformed into a hardened debauchee. As a result, his hand becomes "a black stump" and ultimately he dissolves into "oily unctious bubbles". The reason for his decline is that the white powder was actually an extract from the 'Vinum Sabbati', the evil grail out of which the witches drank, quite possibly a Gnostic brew, for in the *Pistis Sophia* the apostle Thomas asks Jesus: "We have heard that there are men on this earth who take the sperm of men and the menstrual fluids of women and mix them together and eat them with lentils ... Is that allowable or not?" Jesus' reply was in the negative.

Hence Francis relived the myth of the fall, drowning in putrid sexual ecstasy like Adam and Eve, only in more concentrated and virulent form. Although the characters do not rise above mere names, the story is stylistically accomplished and the undisclosed abominations are counterpointed by a view of the universe as "a tremendous sacrament; a mystic, ineffable force and energy, veiled an outward form of matter ..."

Yet even allowing for the stridencies of Victorian morality, it is curious that an author who ably translated Cassanova's memoirs should repeatedly hint that the penalty for sexual indulgence (which, after all, is only part of nature's sacrament) is to become a liquid excrescence. In some ways, Machen's world is a fishbowl of lurid fancies alleviated by a feeling for landscape. Seldom does he depict phenomena in a state of causal innocence. An urge to taint things or apply warpaint too thickly gets the better of him. He achieves his vision by wilfully ignoring that which would seem to disrupt it – by circumventing the more obvious workings of the world. His prose – very fine at its best – appeals to those who value a measured elegance of syntax and Pateresque felicities of phrasing.

Like Crowley and Lawrence, Machen was fascinated by sex in its demonic aspect. He retained *fin de siecle* notions of purple sins and unspeakable practices and consequently we are more tantalised than enlightened as to the precise nature of the 'foul' rites at which he hints. Yet from his stories most readers would gather that orgiastic activity is seriously debilitating and overly sexual types are liable to be reduced to foul slime or primal soup.

Machen defined Pan as "all things mingled, the form of all things but devoid of all form ... " So what accounts for his pathological loathing of this shapeless yet dreadful deity? The genesis of the story, he tells us, was a memory of a landscape: "I saw the lonely house between the dark forest and the silver river, and years after I wrote *The Great God Pan* in an endeavour to pass on the vague, indefinable sense of awe and mystery and terror that I had received."

Machen's real horror was the chemical mire from which men and women evolved, a loathing echoed in a fastidious shrinking from the bodily secretions with which Crowley liked to play during his magical rites. Having no ideal form, the god stood for the denial of necessity and substance. Pan was the void of choice, the annulment of presence and ego-centred striving. In the ethos of such a god, neither murder nor rape nor sexual depravity had heightened significance. Everything was allowed in that formless cauldron in which values and meanings are dissolved.

The Wrong Shape

Surprisingly it was not Arthur Machen but Crowley's old opponent, G.K. Chesterton, who thought so deeply about shapelessness, nothingness and what it implied that he managed to go beyond mere impressionism and translate the problem in fictional terms, as he did in the detective story *The Wrong Shape*, in which Father Brown investigates the murder of the aesthete Quinton who is a collector of weird and vivid Eastern artefacts.

As gripping as the mechanics of the tale is Father Brown's implicit criticism of paganism. For during the course of the investigation, his attention is drawn to an exquisitely-wrought oriental dagger. Father Brown praises the colours but objects to the shape of the implement: "It's the wrong shape in the abstract. Don't you ever feel that about Eastern art? The colours are intoxicatingly lovely, but the shapes are mean and bad – deliberately mean and bad. I have seen wicked things in a Turkish carpet."

What Father Brown is arguing is that Eastern art, with its rich swirls and "blinding embroideries", is 'immoral', an attractive chaos, with patterns that flow into each other. Thus the forms merge, and in that merging all boundaries are dissolved. By analogy, this is like a man who cannot trace the line of separation between good and evil. A further implication is that, in Hinduism, evil does not exist as such, only nothingness and shapelessness, as opposed to Western Catholic Christianity which maintains a strong sense of form or of the 'right shape'. Therefore a deity, like Pan, in whom "all things mingled", is naturally incapable of exerting spiritual authority.

Later Flambeau goes out in the garden. He confronts the mysterious Indian Quinton had employed for some obscure purpose and asks whether he wants anything:

> Quite slowly, like a great ship turning into harbour, the great yellow face turned and, looked at last over its white shoulder. They were startled to see that its yellow eyelids were quite sealed, as in sleep. 'Thank you,' said the face in excellent English. 'I want nothing.' Then, half opening the lids, so as to show a slit of opalescent eyeball, he repeated, 'I want nothing.' Then he opened his eyes wide with a startling stare, said, 'I want nothing', and went rustling away into the rapidly darkening garden.

The Indian – though sinisterly drawn – is quite innocent of the crime, as it turns out, but the impression created is of an unnerving inscrutability.

Separate Stars: Crowley and Lawrence

While writers like Mann, Machen, Conrad, Kipling and Chesterton feared and doubted Pan, or the instinctual, 'shapeless' aspect of man, D.H. Lawrence took the opposite view, writing novels that translate all the nuances and tremors of the awakened senses. Long passages reaffirm the "Dionysiac or Aphrodisiac ecstasy" which he believed modern industrial civilisation had lost. Men had ceased to think and feel with their bodies; the natural flow between the lower and higher sexual centres had been arrested. The end result was either sex-fiends or desiccated intellects. Such behaviour was engendered by fear, and the "root-fear of all mankind" was fear of the phallus. Because of an inability to relate frankly to their animal selves, men had become spiritually warped like Conrad's ivory traders. They should be able to openly embrace the dissolution of the consciousness as it takes a plunge into primitive ecstasy:

> Ah yes, to be passionate like a Bacchante, like a Bacchanal fleeing through the woods, to call on Iacchos, the bright phallos that had no independent personality behind it, but was pure god-servant to the woman! The man, the individual, let him not dare intrude. He was but a temple-servant, the bearer and keeper of the bright phallos, her own.
> (*Lady Chatterley's Lover*)

But Lawrence also recognised that the energy of Pan, collectivised and operating through the wrong channels, can take on a far more dangerous expression. "What I did through individuals," he wrote to Waldo Frank, "the world has done through the war." Lawrence identified in the First World War the spirit of ancient, destructive frenzy on a grand scale. Man was full of phallus-hatred and disgust, so the logical thing to do was to create engines to destroy the temple of the flesh. In fact, all the sadistic ruses of the past, the flagellations, whippings, crucifixions and tortures, expressed the same thing: that man basically hated his body. The First World War was no exception. No catharsis was involved in this collective suicidal gesture, only pyramids of corpses and gas-damaged lungs. Lawrence despised the pointlessness of the Armaggedon of 1914 but hoped that it would sweep away the old order and usher in better times.

He knew all too well that urban man is not intrinsically more evil than tribal man. Soft primitivism, which has its roots in thinkers like Rousseau, is often promoted as a corrective to urban corruption. But many anthropological studies show tribal groups are as hidebound with taboos and stratifications as European or American communities. There is nothing innately good about natives of a jungle or desert, although they may appear more admirable because their power is not technologically extended. When an Aborigine or Kalahari pygmy feels an uprush of instinctual frenzy, the need to express the night-side of his nature, the outcome is contained within a limited framework. When urban-dwellers choose to rehearse their primitive blood lusts, the technology of destruction wielded by the military priesthood on their behalf ensures that the consequences are spectacularly dreadful.

Another problem is that any theory promoting the instinctual drives inevitably has painful social implications. Lawrence's central idea developed into a gospel of evolutionary fascism which states that, "as far as existence goes, that life-species is the highest which can devour, or destroy or subjugate every other life-species against which it is pitted in contest." The argument denies all concept of social justice. Whoever is the strongest is also the best or ennobled by the 'Holy Ghost':

> Vitality depends upon the clue of the Holy Ghost inside a creature, a man, a nation, a race. When the clue goes, the vitality goes. And the Holy Ghost seeks everywhere for a new incarnation, and subordinates the old to the new. You will know that any creature or race is still alive with the Holy Ghost, when it can subordinate the lower creatures or races, and assimilate them into a new incarnation.
>
> (*Phoenix II*, 467)

There is an inherent contradiction of which Lawrence must have been aware. If he believed that the 'Holy Ghost' was destined to dominate, then he might better have placed his faith in the huge corporations and industrial complexes which ultimately devoured the native cultures.

Every Man and Every Woman is a Star

Women in Love has been judged one of the finest of Lawrence's novels, although it never manages to work out in practical terms the problem of how men and women can express their different natures and yet remain happy and complete within a marriage. In one of the interminable discussions between Birkin and Ursula, the latter tries to define his ideal relationship:

> What I want is a strange conjunction with you; not meeting and mingling – you are quite right – but an equilibrium, a pure balance of two single beings: as the stars balance each other.
>
> *(Women in Love)*

Coincidentally or otherwise, Lawrence was expressing the same idea as Crowley or 'Every Man and Woman is a Star', implying individuals were discrete units, each possessing the seed of a unique Platonic 'will' or destiny which required nurturing and pointing. Like Lawrence, his philosophy was a weird mixture of anarchy and authoritarianism. In his volatile, intermittently blasphemous *Book of the Law*, strictures like "the slaves shall serve" grind against notions of the essential "godhead" – no doubt Crowley would argue that certain souls satisfy their deepest needs by running errands for their superiors. At the back of some editions are appended a list of his rulings headed by the Nietzschean statement, 'There is no god but man':

> Man has the right to think what he will:
> to speak what he will:
> to write what he will:
> to draw, paint, carve, etch, mould, build as he will:
> to dress as he will.

The sequence ends ominously, "Man has the right to kill those who would thwart these rights".

Lawrence would have agreed with most of these rulings. He might even have sympathised with the strident tone, for he was inclined to adopt the same when hounded by censorship and prudery. There is a possibility that he met Crowley – perhaps at the house of Gwendolen Otter – but there is no record of any contact between the two. Grace Crawford loaned Lawrence a copy of Crowley's anthology 'Ambergris' (1910) – but he dismissed it with an "Ugh!" It seems he found disagreeable the scattered allusions to things like dyspeptic whales and feline secretions. On the other hand, both authors were highly rated by P.R. Stephensen, a director of the Mandrake Press. 'Inky Stephensen', as he was known, was a young Australian, a likeable, fair-minded apostle of freedom and frankness in literary matters. He published *The Paintings of D.H Lawrence* (1929), creating a salacious splash in the popular press, as well as Crowley's *Confessions*, the novel *Moonchild* and short story collection *The Stratagem*. Crowley dedicated his variations upon themes of Frazer *Golden Twigs* (as opposed to *Golden Bough*) to David Herbert Lawrence although the latter did not seem eager to trade commendations. "I'm a bit sorry you've got Aleister Crowley at such heavy tonnage," he wrote to Stephensen, "I feel his day is rather over."

Ideologically they were close. Like Lawrence, Crowley was deeply concerned with people's psychic make-up. He thought that people's sexuality had been stunted. By suppressing the liberty of the individual, western civilisation had got out of hand and regulations, taboos and pruderies were imposed by such institutions as the Church and State. Resenting moral straitjackets, he finally evolved a religion based upon what he termed life, love, liberty and light. Its central credo 'Do What Thou Wilt' placed emphasis upon the individual discovering his own unique destiny which, being perfectly attuned to his character, is also the will of God.

Contrary to popular opinion, it did not signify unbridled indulgence (although Crowley's own life often epitomises that trait), but that men and women should subject themselves to rigorous personal disciplines and find their own true wills or magical destinies. The objection to this goes: 'Yes, but what if my true will clashes with that of my neighbour?' The answer is that true wills, being intrinsically harmonious, do not collide. Like a star, determined by laws of celestial mechanics, each has its own precise course, hence the 'star' stands for the uniqueness of each separate self.[2] These maxims were the basis for Crowley's own 'ideal' community, the Abbey of Thelema in Cefalu, Sicily which, like Plato's model, was run upon strict, hierarchic lines, although Crowley dismissed contemporary despotic ideologies with thumping alliteration:

> Ferocious Fascism, crackling Communism,
> equally frauds, cavort crazily over the globe.
> They are hemming us in.
> They are abortive births of the Child, the
> New Aeon of Horus.
> Liberty stirs in the womb of Time.
> (*Book of the Law* – Preface)

Adopting Egyptian models to explain himself, he divided history into three periods. The age before the birth of Christ was characterised by the dominance of Isis or the Mother Goddess. The second age was the Age of Osiris when matriarchies vanished and Jehovah or 'God the Father' reigned supreme. The third age, beginning in the year 2000, was the Age of Horus or the Son. Hence Crowley regarded various 20th-century fads – vegan cults, nudism, theosophy and spiritualism – as freak, sportive growths preceding the full definition of the World Spirit, rather like a child adopting and experimenting with various disguises and postures before hardening into adulthood.

Pure Dry Air of Mexico

Seeking to sanctify the sexual act by employing it during religious ceremonies, Crowley was caustic about England, "this god-awful country where one has to sleep with one's penis under one's pillow", for he styled the phallus as the "godhead", the connection between man and the planets, the nodal point at which matter and spirit unite. Lawrence, although not a Thelemite, expressed an identical outlook in *The First Lady Chatterley* (1944). He, too, believed in achieving an intimacy that went beyond personality and reached out to some cosmic principle. "The knowledge of the movement of the stars and the laws of celestial gravitation," he wrote, "is wonderful, but the beauty of the stars in their motion is still more wonderful and it is the penis which connects us sensually with the planets. But for the penis we would never know the loveliness of Sirius or the categorical difference between a pomegranate and an india-rubber ball."

Lawrence means that the penis is the generative power of the cosmos in microcosm and reconciles the intimate with the distant. If his language seems highflown, slightly ludicrous, it is probably because, in the tradition of the west, the penis is regarded as a comic, slightly impudent device – the 'tool' of the clown – and not quite up to all that starry solemnity.

Likewise, in his essay *Pan in America*, Lawrence evokes the phallic image of the pine tree, "fierce and bristling" and "turpentiney" as standing for the complex interplay of forces that the god represents. Even Mellors, the gamekeeper, supported this view, nominating the goat-god as the most suitable divinity for the masses. "They ought to learn to be naked and handsome," he said, "and to sing in a mass and dance the old group dances ... Then they wouldn't need money ... the mass of people oughtn't even try to think, because they can't! They should be alive and frisky, and acknowledge the great god Pan. He's the only god for the masses ..." (*Lady Chatterley's Lover*)

Among other things which he thought appropriate to the New Age, Crowley sought to revive the Dionysiac ecstasy, the dance of Pan, where the consciousness is blanked out, leaving an upsurge of frenzy and exultation:

> Thrill with lissome lust of light,
> O Man! My Man!
> Come careering out of the night
> Of Pan! Io Pan!
> ('Hymn to Pan')

So far as Crowley was concerned, Pan had two aspects, the careless, unscrupulous All-Begetter and the god of "energised enthusiasm", or sexual passion canalised to create vibrations on otherworldly planes. Like Lawrence, Crowley identified a self-regulating aspect to the body which, if mastered, harmonised perfectly with the psyche. Falling apart or succumbing to headstrong behaviour did not matter particularly. It was just indicative of the ebb and flow of the will, sometimes lying low, sometimes surging up and taking over:

His diatribes against modern civilisation resemble those of Lawrence. He was against things like make-up and face creams – anything that created an artificial layering – and preferred nakedness to the lacy enticements of the boudoir. Like Rupert Birkin, the masculine pivot of *Women in Love*, he was drawn to anal intercourse – to exploring "the deepest, oldest shame" and "the root of darkness" – and preferred peasant communities where industry and neurosis had not tainted the psyche and 'Magick' could be effectively harnessed. "In the pure dry air of Mexico," he wrote in his *Confessions*, "with its spiritual energy unexhausted and uncontaminated as it is in cities, it was astonishingly easy to produce satisfactory results."

Lawrence found Mexico equally inspiring. In *The Plumed Serpent* he portrays the religion of Quetzalcoatl as preferable to European models, being sun-inspired, sexually frank, organic rather than mechanical. Quetzalcoatl is god of the lightning, wind and rain, and the Morning and Evening Star. Like Pan, he reaches out to the snake in the body of man and lends him his potency. "Gods should be iridescent, like the rainbow in the storm," Kate says, "but the god-stuff roars eternally, like the sea, with too vast a sound to be heard."

But gods are also demanding of placation and, in common with Crowley, something in Lawrence was drawn to the brutalities of blood-pacts and sacrifice. He once embarrassed John Middleton Murry by suggesting that they become blood-brothers and wrote sympathetically of bull-fighting. This interest is well dramatised in the Mexican story *The Woman Who Rode Away* which begins by describing a couple who live in a barricaded hacienda in a remote province. The woman is married to a hardworking man of principle. He admires her but is spiritually a bachelor. One day she breaks out and rides away to find the Indians who lie behind "those great blank hills".

She locates a lost tribe who solemnly take her in, feed, bathe and clothe her. Fascinated by their grave, reverential attitude, she learns their motives are not only non-sexual but non-chivalric, for she is being nurtured as an offering to the sun. "White people," a young Indian tells her, "they know nothing. They are like children, always with toys. We know the sun, and we know the moon. And we say, when a white woman sacrifice herself to our gods, then our gods will begin to make the world again, and the white man's gods will fall to pieces." There are moments of panic and terror, but the Indians soothe her "with their silent, sexless, powerful physical presence."

During her last hours, she is stripped, washed and fumigated and led to a cave behind a drooping fang of ice. Wrapped in robe of blue, the wind's colour, her destiny is to be ceremonially stabbed in the cave when the sun strikes the icicle. The Indians' eyes remain compassionless – fanatically fixed on the rising orb. The story has been called "a triumph of empathic imagination", which it undoubtedly achieves in its portrayal of the Indians, but there is a disquieting element which hints that the woman at some subterranean level finds such an end acceptable. Her old life had been an ignominious form of sacrifice to a man who never properly understood her; she had ridden away into a new life only to find herself under an immense phallic icicle waiting to be stabbed. Is this any sort of improvement? Lawrence manipulates the reader by prose that is all bewitched acquiescence rather than intellectual analysis, so that becoming a sacrificial pawn in a male-dominated religion seems a logical outcome to a life lacking a strong *raison d'etre*.

If he had been aware of it, the ferocious pessimism of this fable would have struck a sympathetic chord in Crowley, who was himself a fanatical sun-cultist, using women repeatedly in life and fiction as a vessel or instrument. So far as he was concerned, the less volatile and mentally developed they were, the better they would function as mediums between himself and the higher deities. In the main the practices of the abbey at Cefalu consisted of an extended orgy with The Beast crying out at the point of climax, "For the establishment of the law of Thelema!" Even the streak of bisexuality in Lawrence's nature would not have been a source of mystification to Crowley, who well understood the feminine in man, since he possessed it in good measure himself. There was a bumptious egotism in the magician that masked a wounded pride and masochistic desire to debase himself, and Lawrence, too, admired forceful and challenging women like Frieda whose Dionysiac urges seem to have exceeded his own.

Footnotes

[1] Neuburg honoured the goat-god with his muse – his second poetry collection *The Triumph of Pan* was one of the better poetic achievements of 1910.

[2] Marcus Aurelius noted of the Pythagoreans that, first thing in the morning, they would look at the sky, "to remind ourselves of beings who forever accomplish their work according to the same laws and in the same fashion, and of their orderliness, purity and nakedness, for nothing veils a star".

3

Wine of Dionysus
The Poetry of Aleister Crowley

> I bring ye wine from above
> From the vats of storied sun;
> For everyone of ye love
> And life for everyone.
> (Dionysus – from *Orpheus*)

We have glanced at the cult of Pan to show that Crowley was less of a literary leper in his stance and outlook than many might imagine. He explored both the pleasure zones and zones of metaphysical terror implied by the hybrid deity he adopted. If his manner of presenting his ideas was so eccentric as to distract from their relevance, stripped of their magical trappings, the attitudes are not dissimilar to those expressed by characters in the mainstream novels of Lawrence, Huxley and Forster – a 'trust-your-senses' and 'go-back-to-nature-and-healthy-pagan-ways' message that has surfaced in different guises since Rousseau. (The question, 'Did *he* ever achieve the 'good life' he tried to persuade others to adopt?' has already provided a biographer's field day.) In Crowley's ideal community, personal frictions were eliminated, their religion enabling them to harmoniously pursue divergent paths.

This gospel of freedom and inward joy was directed at the whole human race and infuses a great deal of his poetry. Pan was a god of the people and Crowley tried to 'reach' the people, albeit by implausible methods. His esoteric poetry was cast in the 'popular' Victorian manner of plays, dialogues and lyrics. Yet it remains neglected, perhaps owing to it displaying skills literary critics – if not necessarily the reading public – have long ceased to admire: internal rhymes, heavy alliteration and a classically clotted vocabulary guaranteed to find the average reference book wanting. The numerous volumes, sumptuously bound with Japanese vellum wrappers and titles like 'Ambergris' and 'Gargoyles', reveal a fascinating – if somewhat muddy – literary backwater. Poems remarkable for their monotony, variety and invention offset each other in curious fashion. Philosophical musings jostle with squibs of humour. Apocalyptic ravings – wildly staked out with exclamation marks – rub shoulders with highflown mystical lyrics. Naughty old-fashioned drinking songs furnish wry epitaphs on the passionate love sonnets that precede them. What we find is a jarring collusion of impulses which are not always artistically resolved, even in the context of a single poem.

So far, there has been no single sustained effort to place the poetry of Aleister Crowley in a literary context. The subject has been broached by scholars such as Martin Booth and Stoddard Martin in *Orthodox Heresy*, but their judgements have been wary and non-committal, as if they prefer to leave the issue open-ended. In the following pages, I attempt an overview of Crowley's work, accounting for its worst and best elements. The approach will not satisfy the purist who demands that criticism be purely textual, for it will encompass personal aspects of the subject's life. A certain amount of biographical route-work is, I think, necessary.

Inevitably themes overlap and repeat themselves, but if one was to attempt an overview of his poetic œuvre, one can say his early work fits the *fin de siècle* mode: dark, tragic, blood-smeared musings like 'Aceldama' (1898) and 'Jezebel' (1898) mixed with sunnier, lightly erotic material after the manner of Swinburne and religious yearnings, notably 'The Tale of Archais' (1898) and the metaphysical 'Songs of the Spirit' (1898). Later there came a deepening of subject matter with the magical drama 'Tanhäuser' (1902), Browningesque disquisitions on Buddhism, Anti-Christian dialogues and passionate sonnet-sequences like 'Alice – An Adultery' (1905). An Egyptian period was inaugurated by the *Soul of Osiris* (1901), and that mythology became increasingly important to his later choice of imagery and philosophy.

Much was written during this first phase (1895-1905), blasphemous, reverential and erotic, but not always memorable. During the second phase (1905-1915), he achieved what may be seen as his best work, developing a flexible, erratic style, shedding the reverie for a more idiosyncratic voice, rhapsodic, mocking and learned, but often surprisingly 'contemporary' and sophisticated in content, despite using sexual imagery drawn from arcana or anthropological sources. (A fair amount of satiric verse was written at this period, too, but it tended to ram its target like a cockchafer rather than sting it like a wasp.) The quality, as always, was uneven, the morbid, worthless and perverse, set alongside the mellifluous and inspired. Ephemera such as 'Alexandra' (1905) – a mock-courtly tribute to a fashionable princess that is wreathed in coils of gushing exegesis – were clanked through the presses along with sanctimonious posies like 'Amphora' (1908), an assortment of rather well-handled hymns to the Virgin Mary that drew praise from the Catholic press.

Crowley loved to blend the reek of altar incense with scatological gas and the priapic sweat of unadulterated pornography and, in this tendency of his poetry and writing, he reached his apogee in the sonnet-sequence 'Clouds Without Water' (1909), in his marriage hymns 'Rosa Mundi' (1905), 'Rosa Coeli' (1907) and 'Rosa Decidua' (1910), in 'The Scented Garden of Abdullah' (1910), in the Russian poems (1913) that climaxed in 'Hymn to Pan'. Other triumphs were the teasingly paradoxical *Book of Lies* (1913) and the mystery play 'The Ship' (1913) which first appeared in *The Equinox*. Next came the period in America (1914 – 1919), during which he was employed to write propaganda for the German-funded magazines *Fatherland* and *The International*. This gave rise to many essays, both of magical and general interest, notably 'Cocaine', 'Ethyl Oxide' and 'The Old Absinthe House'. To this period belongs the novel *Moonchild*, written in New Orleans in 1918, but not published until 1929. On returning to Europe, he published *Diary of a Drug Fiend* (1922) and his magnum opus *Magick in Theory and Practice* (1930) and the lucid, accessible *Little Essays Towards Truth* (1938) as well as the erudite and innovative *The Book of Thoth* (1944). Owing either to lack of funds or inspiration, the poetry collections petered out and, when he did write verses, they revisited themes of old, with incursions into doggerel, drollery and patriotism.

During the Second World War, he abandoned Germanic affiliations and roundly praised Britain's war effort. Although he remained an occasional poet – his last collection 'Olla' appeared in 1946 – he did not stay abreast of his younger contemporaries, styling them as an assortment of faceless dandies. "Poetry is the geyser of the Unconscious," he wrote, "the intelligible musical expression of the

Real whose mirror is the phenomenal Universe." The fashionable poets had been seduced by the Zeitgeist or the spirit of the age, "a mercurial element corrosive of true gold" that would break down their reputations. "T.S. Eliot, Ezra Pound, W.H. Auden," he concluded, "have log-rolled their heads and their styles until Bloomsbury, Brixton, Balham, Bournemouth and Baaston believe them to be poets. Pedantry and precocity, push and peacockry, are not the stuff of song."

This impatience with poetic standards other than his own had been evident in early works like *The Psychology of Hashish* where, dismissing "superficial twaddlers" like Tennyson and Longfellow, he adopted a brisk laying-down-of-the-law tone, out of sorts with the hedonistic experimentation he elsewhere espoused: "The so-called poet with his vague dreams and ideals is indeed no better than a harmless lunatic; the true poet is the worker, who grips life's throat and wrings out its secret, who selects austerely and composes concisely, whose work is as true and clean as razor-steel, albeit its sweep is vaster and swifter than the sun's!"

Crowley had certainly gripped life's throat but how many immortal lines had resulted from the act of violence is questionable.

Borderlands of Sanity

Up to date, advocates for his poetry have been few. Some writers have dismissed it as entirely lacking in literary quality. Constantine Fitzgibbon called it "execrable verse". John Symonds grudgingly acknowledged some talent, adding that he lacked the equipment for the "higher flights" of poetry. Colin Wilson summed him up as a "fluent poet" who lacked "verbal discipline". Somerset Maugham acknowledged his cleverness and talent but added that he was "grossly imitative" of Browning and Swinburne. Yeats conceded that, amid much cant and bad rhetoric, Crowley had written four lines of genuine verse.

Counteracting dismissals and sprinklings of faint praise are the views of several non-modernist critics who have praised Crowley highly. Some of his work was printed and reviewed in the *The Poetry Review* (edited by Harold Monro and castigated by Ezra Pound) but never on a regular basis. He had to find his own admirers, the most fulsome being the idiosyncratic Major General 'Boney' Fuller who, in a long essay *The Star in the West*, spoke of Crowley in the same breath as Jesus Christ, Bishop Berkeley, David Hume, Wolfgang Goethe and many another demi-god. Calmer and more reliable was the eloquent memoir of Charles Richard Cammell who concluded by saying that, if we discount the unsavoury aspects of Crowley's life, "we are finally left with a poet, fired with an imagination, gifted with an eloquence, singular, vehement and magnificent." Cammell admired Crowley because he embodied the traditional virtues, stepping in "just soon enough to have made himself secure in the history of English poetry before the revolution of crazy theories had created a Reign of Folly ..." Obviously Cammell, an able poet himself, did not admire the work of his avant-garde contemporaries: Eliot, Pound, Wallace Stevens and their imitators. He liked a poetry replete with rhyme, romance and mystic metaphor and, set beside the gorgeous vermilion pantaloons of Crowley's verses, the lines of the moderns seemed grey-suited, drab.

Similarly, the novelist friend of the Powys brothers, Louis Wilkinson, thought the sonnet-sequence 'Clouds Without Water' was "the most real and tremendous love poem since Shakespeare"; he also praised the energy and verve of several shorter pieces. Austin Harrison, who succeeded Ford Madox Ford as editor of *The English Review*, pronounced Crowley to be the finest living metrical poet since Swinburne and, in a sense, during that period Crowley was a very minor literary star. Reviews of his work were often polite, dubiously approving, yet affecting a comical detachment, as if they found his verses overly rapturous or bizarrely out of touch with the modern current.

In the literature of the Edwardian period he is an oddly ubiquitous figure, alternately dismissed and taken seriously. His magical personality had not yet taken hold. He had not established himself as "The Great Beast" or "King of the Shadow Realm" (Symonds). Neither was he the "Clown of the Occult" or "The Emperor of Hocus Pocus" (Richardson) or the founder of an innovative magical system. He was a rich young man about town, a poet and mountaineer who dabbled in Buddhism and the occult.

Even the popular magazine *John Bull*, before they set about the process of vilification, commented favourably on his work:

> Though he has never yet succeeded in catching the long ear of the public, he has been a voluminous writer, and has published works which fill many shelves. 'Konx Om Pax' and '777' have already been noted in this journal. To the uninitiated, they appear like the outpourings of an extremely clever lunatic, now solemnly revealing the secrets of the ancients, now running off into the most delightful nonsense, now assuming the role of preacher, now frankly pulling legs. His chief efforts have been concentrated upon the composition of really remarkable poetry. His rhythm and metre and melody are often quite perfect, and as a lord of language he runs Swinburne very close. Often he goes very near to the borderlands of insanity.

The reference to insanity had been picked up earlier, in a review of 'The Mother's Tragedy' (1899), which described the poems as "powerful, yet it is (we might also say) the power of insanity, so little it is under the author's control, so contorted and spasmodic it is, proceeding by vehement leaps and rushes of speech, abruptly checked by thick and struggling utterance." In other words, Crowley does not use language, but language rushes up and overwhelms him. He is a speck of dust caught up in a rhyming whirlwind and what he says is cloaked in a swarm of words that regretfully obscures rather than clarifies. This is where he fails as a poet. Ignoring Eliot's "intolerable wrestle with words", he grabs what is to hand and hopes it will somehow work out.

The other extreme of his emotional spectrum is a fixation with calm, solitude, absolute stillness, when the poet opens himself to the great without. He establishes an affinity with rocks, streams, empty spaces, an intimate topography of isolation, so that he may better understand his relationship with non-human things. "We come out of the dark and go back into the dark," wrote Thomas Mann, "and in between are the facts of our lives." In an attempt to understand that darkness, the poet, adrift on the earth, becomes the eternal wanderer, thrilled by the icy vastness of the starlit dome, inhaling the breath of God and perpetually craving the inaccessible. He sees the world and its fleeting forms as no more than shadow-play, captivating illusion. The way forward, he believes, is by mingling the solitude in himself with the soul of things or by exploring loneliness so profoundly that it expands into a sense of mystic communion:

> All things which are complete are solitary;
> The circling moon, the inconscient drift of stars,
> The central systems. Burn they, change they, vary?
> There is no motion beyond the eternal bars.
> Seasons and scars
> Stain not the planets, the unfathomed home,
> The spaceless, unformed faces in the dome ...
> ('The Hermit's Hymn to Solitude')

These lines, written beside the Falls of Foyers, show Crowley at his loftiest and most ethereal. Burns had celebrated the waterfall by the shores of Loch Ness nearly a hundred years earlier, but his pithy phrases – all moss, froth and saturation – attain nothing like the awestruck splendour of Crowley's meditation 'The Hermit's Hymn to Solitude', dedicated to his friend Allan Bennett. In essence a Buddhist hymn, it attempts to penetrate a state of spiritual suspension:

> All change, all motion, and all sounds are weakness!
> Man cannot bear the darkness which is death,
> Even that calm Christ, manifest in meekness,
> Cried on the cross and gave his ghostly breath,
> On the prick of death,
> Voice, for his passion bear not dare
> The inter-lunar, the abundant air ...

The poet dismisses any relationship between sorrow and solitude. One is being unhappy with one's loneliness; the other is rejoicing in it. He invokes the spirit of isolation so that the process will perfect and complete him:

> Draw me with cords that are not: witch me chanted
> Spells never heard nor open to the ear,
> Woven of silence, moulded in the haunted
> Houses where dead men linger year by year,
> I have no fear
> To tread the far irremeable way
> Beyond the paths and palaces of day ...

Beyond the impressionistic flourishes, one has little sense of the physical setting as one might get from Wordsworth or Keats. We are given a picture of the poet seated on a promontory taking in the waterfall as background scenery. Where Hopkins or Coleridge would have taken pains to anatomise the clustering flakes and bubbles of foam, the myriad textures of rock and moss, hoping to find some truth or clue, here they frame a self-sealed reverie. So far as Crowley is concerned, nature is a trigger rather than a meaning.

A Poetic Automaton

The 'Hermit's Hymn' is a Shelleyan piece in the sense that it all too quickly deserts the physical scene for interlunar space and, in any judicious assessment, what must be made plain is that much of Crowley's work is imitative of the 'rhapsodic' poets who enjoy being swept up into some ethereal realm or borne aloft on the wings of bliss: Shelley, Swinburne and Browning, the latter accounting for Crowley's deployment of satire and bumping, eccentric rhymes. He ingested the techniques of the first two so thoroughly that he unconsciously tethered his own development by producing a large quantity of superficial 'mood music' and trite pastiche. What he added of his own was a streak of sexual savagery and gloating necrophilia – effects that seldom work on the calm of the printed page. A second point is that his vocabulary is emphatically Late Romantic. He was one of the many who failed to see that overuse can exhaust the potentialities of certain rhymes. Vales and nightingales, kisses and blisses, wine and vine, trees and breeze, gem and diadem – such pairings, perfectly acceptable in 1800, were beginning to fall with a distinctly flat sound by 1900.

When composing satiric verse or heroic couplets, the influence of Browning makes Crowley more adventurous, rhyming 'sperm' with 'worm', 'rumours' with 'bloomers' and 'Aeschylus' with 'fleas kill us' – but this is hardly innovative. Striking a romantic mood, he often proves surprisingly uneven, especially in longer poems where the verses lose their impetus and become tangled and tiresome. For instance, 'Priestess of Panormita' (*Equinox*, Vol.1) begins:

> Hear me, Lord of the Stars!
>   For thee I have worshipped ever
> With stains and sorrows and scars,
>   With joyful, joyful endeavour.
> Hear me, O lilywhite goat!

> O crisp as a thicket of thorns,
> With a collar of gold for Thy throat,
> A scarlet bow for Thy horns!

This seems a vibrant start, and the verses race on, rounding up satyrs and fauns, the rape of a maid, the accidental killing of Hyacinthus by Apollo, until the rhythm becomes degraded and the language fatuous:

> Wherefore reborn as I am
> By a stream profane and foul,
> In the reign of the Tortured Lamb,
> In the realm of a sexless Owl,
> I am set apart from the rest,
> By meed of the mystic rune
> That reads in peril and pest
> The ambrosial moon – the moon!

What does this mean? If Christ is the 'Tortured Lamb', could the Virgin Mary (adopting the role formerly allotted to Minerva) be the 'sexless Owl'? Is the poem's protagonist reborn as Aleister Crowley in the contemporary age? Whatever the explanation, such writing causes confusion in the reader. Briefly, if the poet wants to add layers and meanings – to make it a good deal more than a rhyming exercise – he needs a more sophisticated, less casually improvised structure. The 'Priestess of Panormita' would have been better cast as a short lyric rather than the narrative it purports to be.

In fact, the larger part of Crowley's Shelleyan and Swinburnian poetry is less than enthralling. Primarily the atmosphere is one of language with the objective element – direct observation of nature and human psychology – trimmed or distorted to accommodate rhyme or alliteration. This is not inevitably a bad thing, for a poem subsisting on 'verbal atmosphere' can be as valid if well done as one relying on contact with its subject. Language – as in nonsense poetry – can thrive perfectly well in a context created by itself for itself. Any strict connection with the dictionary will slacken as words take on the imperatives of the author's emphases. In Crowley's œuvre, the noun 'death', for instance, takes on a feverishly dynamic quality that is often explicitly erotic and 'blood' is flaunted as scarlet ornamentation rather than something to avoid shedding.

He acquired this cavalier attitude, not out of perversity, but from an instinctive enjoyment of the euphonious 'boomers' of language, those masters of the curved vowel and clanking consonant who make the doors of each stanza shut with a loud, satisfactory bang. When Crowley wrote in such a way, he tended to reduce poetry to a medley of pleasant noises and picturesque adjectives. And one has to admit that, as far as pastiche goes, it is confident enough, replete with luscious, swooping rhythms, loud with alliterative clamour, but it has the glibness of one who can go on versifying everlastingly, an unstoppable poetic automaton:

> Whence the black lands shudder and darken,
>   Whence the sea birds have empire to range,
> Whence the moon and the meteor hearken
>   The perpetual rhythm of change,
> On earth and heaven deluded
>   With time, that the souls of us kills,
> I have passed. I have brooded, fled far to the wooded
>   And desolate hills.
>
> Like a lion asleep in his fastness,
>   Or a warrior leant on a spear,
> The hills stand up in the vastness,
>   And the stars grow strangely near;
> For the secret of life and its gladness
>   Are hidden in the strength that distils
> A potion of madness from berries of sadness
>   Grown wild in the hills.
>
>   ('The Hills')

Notable, too, is the fact that Crowley's vision is maimed by an inverted religiosity. References to wounds, pain and the Crucified One are far too frequent for any poet not intent on evangelising. Seemingly, he prefers to rehearse the spiritual struggles of his adolescence rather than address a developing world. A *devout* iconoclast, he cannot treat religion lightly and impudently like his contemporary, Bernard Shaw (on whose Biblical scholarship he provided a lively, perspicacious commentary: *The Gospel According to St Bernard Shaw*) but rails, rages, blasphemes and mocks, like a man literally nailed to the cross of his grievance. Rather than embrace a 'godless universe', he substitutes a Greek or Egyptian deity for Christ. Despite pleas to the contrary, his attitude is not that of a scientist who sees religion as a blind alley – a glorious delusion on which great men have frittered their intellects – but of a poet who cannot resist that Aladdin's Cave of ritual enchantments.

Rodin in Rhyme

The three volumes of his *Collected Works* – that bizarre medley of poems, plays, essays and oddities – demonstrate his faults and virtues better than anything. At first glance, it is rather as if an egotistic schoolboy, caught up in the first breath of poetic inspiration, has been allowed to publish every fancy that welled up into his mind. It is indeed, as one non-literary critic remarked, "windy stuff", couched in a language that mingles the Biblical with the Decadent, a synthetic and often awkward patois.

Literary decorum is entirely absent. For instance, his introduction to a series of sonnets on Rodin's sculptures, which he wrote in 1902, is largely taken up with abusing a certain French gentleman who dared to suggest that the poems had more of Crowley about them than Rodin:

> One accepts the lion as a worthy antagonist ... but there are insects so loathsome, so incredibly disgusting, worms whose sight is such an abomination, whose stink is so crapulous and purulent, that, ignoring their malignity, but simply aware of their detestable presence, the heel is ground down in a generous impulse, and the slimy thing is no more ... Such a worm are you, M.D, who once, as above described, voided your noxious nastiness in my presence, trusting to conciliate me by the intended compliment that my poems on Rodin were from myself and not from him, and that any other statues would have done as well.

This is undignified, on par with that of a mayor holding up an official duty, like unveiling a statue, in order to scream abuse at an onlooker. Such indulgences dismayed the reader and lessened Crowley's chance of being taken seriously.

Turning to the sonnets in question, though the sculptor showed a polite appreciation and Marcel Schwob translated two into French,

Rodin did not bring out as much in the young Crowley as he had in Rainier Maria Rilke a few years earlier. The bloated adjectives and lame personifications – "Good breathes and bends into the rosy shell" – read artificially, but there are a few pleasant exceptions. In trying to capture the mingling of human and mineral in Rodin's *Icare*, Crowley shows originality; the overreacher is brought down and the earth embraces him – "Icarus and Gaia kiss". *La Cruche Cassee* – a girl weeping at her broken waterpot – exploits the symbolic gesture plainly and dramatically:

> She knows the utmost now; what waters white
> She held from heaven's crystal fountains; flight
> Of what celestial birds struck down: – Ah me!
> What god or demigod hath struck remorse
> In that close-crouched, cold, and desolate corse,
> Wailing her violate virginity?

Crowley seems to have been most pleased with his sonnet on Balzac:

> Giant, with iron secrecies ennighted,
> Cloaked, Balzac stands and sees. Immense disdain,
> Egyptian silence, mastery of pain,
> Gargantuan laughter, shake or still the ignited
> Stature of the Master, vivid. Far, affrighted,
> The stunned air shudders on the skin. In vain
> The Master of *La Comédie Humaine*
> Shadows the deep-set eyes, genius-lighted.
> Epithalamia, birth songs, epitaphs,
> Are written in the mystery of his lips.
> Sad wisdom, scornful shame, grand agony
> In the coffin folds of his cloak, scarred mountains, lie,
> And pity hides i' th' heart. Grim knowledge grips
> The essential manhood. Balzac stands, and laughs.

It is possible to admire the last line of the sonnet. In the earlier section, it is difficult to guess what is meant by:

> Immense disdain,
> Egyptian silence, mastery of pain,
> Gargantuan laughter, shake or still the ignited
> Stature of the Master, vivid.

In expressing imploded energy, the poem conveys statuesqueness, frozen gesture, petrified vitality, the quality of tension achieved in great works of art – but the verbal overload is intrusive. Too many qualities are enumerated for the reader to form a single impression; also the use of "shake" as a verb may be acceptable, but conjoining it with "still" creates an imbalance, and "vivid" left hanging at the end triumphantly completes the triad of confusion. The threadbare cliché "mystery of his lips" adds nothing either, but the "coffin folds of his cloak" making "scarred mountains" is arresting. The conciseness of the last sentence achieves fine dramatic effect after the excess of inflationary phrase-making.

'Aceldama'

It was his male lover – Herbert Charles Jerome Pollitt – who introduced Crowley to a school of writing "which I instinctively despised, even while I adored it" – referring to the Decadents whose languorous, drug-drowsed affectations seemed made-to-measure. Their attitude of acquiescence – of giving oneself up to whatever was voluptuous, exquisite and sinful – appealed to the hedonist in him. If it were possible to make a brief inventory of attitudes and tendencies promoted by the Decadents, one might discern a preference for the cultivated over the natural; for hothouse flowers rather than Wordsworth's daffodils; a painting of a foaming waterfall and rocky gorge rather than the real thing, craggy and wet, reeling beneath one's feet. A liking for the city over the country and an inclination toward sterile sex, or sex without issue, the erotic rather than the domestic, sensation rather than procreation, allied to a fixation on the figure of the prostitute rather than the soulmate. Add to this, a liking for jewels, perfumes, corsets and accessories – all the condiments of the boudoir – rather than the stark naked body. In other words, the Decadents espoused the artificial as being expressive of the revolt of man against Nature, God and Meaning.[1] This revolt was perfectly epitomised in the figure of the dandy who substituted a buttonhole for a halo and strove to establish himself as a minor social deity.

Not all of this appealed to Crowley. His blunter, masculine side, which craved the rigours of mountaineering and despised the sight of an artificially floodlit waterfall in Sweden, rebuked the tragic posturing implicit in the school. But still he could not resist the steamy, sex-soaked vapours of the French Decadents and attempted to infuse them with his own brands of virility, magic and mysticism. In the preface to 'White Stains' (1898), he pays tribute to "the intolerable long roll of names, all tainted with glorious madness. Baudelaire the diabolist, debauchee of sadism, whose dreams are nightmares, and whose waking hours delirium; Rollinat the necrophile, the poet of phthisis, the anxiomaniac; Péladan, the high-priest – of nonsense; Mendés, frivolous and scoffing sensualist; besides a host of others, most alike in this, that, below the cloak of madness and depravity, the true heart of genius burns." He concludes that the movement represented a tragic, terrible waste; "so many great minds, of which hardly one comes to fruition; such seeds of genius, such a harvest of – whirlwind!"

Crowley promoted himself as an English decadent in his first long poem 'Aceldama' (1898) which was privately published while he was a student at Cambridge. The title derives from the field mentioned in Acts I where Judas met his unhappy end – "And falling headlong, he burst asunder in the midst, and all his bowels gushed out ... that field is called Aceldama, that is to say – the field of blood."

The poem is set in a brothel. Conscious of the indecency laws, Crowley uses the Latin 'lupanar' to render it more appealing. Despite the sordid surroundings, the poet ponders on the mystery of religion, expressing fear at the thought of a vast unmeaning cosmos which appears devoid of form:

> I crept, a stealthy hungry soul, to grasp
>   Its vast edge, to look to the beyond;
>   To know. My eyes strained out, there was no bond,
> No continuity, no bridge to clasp.
>   No pillars for the universe. Immond,
>   Shapeless, unstayed,
> Nothing, Nothing, Nothing, Nothing! I was afraid.

Like Daedalus, he sprouts "white orange wings" and climbs up to the infinite. There he finds peace in that place where "dark and deep light" rejoice "in their strange wedlock":

> I climbed still inwards. At the movement point
>   Where all power, light, life, motion concentrate,
> I found God dwelling. Strong immaculate,
> He knew me and he loved! His lips anoint
>   My lips with love; with thirst insatiate
>   He drank my breath,
> Absorbed my life in His, dispersed me, gave me death.

Not only is this odd, it is confusing to boot. Is Crowley talking of spiritual union with his Creator or simply describing homosexual passion? Probably both. Like Nietzsche, he believed spiritual ascent might be obtained through pure sensation. The body stored the divine spark of spirit like a battery stores electricity. Intimacy of language is in no way at odds with mysticism. God is depicted as an agent of physical union. There are allusions to self-denial and straining for the ultimate, yet they are overwhelmed by the louder strains of masochism, homo-eroticism and coprophilia. The Deity is upstaged by naked writhing women, images of torture, ordure and abasement.

To resolve the paradox of being simultaneously god-mad and sex-mad, the poet re-defines the Creator in his own terms and finally evolves a philosophy based on sampling everything, however disgusting or disabling. Man must break "the golden image with the feet of clay" – an image of the body – to experience spirit in its pure force:

> No prostitution may be shunned by him
>   Who would achieve this Heaven. No satyr-song
>   No maniac dance shall ply so fast the throng
> Of lust's imagining perversely dim
>   That no man's spirit may keep pace, so strong
>   Its pangs must pierce;
> Nor all the pains of hell may be one tithe as fierce.
>
> All degradation, all sheer infamy,
>   Thou shalt endure. They head beneath the mire
>   And dung of worthless women shall desire
> As in some hateful dream to lie;
>   Woman must trample thee till thou respire
>   That deadliest fume;
> The vilest worms must crawl, the loathliest vampires gloom.

A truthful, albeit curious statement for a young man of 23. Odder still is the fact that he kept faith with this philosophy. Crowley literally explored "the every self", mapping out avenues of recondite perversion with the enthusiasm and ardour of an explorer in virgin territory. In his view, forcing himself to partake of every vice was as much a discipline as totally denying himself. Satiety and asceticism were extremes of the spirit's pendulum and, in 'Aceldama', the mixture of spirituality and corruption recalls Baudelaire, but it lacks the Frenchman's conciseness and visual exactitude. Baudelaire took his diabolism seriously and the young Crowley quaffed down his verses like black wine. He must have thrilled at *Litanies of Satan* wherein the Arch Deceiver is invoked as the true helpmate to those whom God has abandoned:

> O Prince of Exiles, who have suffered wrong,
> Yet, vanquished, rise from every fall more strong,
>   Satan have pity on my long despair!
>
> To lepers and lost beggars full of lice,
> You teach, through love, the taste of Paradise.
>   Satan have pity on my long despair!
>
> You who give suppleness to drunkards' bones
> When trampled down by horses on the stones.
>   Satan have pity on my long despair!

By the end of the 1890s, however, the Satan and Damnation cards were played out and the blood, wine and roses brigade was beginning to look a little anaemic. This did not leave Crowley poetically bankrupt – for he had reserves of philosophy and arcane lore to sustain him. He could also try to be sexually franker, and these things he did, yet sticking to traditional verse forms, never realising that such conduits can prove restrictive if anything new is to be said. When Crowley used the strophes and metres of Swinburne, he was liable to end up saying similar things.

'Orpheus'

Precocious and promising though much of it is, 'Aceldama' is marred by an artificial vocabulary and an overuse of hysterical adjectives –

deadliest, hateful, ghastly, foul, horrible, shameful. Worse still is the long poem 'Orpheus' which he began in San Francisco in 1901 when involved in ceremonial magic and carried on years later, picking up new ideas and weaving them in, until the hotchpotch left him giddy and bewildered. His original aim was to do the "biggest thing ever done in lyrics", but the result was an epic of awesome tedium, of a mellifluous and irrepressible banality. The problem is that nothing happens. Orpheus sings and describes. Various voices whirl around him – Minos, Rhadamanthus, Persephone, Agave, Calliope – adding to the boredom and confusion.

It would not be so bad if Crowley's craftsmanship was uproariously inept like William McGonagall's – but instead it is gliding and fluent, often technically adept, with varied rhyming schemes. The horror of 'Orpheus' is the horror of gushing competence, a regime of remorseless rhymes, an agony of alliteration. Even when the musician's head has been torn from his body, there is no release – a chorus of nature spirits strike up the same familiar monotony! As Stoddard Martin has remarked, "passionate pursuit of yesterday's models" left Crowley bankrupt as a poet. 'Orpheus' is the last nail in the coffin of Romantic Hellenism.

To be absolutely fair, Crowley's preface admits that the volume lacks architecture. It is all "feet and face"; the narrative is minimal; the philosophy is blurred; yet such was his concern that a masterpiece should not be lost to the world, he issued it in hard covers, partly to obviate the need for further tinkering:

> One should bury him decently in fine fat type, and erect nice boards over him, and collect the criticisms of an enlightened press, and inscribe them on the tomb ...

> Old Man of the Sea, these three years you have drummed your black misshapen heels upon me; I have had no ease because of you; I am bepissed and conskited of your beastliness; and now you are drunk with the idea that you are finished and perfect, I shall roll you off and beat your brains out upon the hardest of flints, the head of the British Public.

The jocular tone conceals a gigantic conceit which rendered him oblivious to his faults and excesses.

A further delusion of Crowley's was that asserting several

viewpoints was akin to being possessed by different people. Assertion, however, is only assertion and not a substitute for imagination and empathy. In the preface to *Olla* (1946), he explains that his poems could be regarded as a series of voices. "Thus 'Amphora'," he wrote, "records the devout yet (unconsciously) passionate outbursts of a Catholic Christian woman; 'Alice' of a romantic boy in love, the seed of doubt and disillusion beginning to sprout; 'Clouds Without Water', of a sexual maniac who is also a man of the world, a sardonic jester, and a mystic. Such impersonations are almost as frequent as the ecstatic moods of Our Lady, of many-minded, many-throned Aphrodite, weaver of wiles."

This is typical. On no account let the reader decide – instead devise strategies and criteria by which one's own productions can be viewed as excellent. Despite Crowley's shameless drawing in of credits, the poems are a series of utterances and signals rather than fully-formed voices or – as Fernando Pessoa called them – heteronymns. A personality is more than an articulated attitude. A Catholic woman does not merely harp about Our Lady's tears and birth pangs. The "romantic boy in love" is suspiciously close to the scheming magician with his sigils and talismans. The "sexual maniac" of 'Clouds Without Water' poses few problems of identification either. So the 'voices' are less bewilderingly varied than Crowley would have us believe. Everything he writes bears his intrusive stamp.

The Rose Quartet

Scottish poet and biographer of the Duke of Buckingham, Charles Richard Cammell, reserved his highest and most ungrudging praise for the sequence of four poems Crowley dedicated to his wife, Rose Kelly, tracing the course of their marriage, from the first flush of love to disillusion, satiety and near-hatred. The first of the quartet 'Rosa Mundi' has been commended by various people. According to Crowley, even the mountaineer Oscar Eckenstein, who did not like his poetry, considered it so precious a document that he thought it would be better found among his papers after his death. Crowley agreed; but nobly decided that he should publish it in order to make the world a "holier place".

The Rosicrucian image of the Mystic Rose, uniting virginity and grace, sensuality and seduction, along with the pleroma, mortal perfection and the union of fire and water, was used by Blake and many another visionary. Furthermore Crowley's old rival, W.B. Yeats, utilised the image with some success, and it is possible that he was attempting to outdo or 'out-exult' the Irish laureate of dreamy sensuosity and faerie flirtation rather than the harder, more politically-aware poet beginning to emerge. Whatever the original intention, the self-praise heaped upon the poem is gushing. 'Rosa Mundi' is far from a masterpiece of sustained sublimity. It relies too heavily on conventional images drawn from the 'beautiful' end of the spectrum:

> Rose of the World!
> Red glory of the secret heart of Love:
> Red flame, rose-red, most subtly curled
> Into its own infinite flower, all flowers above!
> Its flower in its own perfumed passion,
> Its faint sweet passion, folded and furled
> In flower fashion:
> And my deep spirit taking its pure part
> Of that voluptuous heart
> Of hidden happiness!

But it is briefly redeemed by moments of dignity where the diction becomes tense and terse:

> I am a ship whose anchors are all gone,
> Whose rudder is held by Love the indomitable
> Purposeful helmsman. Were his port high Hell,
> Who should be fool enough to care? Suppose
> Hell's waters wash the memory of this rose
> Out of my mind, what misery matters then?
> Or, if they leave it, all the woes of men
> Are as pale shadows in the glory of
> That passionate splendour of Love.

Again, in verse twelve, Crowley evokes an Indian scene with a "bare-legged village boy" and a "grey snake" in the undergrowth. The snake does not pose a threat. Those who stride forth, fearless and unprotected, the poet implies, seldom end up as life's victims. Honesty strips away falseness and deceit, and this timeless, open-to-the-world quality is exemplified in the gods of Egypt (who bring to mind Rilke's angels) in that they abide at the calm centre, apparently indifferent, yet knowing the patterns to which humans assign values will ultimately pass:

> I have seen the eternal Gods
> Sit, star-wed, in old Egypt by the Nile;
> The same calm pose, the inscrutable, wan smile
> On every lip alike.
> Time hath not had nor hath will to strike
> At them; they abide, they pass through all.
> Though their most ancient names may fall,
> They stir not nor are weary of
> Life, for with them even as with us, Life is but Love.
> They know, we know; let, then, the writing go!
> That, in the very deed, we do not know.

In 'Rosa Inferni', the second and shortest of the odes, a note of disillusion and cynicism can be heard. Most biographies state how destructive and unmanageable Crowley was as a husband, but there is a suggestion here that Rose was quite capable of exerting power over him – of arousing jealousy and taking sexual revenge. He hints she was unfaithful to him with a certain young man, whom he, with more pride than charity, refers to as a "sodden youth":

> Some Yankee yelled – I tag it to a rhyme –
> "You can't fool all the people all the time."
> So he of politics; so I of love.
> I am a-many folk (let Buddha prove!)
> And many a month you fooled the lot of us –
> Your spell is cracked within the ring! Behold
> How Christ with clay worth more than any gold
> Cleared the man' eyes! So the blind amorous
> Is blinded with the horror of the truth
> He sees this moment. Foolish prostitute!
> You slacked your kisses upon the sodden youth
> In some excess of confidence, decay
> Of care to hold him – can I tell you which?
> Down goes the moon – one sees the howling bitch!
> The salmon you hooked in fin and gill
> You reel unskilfully – he darts away.
> Alas! you devil, but you hold me still!

Again we have an uneasy blend of the colloquial and grand; "you fooled the lot of us" set beside the Biblical sonorities of "Behold". Later he sees Rose as a vampire, a scheming, shape-shifting temptress and laments the dominance she has over him:

> Aha! the veil is riven!
> Beneath the smiling mask of a young bride
> Languorous, luscious, melancholy-eyed;
> Beneath the gentle raptures, hints celestial
> Of holy secrets, kisses like soft dew,
> Beneath the amorous mystery, I view
> The surer shape, a visage grim and bestial
> A purpose sly and deadly, a black shape,
> A tiger snarling or a grinning ape
> Resolved by every devilish device
> Upon my murder.

As well as being feeble, this is patently inauthentic. Seemingly the poet cannot relax into everyday, intimate observation. He has to lay on the colours thickly, to work his beloved into a morbid caricature, a gothic ripple.

The third of the odes, 'Rosa Coeli', is exultant, affirming the power and depth of his passion. Lush, sacramental, steeped in arousal and anticipation, few instances of pain and vulnerability disrupt this rapturous ramble in the groves of full-blown womanhood. The imagery is as richly carved as section two (A Game of Chess) of *The Waste Land*. Using coy anachronisms like "ree" and clumsy ones like "ensanguine", the poet ransacks and twists language into awkward shapes and gestures. The erotic hymn enweaves the beautiful and the grotesque in its sensuous embroidery, drawing in blue gentians, honey-coloured doves, jackals, crags, lotus gardens, crooked-spined dwarfs and bat-eyed newspaper-besotted men. With all the variousness and diversity, no focused portrait of a woman is achieved but rather Rose is converted to the Eternal Womanly, a mistress of the universe, accommodating the complexities of legend, myth and fancy in the star-chart of her body. As a chronicle of rapture, had it been written a hundred years earlier, 'Rosa Coeli' would rate very high indeed, but out-Shelleying Shelley just before modernism is about to re-fashion literary taste is hardly good timing. Besides, the attractive imagery has been eroded by over-use and forfeited its connection. Mythology no longer affiliates with the intimate lives of men and women.

> Only the one sun on the stepped snows;
> Only the one star of the sister seven;
> Only the one moon in the orchard close
> In the hour that unto love is given
> Of all the hours of bliss;
> Only the one joy in a world of woes;
> Only the one spark in the stormcloud riven;
> Only the one shaft through the rose-dawn driven,
> Thy shaft, Eros!

The lines pour forward impulsively, enraptured by their own fluency. When they strive to break the mould, or communicate a frantic, phantasmagoric state, they get syntactically knotted, so that images clash and cancel each other out. Seemingly the emotions are so strong they cannot be organised but break down into a series of cries or disjointed utterances:

> Rose of the World. Your mystic petals spread
> Like wings over my head.
> The tide of burning blood upon my face
> Drowns all floating images
> That dance their spectre saraband
> In Bacchic race, phantastical embrace,
> Upon the sepulchres, the dizzy seas
> Of this my mind, Sabbatic rout that spanned
> These straits my soul! Ay, they are dead and drowned
> (And damned, I doubt!). Ah God! I am exhaust
> In the red moon's holocaust!
> God! God! The chasms secret and profound
> Suck down the porphyr flood
> Of you maniacal, ensorcelled blood
> That maddens and bewitches.
>
> My life is suffocated – now I swoon –
> I die! I am in hell, red hell, red hell,
> And all the immortal in me itches
> To grip the immortal ...
>   ('Rosa Coeli')

There is a problem when this type of material is transcribed, language being a 'cooler' medium than direct experience. In recalling a past event, an element of reflection – of evaluation – is liable to come into play. Trying to resurrect ecstatic or despairing states is far more difficult than setting down plain narrative or emotion recollected in tranquillity. If one asserts anguish or arousal, using exclamation marks as emphasis, the effect may seem hysterical, as if the writer is trying to force language to perform what only flesh can. This is a core weakness found in much of Crowley's work. He bullies and shoves around words in too crass and authoritarian a manner. He makes them rhyme and chime rather than move the reader.

Nevertheless, 'Rosa Coeli' is probably the best of the four odes, effectively mixing the playful and preposterous. Rose's body releases the dreamer and fantasist in the poet. Seeing her naked against the "jetty silk", he thinks of the milky way shining in the darkness of the sky and of the zodiac:

> A poet is at ease
> In all such voyages:
> Why, as a boy I steered
> Up to the Scorpion and tweaked his tail,
> Plucked foolish Capricornus by the beard
> And kissed the Blessed Damozel that leaned upon the golden rail.
> Drunk from the glad rim of the grail
> Or soothed the squally Twins (for they would weep!)
> And while I smiled "In Heaven how safe I am!"
> Found myself in my little bed asleep
> Having been butted thither by the Ram.

Crowley believed that such images deepened his work and rendered it a palimpsest. "For instance, if I mention a beetle," he explained, "I expect the reader to understand it as an allusion to the sun at midnight in its moral sense of Light-in-Darkness; if a pelican, to the legend that she pierces her own breast to feed her young; if a goat, to the entire symbolism of Capricornus, the god Pan, Satan or Jesus (Jesus being born at the winter solstice, when the sun enters Capricorn); if a pearl, to the correspondences of that stone as a precious and glittering secretion of the oyster, by which I mean that invertebrate animal life of man, the Nephesch."

This is a way of saying 'pearl' signifies semen. Writing as he was in Edwardian England, Crowley cannot be rigorously anatomical, so he masks his lovemaking by exotic imagery. In Egyptian mythology, light or 'gnosis' was born out of the coupling of earth and sky, and Crowley attaches to the act a similar celestial grandeur. Evoking the secrets of his wife's body, he cannily resorts to landscape symbolism and metaphors of heat and burning:

> Another time I passed the holy well
> And plunged (as Phoebus in the western ocean)
> Into a forest of flame that crowned
> The holy hill; all was enchanted ground,
> The flames like scented tendrils of a vine
> Or sensitive rays that spell
> Strange curves to match their master-god's emotion.
> And ever nearer to the scarlet slash
> I clomb, where the strange perfumes struck me like a lash
> And the dread fire scorched up my life.
> There, O insufferable delight
> I mock with the weak word of wife,
> I was sucked down into the crater rim,
> Into the crimson damask dim
> Candescent cave of night –
> O then I mock myself with words!

Crowley was a mountaineer who knew full well that, after attaining the topmost pinnacle of the spirit, one has little choice but to peg one's way down again. This is not exactly what he did – in fact, his descent appears more like a suicidal leap. For if we place 'Rosa Decidua', the most violent and bitter of the quartet, side by side with 'Rosa Coeli', we are shaken by the contrast. The poem is dedicated to Lord Salvesen who presided at the divorce trial and prompts the reader to ask: How could Rose have changed so? Was she alone responsible? Such personal questions would not normally arise from a literary text, but as Crowley specifically cited the circumstances of his divorce, the reader can only focus on whatever suspicions arise. Crowley regarded 'Rosa Decidua' as the high-water mark of his realism and Frank Harris – out of diplomacy or enthusiasm – agreed, "Astounding realism raised to art by perfect artistry."

The tone is harsh, jarring, yet maintains a strict metre throughout. Briefly, the gist of it is that Rose has become a dipsomaniac; her complexion and poise have utterly departed. Bitterly, the poet observes her as she waddles around picking up bottles and draining them dry while he, the concerned husband, sinks into a mire of remorse and recrimination. Sadistically he sets down the details:

> Come, look at it! This leaden skin
> With ochre staining its amorphous grey;
> All that elastic brilliance passed away;
> Minute invading wrinkles where the flesh
> Is soaked away by the foul thing within
> Her soul; the bloom so faint and fresh
> Smudged to a sunset glow as one may see
> At sunset in Factory lands ...

This loud anguish makes it oddly compulsive, but also unsatisfactory and difficult to assess. Using one's command of rhetoric to insult one's sick wife is neither chivalrous nor appealing – hence the passages highlighting the poet's grief are more acceptable than the denunciations:

> This would corrupt God's body with a breath.
> I see Him sicken and swoon; I see Him rot
> Through, though his tabernacle be
> Eternity.
> This makes a man catch hold of death
> Greedily like a harlot in the street
> That plucks by the arm some sot.
> Death shakes me off with a harsh curse.
> Tied to this woman, his beneficience
> Were too like heaven ...

The language becomes coarsely physical and abusive – "I reel back beneath the blow of her breath" – as he describes drunken rages and attempts to win back his affection. He plummets into the pit of despair and dazedly wanders around rehearsing the details of their once-happy life. He claims to be rid of her memory but it is pervasive, insistent, mocking. His mind orbits the centre of its pain, yet finds no reserves of emotion:

> Cry like a dog and run about the city!
> There is no word left, now the deed is dead!

No thought of me is in her; I am a stranger
To all that dream of danger
And bliss Rose was. The green shoots
Of life that spring in me are fed
Not even on the mire of her decay.
They spring from other roots.
Now I am cleansed of her, I am so to say
A man part paralysed. One limb is dead
In feeling as in motion. This remains
To ask: Will all catch death – how soon? This head
Excites its miserable brain
To think the word it knows by intellect
To be the right word – pity! Then reflect:

Pitiful! pitiful! most pitiful!
The pity of it! Think of the love past,
Blossoms too beautiful!
Think of the hardships conquered comrade-wise!
Think of the babe and its most piteous end!" –
All these things sound like lies.
I do not comprehend
Anything of them – Pity! pity! pity!
'Tis like the drippings of some stagnant rain
From the housetops of a ruined city
Upon the flagstones. Not one petal clings
Upon the stalk of memory. Stain
Not one pale thought with blushes; my soul's dead
As a corpse flung tideways on
The stinking flats of London mud ...

'Rosa Decidua' is not a masterpiece, being too high-pitched and nakedly expostulatory, but it is interesting and has felicities of phrasing, memorable passages and a wild despairing music all its own. In its abrupt transitions, its mingling of the sordid and sumptuous, it anticipates the juxtaposition of the lyrical and the despairingly brutal found in T.S. Eliot's *The Waste Land*, down to imagery of dying vegetation and "the stinking flats of London mud". Unpleasant though much of it is, Crowley at least manages to break away from his favourite mannerism – the flatulent rhetorical flight culminating in an exclamation of bliss – and use a balder, more basic vocabularly which he normally reserves for his profane poems like the truly shocking 'Leah Sublime'.

The Heart of Holy Russia

The most influential of Crowley's contacts in the literary world was the editor of the *English Review,* Austin Harrison, son of Frederic Harrison, philosopher, social critic and friend of George Gissing the novelist. Crowley and Harrison played golf together; the latter printed several leading contributions by Crowley including 'Morphia', 'The City of God', 'Hymn to the American Republic' (in which the United States is serenaded, one reviewer remarked, in a similar language to one of Mr Swinburne's "girl-harlots"), an insightful centenary article on Shelley, a discussion of the "Jewish problem" (hindsight sees this more as a Gentile problem), some acute and foolish ruminations on drug-taking, a short story *The Strategem* and other assorted pieces. He admired Crowley's mystical verse but fought shy of some of the more starkly morbid offerings like 'To Any Unborn Child' beginning:

> On that intolerable planet
>   Whose nature and whose name is Hell,
> There slants a path of polished granite
>   Straight to the scaffold from a cell.
>
> With lids cut off and fettered hands,
>   Each shoots the inexorable slope
> To where the hooded hangman stands,
>   His fingers ready on the rope.

Rejecting this effusion, Harrison told Crowley that he thought it rather "hard on the kid" condemning him to such a grim future. Crowley saw the remark as evidence of Harrison's mendacity, but one suspects that Harrison wanted to lightly avoid such doom-laden barkings. A longer poem which did impress Harrison – he printed it on the opening pages of *English Review* in January 1914 – was 'The City of God', evoking Moscow as "a hashish dream come true." Crowley had recently returned from the city where he had been acting the part of a theatrical impresario, managing a troupe of women called 'The Ragged Rag-Time Girls' about whom he amusingly commented:

Leila Waddell was the only one with a head on her shoulders. Of the other six, three were dipsomaniacs, four nymphomaniacs, two hysterically prudish, and all ineradicably convinced that everyone outside England was a robber, ravisher and assassin. They all carried revolvers, which they did not know how to use; though prepared to do so on the first person who spoke to them.

Crowley explored Moscow culture and low-life with zest and intrepidity. After a while, he began to believe that he had gained profound insights and accordingly set them down. The results were 'The City of God' and a prose pendant *The Heart of Holy Russia* which "struck many Russians competent to judge as nearer the soul of their country than anything out of Dostoyevsky."

Unfortunately this is self-congratulatory fantasy and *The Heart of Holy Russia* might be better named *The Heart of Holy Crowley*, in that the author intrudes a great deal of himself in it. Yet the essay possesses an attractive eloquence and panache and, in some respects, anticipates Hermann Hesse's collection of essays 'In Sight of Chaos' (1919), the subject of which is ostensibly the novelist Fyodor Dostoyevsky. Analysing the latter's characters, Hesse identifies 'Russian Man' as a breed apart, a lunatic, criminal and drunkard, "the unpredictable man of the future" for whom morality amounts to no more than convention, and eccentricity and revolt are as natural as breathing. T.S. Eliot was so inspired by Hesse's essay that he worked parts of it into *The Waste Land*, but he might have been equally affected by Crowley's which makes the same points. In Hesse there is a hint of warning, a fear of this wild, impetuous, anarchic beast, while Crowley openly admires the Russians for their passionate impetuousness, their ragged unpredictability, their lawlessness and spontaneity – in fact, for their un-Englishness:

> The Russian understands suffering as a thing to observe, not to feel. He accepts the hardship of his lot as God's experiment with man. The means is nothing, the end is all. Hence the patient longing of his dog-like eyes, and the beatitude glimmering from his pale cheeks. Hence the joy in sorrow and sorrow in joy of his whole mental composition. Hence his long-suffering and his fierceness, his tenderness and his brutality. The Great Mean is realized by the exhaustion of the

extremes. It is the Chinese Taoist philosophy in practice and at the same time the antithesis of that plan of achieving everything by achieving nothing.

It is difficult to assess how useful such stereotypes are, but the details make up a recognizable portrait of a strongly defined type who is of a piece with the barbarous, fantastic architecture and ambience of the place. Fertile, erudite and ablaze with enthusiasm, *The Heart of Holy Russia* survives as one of the more inspiring travel documents of the period, using spectacular resources of allusion and framed in cadences that rise to carefully orchestrated crescendos. In trying to evoke what literally 'beggars description', the prose, by curious paradox, aspires to an eloquent speechlessness, especially in its response to the Kremlin and St Basil's Cathedral:

> It is the imagination incarnate in metal and stone. It is the absurd in which Tertullian believed. It is a storm of beauty, a mad poet's idea of heaven. It mocks human reason. It belongs to no school or period; it could not be imitated or equalled, because the mind of even the greatest artist has limitations, grooves of thought; and in Moscow, it is the unexpected which always happens. Happens: the Kremlin is an accident. The town itself is an accident. There is no particular geographical reason for it being where it is. As to natural advantages, it has none. There is a small river, perhaps half as wide as the Harlem River or the Thames at London Bridge, and a hill no higher than Morningside or Ludgate Hill. Go to the top of Ivan Veliky one clear day and you can see but vastness of plain all ways to the horizon, save for that low mount-line whence Napoleon first saw the city. It has no Vesuvius, no bay of blue, no crested Posilippo. It has no seven hills. It has no mountain setting, no mighty river, no possibility of background but the sky. And there it is, unassailably magnificent, sheer warlock's work. It is the sudden crystallization of one of those 'barbarous Names of Evocation' of which Zoroaster speaks. It is the efflorescence of a Titan vice, the judgment of God that turned Lot's wife into a pillar of salt upon a spinthria of the whole race of giants. For, like the Thrysus around whose spear twist vine tendrils, every dominant form of the Kremlin is a fantasy upon one theme, and that a theme of which the sun himself is but the eidolon. It is the Lord of Life, the Giver of Life, the bountiful,

the single, the master of ecstasy, the fulfiller of promise, the witness of the invisible, the viceregent and arbiter of the godhead, the mainspring of manhood, the compeller of destiny, that is commemorated in this wilderness of wonder.

After working the rhetoric to bursting point, Crowley sums up the church as "the solution of the plastic antimony of the Many and the One" in that none of the spires are precisely alike, and yet the identity of each is endowed with a special quality that is indebted to the sheer multiplicity: "here is perpetual motion in unmoving stone; the volatile is fixed, the fixed is volatile ..." Accompanying this awesome spectacle comes the sound of the bells of Moscow, "as wonderful to the ear as the city to the eye", and the mystic is swept up into the empyrean and his ego extinguished in a moment of bliss.

'The City of God'

As for 'The City of God', a poem praised by John Symonds and several other students of Crowley, this turns out to be a pot of language spilled over the page. It is like sightseeing through satyr's spectacles, a poem which refuses to 'listen' yet exults in the bombastic grandeur of its proclamations.

A nameless narrator opens the poem. We learn that he is one of a caravan crossing a dreary plain. They reach the fabled city as the dawn sun strikes the spires and rooftops. At this the narrative topples over a cliff and gasps its last as the glory becomes too much to bear. The spectacle unmans them. They cannot proceed or think. Light breaks over the city, kindling its strange, bulbous outlines and, instantly, they are swept up into a ecstatic state in which they glimpse the Godhead through the suggestive, highly-coloured architecture:

> Dome upon dome, cupola beyond cupola,
> Great gland, sun, moon, cross, crescent, breast
> And mightier breast and gland and vesica
> Heaving with natural and unnatural longing,
> Crowding, coalescing, thronging,
> Mixing their magic, clouding over all
> With pale, pure gold, the spring sun's thrall
> Thrilling with ecstasy to burst the blue –
> Oh! all our hashish dreams came true

> When we beheld the jewel of the city,
> Its nine glands covered like all manner of fruit
> And flowers with stripe and trellis, whorl and spire,
> Even like all manner of beast and bird that be,
> And every gland stood bare, disdaining pity ...

Presumably, as in *The Heart of Holy Russia*, this evokes the plethora of copper-capped onion domes, cupolas and turrets adorning buildings like St Basil's Cathedral, translating them as a kind of sacred marriage of forms. The gaudiness of the concept – the violent concatenation of shapes and textures – recalls the unsettling 'astral' paintings of C.W. Leadbeater, who dictated to artists what he saw during his peregrinations beyond the physical. The building has nine glands or domes, nine being the greatest of all primary numbers, enabling a magician to control the forces of nature. Nine is also the number of Buddha's meditational stages of attainment before his entry into Parinirvana, the final 'nirvana' or state of perfect bliss obtained after death.

The vision of the City violently assaults the senses (so violently, in fact, that we are not even certain of the time of day, the dawn sun unloosing "a river of sunset blood") and produces a blaze of Turneresque effects. As in Buddha's 'Fire Sermon', the eye is on fire, the nose is on fire, the mind ablaze and the ear aflame. "Perceiving this, O priests," the master concludes, "the learned and noble disciple conceives an aversion for the eye, conceives an aversion from forms ... And in conceiving this aversion he becomes divested of passion, and by the absence of passion he becomes free."

But Crowley never wanted to shed his passions, save perhaps to achieve short-term effects. He believed that orgiastic abandon acted as a kind of trampoline to launch the soul into the empyrean of higher magic, and despite its free employment of fiery and incandescent imagery, 'The City of God' is no baptism of fire, an attempt to incinerate all impure cravings, but rather a hymn to the higher lust, a solar-phallic reverie.

Nevertheless, it is of limited use erecting a scaffolding of significances around a building which is basically unsound. If examined critically, 'The City of God' cannot be considered a success. The esoteric embroidery fails to awaken the inner eye or attain lucidity. The imagery is giddily excessive and, rather than an organised poem, we have an impressionistic cannonade. Architecture is portrayed in a state of violent sexual arousal – a Daliesque orgy of inanimate desires – which might be more acceptable as a witty conceit. Crowley reminds one irresistibly and charmingly of Mr Mybug in *Cold Comfort Farm*, the poet who cannot go on a simple country walk without working himself into a frenzy by reading phallic connotation and sexual dalliance in each budding crocus and flowering twig.

The 'City of God' ends with a fanfare. The poet finds himself swooning into non-existence, followed by trumpet blasts and weird burning shapes preceding the appearance of Horus, the hawk-headed god, symbol of Crowleianity and solar power:

> And in that heart of hearts was no more I,
> No more the heart; but, sobbing through the sky,
> Came trembling the more awful beat, the blast
> Of a million trumpets blazoning the past,
> Heralding the to-be, and on their wings
> Whirred incommunicable things.
> And in their wake, tremendous and austere,
> A form of fear,
> Awe in the shape of the Most Holy One,
> A globe, an eye, a hawk, a lion, a lord,
> A bowl of brilliance, a winged globe, a sword –
> All these in one, and one beyond all these,
> Mute ithyphallic, caryatides
> Like gods about his car, came crested on
> The one true God, the Sun!

(The only other poet who raved as improbably as this was Francis Berry, author of *Poetry and the Physical Voice* and a series of eccentric volumes, drawing upon many cultures and mythologies, culminating in the collection *The Galloping Centaur*. Berry seems to have been a weird blend, half-Christian, half sun-worshipping pagan, and his long poem 'The Iron Christ', much-admired by Professor Wilson Knight, ends with a similar shattering blast of solar pyrotechnics.)

Apart from 'The City of God' and 'The Fun of the Fair', while in Russia Crowley wrote 'Hymn to Pan' (regarded as his poetic logo), 'A Moscow Night's Entertainment' (verses evoking a street murder at night beneath the Kremlin walls) and 'Ivan, the Unconquerable

Tsar' which he called an "anti-Lepanto" (never having exorcised the spectre of Chesterton's success), a melodramatic poem on morphia addiction (quoted in *Diary of a Drug Fiend*), a religious 'drama' 'The Ship' (incorporated into the Gnostic Mass), a novel entitled *The Lost Continent* (a Utopian or Atlantean tract, in the manner of Francis Bacon, with dashes of Swiftian satire) – all of which eventually appeared in the 'The Giant's Thumb', intended to be published in America in 1915 but not appearing until 1992 in facsimile form. So his holiday may be seen as intensely productive, a creative detonation that he was never able to match again.

'The Fun of the Fair'

More approachable, less pretentious than 'The City of God', is 'The Fun of the Fair', a breezy, chatty, rambly account of the Great Fair at Nijni Novgorod, a town 255 miles east of Moscow, set at the confluence of the Oka and Volga rivers. The fair, traditionally held between 15th July and 1st September, used to draw a vast number of traders and customers, the main products sold being cotton, woollen, linen, tea, silk, metalware, furs, leather, porcelain, earthenware and glass. Having read about this marvellous fair as a boy, Crowley decided to capture its atmosphere in verses reminiscent of Charles Churchill.

The poem was scheduled to appear in the *English Review* during the autumn of 1914 but its appearance was delayed to make room for the more timely 'Appeal to the American Republic'. Publication had to wait some 28 years, until 1922 when the O.T.O. (Crowley's own press) issued it with an introduction by Louis Wilkinson who naturally over-praises his friend's work:

> Here is a dish of caviar. Caviar à la Crowley. No one else could serve such a feast in such a manner. The qualities of this 'Reportage' – wit, irony, vigour, vividness, raciness, and verve – are all Crowleianized, all are plentifully endowed with that Crowleian surprisingness so alluring always to some and so infuriating always to others. Under the Byronic surface of this verse there show clearly the living shapes of that singular identity glancing and flashing like a fish, strangely-finned, strangely-hued, strangely-tailed.

Sociologically interesting as a portrait of pre-Leninist Russia, 'The Fun of the Fair' has the note-taking immediacy of a flippant diary. Written in irregular couplets, it describes the train journey to the fair, the weird mixture of races, the droskies, the hotel room, the freaks on display, a romantic interlude with a Tartar lass and the distant view of the Caucasus. Drinking and eating customs are dealt with in detail and it is obvious that Crowley prided himself on being both connoisseur and gourmet:

> Note for the gourmet. If your lips grow scorny
> Over the Russian black-bread, yclept Chorny,
> You err. As nothing else its taste combines
> With caviar. And when you read these lines,
> Further observe that caviar best walks
> On stilts of finely chopped green onion stalks.

There are the usual emotional switchbacks. Facetious passages are set beside rhapsodic bouts of lovemaking and, towards the end, the mood darkens as the sun sets over the river and the poet dwells on mortality:

> A blue-grey gleam
> Subtly enfolds the steppes. Soft clouds lie grey
> About the north: earth's noises die away:
> Heaven's anthem wakes – 'tis but a hush increased!
> Great flights of birds come flickering from the east
> Like dead leaves down the wind; the Volga shines
> More silver-rose, still subtler grow the lines
> Of all the landscape; a vermilion haze
> Surrounds the sun, that still shoots out his rays
> Venomous, as a warrior in his death
> Spends utmost malice in the utmost breath.
> And now all suddenly goes blue. The sky
> Flames into green and orange. Must thou die,
> Beloved? This is the extreme of fate.
> The whole world goes incalculably slate.
> The wind comes chill; the sun is dead. Oh death,
> I feel the first faint fondling of thy breath
> Even now. Bring wine! Bring food! Bring anything!
> It matters nothing: man must meet his king.

The writing achieves a Pharonic dignity. As the sun goes down, so does one's inner certainty decline. Dr Johnson stated how each small ending or cycle of completion brings one closer to the great termination or "the secret horror of the last". Food and the wine are the consolations of physical existence. They make a bridge between the two worlds and must be consumed as a preparation for a journey that will be without nourishment or precedent.

'Alice' and 'Clouds Without Water'

Crowley enjoyed the sonnet form. However, he never used it as an extended narrative until he wrote 'Alice: An Adultery' (1903), a vivid, passionate account of a shipboard affair between a young Englishman and a married woman. The former was Crowley and the latter, Alice Rogers, wife of an American lawyer. The two met in May 1901 in Waikiki and later boarded a vessel together for Japan. From the start Crowley pressed his attentions on her, and eventually she succumbed.

Like many Crowley texts, 'Alice' is ornamented with footnotes and prefaced by a mock introduction anticipating its virtues and deficiencies: "Brutal truth-telling humour, at times perhaps too Rabelaisian; lyrics, some of enchanting beauty, other painfully imitative; sonnets of unequal power …"

There is value in these comments, save that little in the sequence would offend anyone. But some of the actions were mildly shocking today – for instance, entering his mistress' cabin and making love to her while her child was sleeping nearby – though the language stays demure and arcane:

> She dared not come into my room to-night.
>   So? I was acquiescent, sharp despair
>   And nervous purpose mixing in me there
>   The while I waited: then I glided light
> (Clad in the swart robes of an eremite)
>   Across the passage. Now, all unaware
>   My kisses underneath the veil of vair
>   Woke her: she turned and sighed and held me tight.
>
> Her child slept gently on the farther side.
>   But we took danger by the throat, despised
>   All but the one sole splendour that we prized;

> And she, whose robe was far too slight to hide
> The babe-smooth breasts, was far too frail to cover
> Her heart's true fire and music from her lover.

Elsewhere the daring subject matter is encumbered by glib alliteration "splendour of sin", "divider of the dawn's divinity", "secret sea" – and a plethora of tried and tested metaphors. (Ironically the *English Review* praised the stanzas of 'Alice' for "their singular disseverance from the things of the day, their entire lack of what is called 'The Modern Note' in poetry.") There are too many clichés, "the soft wind sighs", allusions to lilies and roses, decorous hints of arousal, "as dewy spheres glow", and phrases that strain after fate, doom and sexual guilt, "broken kisses and stained cheeks of love." To add a dash of Scotch to the slightly bland soda, Crowley occasionally inserts a dramatic statement – "I drew a hideous talisman of lust" – and broaches psychological complexities, such as that troubled feeling when erotic reverie is forced to awaken to itineraries and obligations. Studding the narrative are lyrics that endure as agreeable celebrations of romantic passion, notably 'Alice':

> The stars are hidden in dark and mist,
>   The moon and sun are dead,
> Because my love has caught and kissed
>   My body in her bed.
> No light may shine this happy night –
> Unless my Alice be the light.
>
> So silent are the thrush, the lark!
>   The nightingales at rest,
> Because my lover loves the dark,
>   And has me in her breast.
> No song this happy night be heard! –
> Unless my Alice be the bird.
>
> The sea that roared around the house
>   Is fallen from alarms,
> Because my lover calls me spouse,
>   And takes me to her arms.
> This night no sound of breakers be! –
> Unless my Alice be the sea.

Despite 'Alice's' sporadic merits, arguably Crowley's most sustained sonnet sequence is 'Clouds Without Water' (1909) which appeared during his middle or 'Equinox' period (1908) when much of his best work was accomplished. Compared with 'Alice', this is original Crowley rather than "Swinburne and water" and has a robust and varied vocabulary, mingling Greek, Latin and Egyptian tags, and creating a voice which is brutally forthright yet at the same time mocking and darkly erotic. With predictable Crowleian irony, it is introduced by an Anglican minister, the Reverend C. Verey, who feels compelled to edit the "atrocious manuscript" and set it before the public as a dire warning to all those who indulge in Atheism and Free Love. It ends with a prayer wherein the fervent cleric implores the Almighty to confer on him "a double portion of Thy holiness."

This *is* funny, anticipating the Nabokov of *Pale Fire*, except Crowley's poem is superior to the rather tedious pastiche of the latter. But still one begins to see something self-protective in the number of times he presents his work as a lavish, jocular whim. He seeks praise and adulation, yet hopes by assuming varied colorations and disguises, he will baffle the critic and be rendered immune from barbs of the sharper kind. Of course, the 'exploding text' had already been touched on by writers like Lawrence Stern and Lewis Carroll, but Crowley introduced innovations of his own and was far more daring in his sexual content.

Crowley gives a background account of the poem in his *Confessions*, stating that he was inspired by a beautiful English girl named Vera, an exotic Highland sculptress [Kathleen Bruce: later she married the Antarctic explorer Captain Robert Falcon Scott!], who was studying under Rodin and "took delight in getting married men away from their wives", and a society woman [almost certainly Ada Leverson], who was a writer of subtlety and distinction and a loyal friend of Oscar Wilde. The latter attracted Crowley by filling him with "fascination and horror" and reminding him of a "devourer of human corpses, being herself already dead." A bout of "fierce and grotesque" passion sprang up between them and helped provide the dark, hysterical climax to the poem.

'Clouds Without Water' chronicles a very physical, very ecstatic love affair with a woman named Lola.[2] The lovers enjoy an adulterous liaison, flout social mores, indulge in every variety of sexual experiment, catch syphilis and commit suicide with an overdose of laudanum. Despite the grimness of the subject matter, the tone is one of absolute abandon..

It is divided into eight sections, all of which bear occult names appropriate to the changing moods and fortunes of the lovers: 'The Augur', 'The Alchemist', 'The Hermit', 'The Thaumaturge', 'The Black Mass', 'The Adept', 'The Vampire', 'The Initiation'. 'The Augur' contains the intimation that the lover's lot will be tragic ("no happy end") while the 'The Alchemist' praises the wine that transmutes their guilt and sense of sin. 'The Black Mass' hints at various masochistic and sadistic variations on the act of love. Extremes of pleasure and pain create a non-human nightmare realm:

> So in this agony of enforced silence
> The sober song breaks to a phrenzied scream;
> The shattering brain admits the mad god's violence,
> And wild things course as in an evil dream;
> Devils and dancers, druid rites and dread,
> Horrible symbols scarred across the sky,
> Invisible terrors of the quick and dead,
> Impossible phantoms in mad revelry
> Conjoined in spindthriae of bestial form,
> Human-faced toads and serpent-headed women,
> All lashed and slashed by the all-wandering storm
> Caricature of all things holy and human –
> Such are the discords that absorb the strain
> As this wild threnody dissolves the brain.
>   ('The Black Mass' XII)

'Clouds Without Water' has a strong theme and shows a progression of feeling. Formally speaking, it is far from perfect. (Erotic imagery, for instance, is so insistently 'molten' that one is left with the impression that being kissed is like getting attacked with a branding iron!) But at least the execution is reasonably artistic. In this ecstatically sustained sequence, the poet preaches, 'Forget society, respectability, middle-class morals, live and die for the white-hot moment.' Esoteric plumes are flaunted and gratification is elevated to the level of religion. As for the magical terms, so irritating in other contexts, here they energize and refresh.

Between bouts of sexual frenzy, there are dignified meditative patches where the mystic anticipates the completion of his spiritual voyage:

> Even as the holy Ra that travelleth
>   Within his bark upon the firmament,
>   Looking with fire-keen eyes on life and death
>   In simple state and cardinal content:
> Even as the holy hawk that towers sublime
>   Into the great abyss, with icy gaze
>   Fronting the calm immensities of time
>   And making space to shudder; so I praise
> With infinite contempt the joyous world
>   That I have figured in this brain of mine.
>   The sails of this life's argosy are furled;
>   The anchor drops in those abodes divine.
> Master of self and God, freewill and Fate,
>   I am alone – at last – to meditate.
>   ('The Adept' I)

Not only is Ra invoked but Pan also, not as an orgiastic goat-god, but as the ever-abiding presence behind all phenomena, dignified, fierce and inscrutable. "To be god is to be lost to God," Crowley observed in an earlier sonnet. Thus, in order to make himself immortal, he has to be absorbed by the greater radiance:

> Yet I abide; for who is Pan is all.
>   He hath no refuge in deceitful death.
>   What soul is immanent may never fall;
>   What soul is Breath can never fail of breath.
> The pity and the terror and the yearning
>   Of this my silence and my solitude
>   Are broken by the blazing and the burning
>   Of this dead majesty, this million-hued
> Brilliance that coruscates its jetted fire
>   Into the infinite aether ...
>   ('The Adept' V)

Chesterton or Belloc would have enjoyed this sonnet praising wine, despite the fact that the vintage has been strained through *The Golden Bough* and assumes a little too confidently that the reader is acquainted with the elements of Egyptian myth:

> This wine is sovereign against all complaints.
>   This is the wine great king-angels use
>   To inspire the souls of sinners and of saints
>   Unto the deeds that win the world or lose.
> One drop of this raised Attis from the dead;
>   One drop of this, and slain Osiris stirs;
>   One drop of this; before young Horus fled
>   Thine hosts, Typhon! – this wine is mine and hers.
> Ye Gods that gave it! not in trickling gouts,
>   But from the very fountain whence 'tis drawn
>   Gushing in crystal jets and ruby spouts
>   From the authentic throne and shrine of dawn.
> Drink it? Ay, so! and bathe therein – and swim
>   Out to the world's everlasting rim!
>   ('The Alchemist' IX)

What is to be admired about 'Clouds Without Water' is that the imagery takes on the chameleon hues of emotion. At one point Crowley is the corrupt, ecstatic satyr; the next the magician, grave, pontifical and wise; then the anguished lover, "his soul like the savage upland plains in Tartary"; then a genial man of the world who accepts his lot gratefully and then a gasping sex-crazed satyr on the brink of orgasm:

> Which? All's the same. Go on. No – what is this?
>   Why dally? To the hilt! Ah mine, ah mine!
>   Kiss me – I cannot kiss you – kiss me! Kiss!
>   Oh! God! God! Oh God! Forgive me; I am thine –
> Horses and chariots that champ and clang!
>   The roar of blazing cressets that environ
>   The form that fuses in the perfect pang.
>   A blast of air through the molten iron –
> One scream of light. Creating silence drops
>   Into that silence when creation – stops.
>   ('The Vampire' XIV)

A jerky, breathless, entreaty-riddled syntax echoes the rushes and jolts of passion and the smithy metaphor – "blast of air through the molten iron" – brings the proceedings to a total eclipse. Not only does Crowley replicate the physical urgency of the moment, he also buoyantly hymns the phenomenology of love. In Sonnet IV ('The Thaumaturge'), for instance, he shows a London transformed by the alchemy of Venus. Generosity spills over from the happy couple and gilds the bustling commercial world:

> We knew enough to wake a choral rapture
> All answering Nature: I will swear the sun
>   Came out; you saw the moulting trees recapture
>   Their plumage, and the green destroy the dun.
> Nothing could jar; the British workman took
>   A kindly interest in our caresses;
>   The loafing nursemaids and the musing cook
>   Agreed with us entirely. Love impresses
> Its seal upon the world; is skilled to wake
>   The sympathy of everything that lives.
>   Kindness flows, not venom, from the snake;
>   The trodden worm dies duly – but forgives.
> The cabman asked four shillings for the job,
>   And almost boggled at my glad ten bob.
>   ('The Thaumaturge' IV)

If we compare 'Clouds Without Water' to Rupert Brooke's contemporaneous sonnets, we find the robust, affirmative tone entirely absent in the younger man. Brooke is lost, petulant and emotionally confused:

> Love is flung Lucifer-like from Heaven to Hell.
> But – there are wanderers in the middle mist,
>   Who cry for shadows, clutch and cannot tell
> Whether they love at all, or, loving, whom:
>   An old song's lady, a fool in fancy dress,
> Or phantoms, or their own face on the gloom;
>   For love of Love, or from the heart's loneliness.
> Pleasure's not theirs, nor pain. They doubt and sigh
> And do not love at all. Of these am I.
>   ('Sonnet')

Contrast this with Crowley's:

> For truth it is, my maiden, we have had
>   Already more than our fair share of pleasure.
> The good god Dionysus ivy-clad
>   Hath poured us out a draught of brimming measure.
> Let us rather give the lustiest praise
>   Our throats can sound than pray for further favour;
>   Even though our sorrow, eating up our days,
>   Devour us also. Gods enjoy the savour
> Of Man's thanksgiving ...
> ('The Hermit' XIII)

Where Brooke is doubting and muddled, Crowley is grateful; he shows "a proud glad face" and thanks the gods for his good fortune. Both responses are perfectly valid and Brooke's sonnets are delightfully accomplished. However, while the soldier-poet's love-sighs have gone through many popular editions, Crowley's spirited chronicle of sacred and profane love is unknown. A niche should be found in English poetry for these round and ringing sonnets which appear to have never been properly read or acknowledged. Even Crowley's biographer, John Symonds, has little to say about 'Clouds Without Water', finding it dull save for two lines which struck him as funny:

> The British public grunts and growls and grovels,
> Swilling its hogwash of neurotic novels.

As for the death of the lovers at the end, Crowley was forced to consider why he ended on such a tragic note. "The powers of life and death," he observed, "combine in their most frightful forms to compel the lovers to seek refuge in suicide, which they, however, regard as victory. 'The poison takes us ...' The answer is that the happy ending would have been banal. The tragedy of Eros is that he is dogged by Anteros. It is the most terrible of all anticlimaxes to have to return to the petty life which is bounded by space and time."

> Lola, dear Lola, how the stillness grows!
>   How drowsy is the world, that folds her wings
>   Over us, folding like a sunset rose
>   Her crimson rapture to the night of things!
> How all the voices and the visions fail

> As we pass through into the silent hall
> Beyond the vapours and beyond the veil,
> Beyond the Nothing as beyond the All!
> ('The Initiation' XIII)

If he had been more adept at expressing "the petty life which is bounded by space and time," Crowley might have been a better poet, but subtle gradations of sensation evade him. He pitches himself at the outermost poles, either groaning with despair or shrieking with joy. Hence the closing sequence is less absorbing than what has preceded it. The poet indulges his obsessions – disease and physical deterioration are gloatingly detailed; the language becomes coarse and commonplace; an inevitable pollution of sensibility takes hold. In contemplating a hellish extinction, the poet wastes too much breath belabouring "meal-mouthed mountebanks, that prate of Jesus, ethics, faith and reason," deliberately piling up more enemies than necessary and then encumbering them with irrelevant coprophilic imagery – hinting, possibly, at some profound link between constipation and middle-class values:

> O costive crapulence!
> They ache and strain within the water closet
> Of church and state, their shocked bleat of offence:
> "The poet's life was such a failure." Was it?
> ('The Initiation' VI)

At least, the final sonnet ends happily as the lovers anticipate the Elysian groves and bowers that await them:

> Farewell! O passionate world of changeful hours!
>   Come, Lola, let us sleep! Elysian groves
>   Await us and the beatific bower
>   Where Love is ours at last where we were Love's.
> Come, with our mouths still kissing, with our limbs
>   Still twined, relax the ecstasy! pass by
>   To the abyss of night where no star swims!
>   On to the end beyond prophecy!
> Ah Lola mine! "No happy end is this" –
>   I love you – ah! you love me – you love me!
> For we have passed beyond imagined bliss

> Into the kingdom of reality,
> Where we are crowned with flowers – yet closer creep!
> Sleep, Lola, now! I love you – sleep – ah, sleep!
> ('The Initiation' XIV)

As a sequence of love poems, 'Clouds Without Water' is unique in English literature. It graphically depicts a catalogue of sexual peccadilloes in a remarkably unabashed way for Edwardian England. One would normally expect a mood tapestry ranging from stately devotion to gentle melancholy, garnished with wistful recollection and pangs of loss. Instead we are confronted with a vigorous, persistent note of passionate affirmation; the emphasis is on raging excess – excess of ardour, of bodily pleasure, of religious intoxication. To maintain such a tone, and at the same time provide a banquet of wit, erudition and metaphysics, is an achievement of a high order.

Invocations to Pan and Other Entities

Few of Crowley's longer works achieve the unity and cohesion of 'Clouds Without Water', but incidental felicities are scattered throughout the many other volumes. Major General Fuller, who thought him "one of the greatest of English lyric poets", praised 'Alice', 'Clouds Without Water', 'Rodin in Rhyme', 'Gargoyles', 'The Winged Beetle', the four 'Rosas' and 'La Gitana', adding that "Much of the rest of it is Hudibrastic satire, and some of it is swill."[3] While Fuller was a man of taste and broad scholarship, he did not gallop happily amid the badlands of modern verse. This made him impervious to the fact that Crowley was maintaining a tradition rather than taking language forward. But he did recognise that many of Crowley's better moments occur in the context of longer pieces or as isolated verses set amidst a matrix of prose or drama.

Even patches of his magical writing have a florid glamour well-suited to radio or stage. In 1909, along with his magical assistant, Victor Neuberg, he set up camp in a desolate spot in the Moroccan desert, drew a pentacle and circle in the sand and summoned a succession of benign and baneful entities, the most terrifying of whom was the demon Chronozon. He recorded their responses in *The Vision and the Voice* (1911), a document as disquieting as anything produced by the Elizabethan magician, Dr John Dee, who had originally devised the 'angelic language'. Plays have been written around Crowley's life and antics (notably two by Snoo Wilson), and the Royal Shakespeare Company could well adapt *The Vision and the Voice* – particularly the Chronozon sequence – and patch together a Marlovian pantomime around the relationship of Crowley to Neuberg, the preparatory invocation and the denunciatory rhetoric of the demon – for he spares Crowley no criticism:

> O thou that hast written two-and-thirty books of Wisdom, and art more stupid than an owl, by thine own talk is thy vigilance wearied, and by my talk art thou befooled and tricked, O thou that sayest that thou shalt endure. Knowest thou how nigh thou art to destruction? For thou that art the Scribe hast not the understanding that alone availeth against Chronozon. And wert thou not protected by the Holy Names of God and the circle, I would rush upon thee and tear thee. For when I made myself like unto a beautiful woman, if thou hadst come to me, I would have rotted thy body with the pox, and thy liver with cancer, and I would have torn off thy testicles with my teeth. And if I had seduced thy pride, and thou hadst bidden me to come into the circle, I would have trampled thee under foot, and for a thousand years shouldst thou have been but one of the tape-worms that is in me. And if I had seduced thy pity, and thou hadst poured one drop of water without the circle, then would I have blasted thee with flame. But I was not able to prevail against thee.

The swagger and opulence here could be made to work dramatically if properly pitched and controlled, but that is hardly the point. Crowley regarded *The Vision and the Voice* as a sacred text rather than an entertainment, unlike the poetry which was meant to be disseminated and judged critically. If we had to select individual poems for evaluation, a general agreement might be reached on the virtues of 'Hymn to Pan', 'Pan to Artemis', 'The King-Ghost', 'Hong Kong Harbour' and a speech of Young John from his mystery play 'The Ship'. In the course of the next few pages, we will consider these and other thematically similar poems, diverging here and there in order to illustrate a point or expand an idea, and then move on to the drama and pornography, ending with some brief comments on Crowley's views regarding the afterlife.

The first – an invocation to the goat-god – compares favourably with Keats' poem on the same subject. If, as Dennis Diderot observed, constraint can be seen as annihilating the grandeur and energy of nature, then Crowley's 'Hymn to Pan' stands as a gesture of almost violent complicity. Instead of working up to a climax, it rides on the shattering surge of its capitulation. An ecstatic ferocity is reflected in its bucking, attenuated rhythms as the poet taps the black springs of the subconscious and allows them to well up and submerge the ego. The "lissome lust of light" is the same force that intoxicated the Berserkers, the warriors of Odin, before they went pillaging and rampaging. It is the same *ekstasis* which overwhelmed the followers of Dionysus and set them blood-letting and flesh-tearing.

As acknowledged in *Magick*, the primary source of inspiration is the scene in Sophocles' play *Ajax* where the sailors of Salamis, believing their king has recovered his sanity, start to dance and rejoice: "I shivered with love, in my joy I took wing. Io, Io Pan, Pan! O Pan, Pan! Who wanders the sea, from snow-covered Kyllene, your rock peak, appear, O lord of the dances of the gods, so that you may be with me and draw me into the spontaneous dance of Mysia and Knossos."

Crowley observed in *The Book of Thoth*, that "the sign of Capricornus is rough, harsh, dark, even blind; the impulse to create takes no account of reason. It is divinely unscrupulous, sublimely careless of result ... For pure will, unassuaged of purpose, delivered from the lust of result, is in every way perfect." In other words, a volcanic eruption or a forest fire is perfect because it acts purely from its own volition and has no intention beyond manifestation.

The goat, whose blood was hot enough to dissolve diamonds, was insatiable in its lust – an amoral attitude striking back to a time before constraint and family values. Crowley's Pan is the undifferentiating pulse of nature, akin to the Spanish duende, the puckish earth-spirit, who can turn malevolent or dangerous, in the same way a party can turn nasty when everyone has drunk too much. But it needs be emphasised that the frenzy is streaked with despair. For the anonymous vessel, who constitutes the voice of the poem, is imploring the god to take him over. Unhappy in human bondage, he wants to leave the pain and fragmentation of the world and re-unite with the cosmic All-begetter:

> I, who wait and writhe and wrestle
> With air that hath no bough to nestle,
> My body, weary of empty clasp,
> Strong as a lion and sharp as an asp –
> Come, O Come!
> I am numb
> With the lonely lust of devildom.
> ('Hymn to Pan')

Finally the god tears into his body and possesses him. The poem ends in madness that will, inevitably, succumb to the pang of gravity. For each passion hoards the echo of its death. The blood has to ebb back to the lower centres and, similarly, the spirit to a foredoomed earth in which pleasure is reined to mortality, and duty and responsibility dominate. For, taking Swinburne's view, this is not the carefree realm of Pan but of Christ, Saviour and law-giver:

> Thou hast conquered, O pale Galilean; the world has grown
>   grey from thy breath,
> We have drunken of things Lethean, and fed on the fullness
>   of death.
> ('Hymn To Proserpine')

Similarly the address of 'Pan to Artemis' (a favourite, incidentally, among neo-pagan lovers of poetry) shows alliterative ebullience and a confident use of those clarion rhymes utilised by Swinburne, Poe and their imitators. The Lord of the Forest invokes the Moon Goddess – a classic mingling of beauty and beast – and recalls their intense union. This poetry of costume and stage effects would make a superb opening to a Dorian fantasia. The imagery – threateningly rather soothingly pastoral – takes a lightning-leap into a region of pines, volcanoes and moody, moonlit shores. The element of danger, of frustrated raving, is neatly tethered by octads that retain the inner tension. Like Southey's poem on the Lodore Falls, the lines cascade over a series of short drops, a mountain torrent trailing a wake of swirling, euphonious bubbles. They include two ("The sentinel sadness/Of cliff-clinging pine") that exhibit an alliterative brio worthy of the best of Crowley's romantic forbears:

> Uncharmable charmer
> Of Bacchus and Mars
> In the sounding rebounding
> Abyss of the stars!
> O virgin in armour,
> Thine arrows unsling
> In the brilliant resilient
> First rays of the spring!
>
> By the force of the fashion
> Of love, when I broke
> Through the shroud, through the cloud,
> Through the storm, through the smoke,
> To the mountain of passion
> Volcanic that woke—
> By the rage of the mage
> I invoke, I invoke!
>
> By the midnight of madness:—
> The lone-lying sea
> The swoon of the moon,
> Your swoon unto me;
> The sentinel sadness
> Of cliff-clinging pine,
> That night of delight
> You were mine, you were mine!

At a far lower pressure of intensity, Crowley wrote revelling verses which – if one has a limited fondness for unremitting phallic marathons, drinking and drug-taking – can prove tiresome, a reaction perhaps intensified by the insertion of Ohs! and Ahs! and similar orgasmic exhalations. Sometimes the voice is drowsy and decadent and on other occasions conceitedly blunt:

> A room I dare scarce wag a limb in!
> Damn these respectable women!
> Give me the ocean to swim in!
>
> Passion – their lamps only sputter!
> Mustard is better than butter;
> Give me a girl from the gutter!
> ('In My Harem')

'Chicago May'

The appeal of prostitutes and casual sexual encounters lay in their undemandingness. Crowley maintained that cheerful tarts, robust negresses or uncomplicated sensual mistresses, generated more potent magical charges than cultured society women, thereby assisting access to the astral plane. However, this facility seems not to have applied to 'Chicago May' (1914), a woman with whom Crowley became briefly embroiled and imposed upon the name of the notorious Irish-American gangstress. He celebrated their liaison in a long poem which in general intention – though hardly in skill or achievement – exudes a frisson of relished disgust on par with Swift's lines to 'A Beautiful Young Nymph Going to Bed' or 'The Lady's Dressing Room'.

But whereas Swift witheringly detaches himself from the object of focus, Crowley is *in there* as the disenchanted paramour. With none-too-dazzling irony, it is labelled 'a love poem', but is actually an epic of abuse, pointing out how May is fat and undesirable and will not allow her lover to stray an inch. Opening unflatteringly – "This is my hour of peace; the great sow snores" – a ramshackle conveyor belt of insults whisks through the uncharitable stanzas. Gross, malodorous and lustful, May longs to be loved and serenaded, but her "loose bulging belly" and "sagging teats" are at odds with the simpering poises she adopts. Yearning for stability and tenderness, she nervously pursues her lover, wherever he is, holding vigil outside the lavatory door:

> She never lets me from her sight an hour.
>> On one excuse, five minutes and no more!
> And then – even then! – she fears to lose her power.
>> I hear her heavy breathing at the door:
> She listens: 'What's he doing?' One confesses
> That must leave you to a pair of guesses.

The Roman poet Horace wrote a work called the *Epodes of Horace* (30 BC) that records a dialogue between he and an Italian witch called Canidia. Echoing the classical satirist, Crowley evokes the same ugly sorceress, who had the power of raising the dead, yet whose range of potions cannot rival the oils, powders and cosmetic plasterwork employed by May to scaffold the crumbling lineaments of her attraction. Inevitably the application only increases the lardage:

> Upon the toilet-table stand in rows
> Potamums that had made Canidia queasy.
> Now we must change the proverb, I suppose:
> 'Sweets to the sweet' for 'Grease to the greasy.'
> Yet how can one go on adding grease to that
> Which is the fount and archetype of fat?

May adorns herself with jewellery, but the effect is inevitably displeasing:

> Ah, but the monstrous jewels that you wear,
> Until you look like a shop window struck
> By lightning, its white velvet soaked – these flares
> Pure sparkles kindled in a mass of muck
> By the great light – O God! – of the pure Sun,
> Which you avoid 'because it freckles one.'

In deflecting the ravages of time upon its female scapegoat, 'Chicago May' tries and sentences by dint of the savage criterion of physical appearance. It connives in the deception that ageing is a selective disfiguration rather than a legacy all must endure. (Crowley, nudging forty, glimpsed in May the reprisals wrought by the excesses to which he was prone: heavy drinking, elaborate meals and ceaseless sexual experiment.) Meanwhile May secures for herself a younger lover, releasing Crowley, who journeys across the seas to meet his true love 'Laylah'. In woeful switchback, he ceases seething cyanide fumes and starts blowing mystic honey bubbles of true love, ending with a Hollywood-style embrace on a moonlit beach:

> These dunes, these stars, these holy trees
> That sentinel our sleep, the moan
> Of the tired sea, the birds and breeze,
> The moon, all these things are our own.
> We made them for our love! our home,
> Our palace of eternal rest: –
> Here, by the starlight and the foam,
> Fold me, a flower to your breast!

Shrill in tone, blithely and crassly autonomous, there are probably more ill-judged things in literature than 'Chicago May', but few spring to mind.

At the other extreme, Crowley involved himself with psychically fragile 'borderline' females, teetering on the verge of breakdown or insanity, believing their instability rendered them more plastic and 'astral'. If their personalities did not touch his deepest feelings, so much the better – he did not want to get psychologically enmeshed. In that way, they would not hold up his religious crusade or taint his soul with emotional impurities. His sonnet 'Penelope' celebrates the harlot at the expense of the faithful soul-mate:

> Ulysses 'scaped the sorceries of that queen
>   That turned to swine his goodly company,
> And came with sails broad-burgeoning and clean
>   Over the ripples of his native sea.
> Yet for the shores his eyes had lately seen,
>   He kept a half-regretful memory;
> And thought when all flower-strewn ways were green,
>   'Better love Circe than Penelope!'
>
> Yes. A good woman's love will forge a chain
>   To break the spirit of the bravest Greek;
> While with a harlot one may leap again
> Free as the waters of the western main,
>   And turn with no heart-pang the vessel's beak
>   Out to the oceans that all seamen seek.

The "oceans that all seamen seek" is the expansion of potential that comes with finding the "True Will" – a notion Crowley erratically pursued all his life. But discourtesy to women is only one side of the emotional coin. The dismissal is a shade too strident; the arrogant, bullying air contrasts with other poems where Crowley sees himself abased before some Kali-like figure who derives pleasure from being cruel to male supplicants. In 'Jezebel' the prophet becomes infatuated with the Scarlet Woman and naturally there is a pronounced moral deterioration:

> Now let me die, at last desired,
>   At last beloved of thee my queen;

> Now let me die, with blood attired,
>   Thy servant, naked and obscene;
> To thy white skull, thy palms, thy feet,
> Clinging, dead, infamous, complete.
>   ('Jezebel')

This is lurid and unappealing. It failed to charm Mario Praz who, in *The Romantic Agony*, wrote contemptuously of Crowley's slavish imitation of Swinburne and the blood-and-pain school. Written off the top of the head, unchecked by stops or inhibitions, this is verse rather than poetry, brash overstatement instead of a willingness to sensitively chart the more spectacular extremes of abasement.

'Leah Sublime'

Perhaps a more honest expression of such pathology is found in 'Leah Sublime', addressed to his mistress and Scarlet Woman, Leah Hirsig, and the most blatantly obscene poem Crowley ever wrote. Unlike Yeats, for instance, who kept his mask in place and consistently dignified his passions with hewn language, myth and symbol, Crowley was prepared to tear away the veil and expose himself as human and contemptible, to turn his shame inside out and present it for others. An astonishing risk, for who, one might ask, would turn to or respect a religious leader who wrote these lines?

> Leah Sublime,
> Goddess above me!
> Snake of the slime
> Alostrael, love me!
> Our master, the devil
> Prospers the revel.
> Tread with your foot
> My heart till it hurt!
> Tread on it, put
> The smear of your dirt
> On my love, on my shame
> Scribble your name!
> Straddle your Beast
> My Masterful Bitch
> With the thighs of you greased
> With the Sweat of your Itch!

The invocatory first verse prepares us for something along the lines of Baudelaire's dark amours. But what follows is quite different, not an erotic collaboration, but a venomous rebuke:

> Cunt! you have harboured
> All dirt and disease
> In your slimy unbarbered
> Loose hole, with its cheese
> And its monthlies, and pox
> You chewer of cocks!
> Cunt, you have sucked
> Up pricks, you squirted
> Out foetuses, fucked
> Till bastards you blurted
> Out into space –
> Spend on my face!

The blend of masochism and disgust explodes in a sexual rage. Short, stabby lines ram against each other making an inventory of obscenities, a queue of abuses:

> Choke me with spilth
> Of your sow-belly's filth.
> Stab your demoniacal
> Smile to my brain!
> Soak me in cognac
> Cunt and cocaine;
> Sprawl on me! Sit
> On my mouth, Leah, shit!
> Shit on me, slut!
> Creamy the curds
> That drip from your gut!
> Greasy the turds!
> Dribble your dung
> On the tip of my tongue!

The poem persists at this pitch of degradation. Potently disintoxicating, it is so intensely personal that, one feels, in reading it, a pact is being broken; there is injury to the intimacy. No radiations of love and romance, no hidden symbols, no mystic images substituted for physical fact, only the 'soft machine' exploring the more savage shores of its possibilities. With its leaking orifices, odours and rank exudations, we are shown the awakened flesh in all its glory and disgust. The blunt clarity of the language seems an act of violence in itself. But after the words have been spat out, language can do nothing, save re-gather its patches of dignity and take up new bearings amid the smoke and shrapnel of the exploded taboo. The problem is: why should 'Leah Sublime' be so disturbing? Why should there be such shame-charges attached to these words and acts? Is it because of the implied humiliation? Is it because of the heartless abuse? To have such an effect, it must locate a network in the reader in which these voodoo-like initiations already have a guilty presence. 'Leah Sublime' is biliously, disturbingly human, but its frankness aspires to therapy rather than art: a determination to state the unsayable in the hope that the effort will, obscurely, emancipate or 'release' the writer.

The Eternal Moment

Between braggadocio and masochism, a balancing point can be located in the many reflective poems, usually focusing upon a mystical experience or a direct intimation of the divine. Judging from the number of the poems wherein he describes himself transported into some ineffable realm, Crowley's spiritual exercises must have been remarkably effective. 'Aha!' (1909), written in couplets that are surefooted as they are soporific, is cast as a dialogue between pupil and master and takes aboard such doctrines as passive attention and waiting, the emptying of the soul, the destruction of the ego, the eight limbs of Yoga, and the unwinding of the fabric of the mind as reason is destroyed and substituted with trust:

> Blind horror catches at my breath.
> The path of the abysss runs through
> Things darker, dismaller than death!
> Courage and will! What boots their force?
> The mind rears like a frightened horse.
> There is no memory possible
> Of that unfathomable hell.
> Even the shadows that arise
> Are things too dreadful to recount!

Only with the surrender of the intellect does the will recover its joyful impetus:

> Then I dropped my reasoning.
> Vacant and accursed thing!
> By my Will I swept away
> The web of metaphysic, smiled
> At the blind labyrinth, where the grey
> Old snake of madness wove his wild
> Curse!
>
> ('Aha!')

Like a Buddhist priest, Crowley hymned not only the shedding of the intellect, but also the bliss of non-existence – a predilection that invites some scepticism. Why did such an egotistical man advocate the goal of non-being or self-extinction? Probably the answer lies in his tendency towards hyper-activity. In the *Confessions*, he admits that he could not eat without reading for fear of wasting time. Throughout his motley career, he was furiously engaged, travelling, climbing, hunting, painting, chess-playing and debauching. By immersing himself in all-absorbing activity, he coiled his spiritual spring very tight: hence, when he did relax and meditate, he found himself almost violently catapulted out of his body. Frantic activity intensified the pressure of the release mechanism:

> Only by energy and strife
> May man attain eternal rest,
> Dissolve the desperate lust of life
> By infinite agony and zest ...
>
> ('Kali')

Parallel to possessing inexhaustible energy is often a desire to be released from the ache of having to expend it. It is hardly surprising therefore that many of Crowley's poems posit the idea of perfect stillness – when the individual self is blanked out and liberated from the pressure of immediate sensation. There is, too, a hankering after Nirvana or immaculate extinction:

> O night!
> Fade, love! Fade light!

> I pass beyond Life's law.
> I melt as snow; as ice I thaw;
> As mist I dissipate: I am borne, I draw
> Through chasms on the mountains: stormy gusts
> Of ancient sorrows and forgotten lusts
> Bear me along: they touch me not ...
> ('Orpheus' Vol. III)

One finds a less tempestuous version of the same in 'Why Jesus Wept':

> Thy flower-life is shed
> Into eternity,
> A waveless lake.
> ('Why Jesus Wept')

Exponents of Zen have bequeathed to us a vast literature about this passive pulling into emptiness. Kosen Imakita, a famous monk of the Meiji era, described a night when he was immersed in meditation: "I suddenly found myself in a very strange condition. There was no before and no after. Everything was as though suspended. The object of my own meditation and my own self had disappeared. The only thing I felt was that my own innermost self was completely united and filled with everything above and below and around. An unlimited light was shining within me. After some time, I came back to myself like one risen from the dead. My seeing and hearing, my thought and my motions were quite different from what they had been until then. When, gropingly, I tried to think of the truths of the world and to grasp the meaning of the incomprehensible, I understood everything. Everything seemed to me quite clear and real. Spontaneously, I threw up my arms in an excess of joy and danced."

Crowley repeatedly evokes this enlightened state. In the admirable 'Hong Kong Harbour', he shows the mind released from all passions and allowed to wander, discarnate and bodiless, between the moon and the sea:

> As one who standing on the moon
> Sees the vast horns in silver hewn,
> Himself in darkness, and beholds
> How silently all space unfolds

> Into her shapeless breast the spark
> And sacred phantoms of the dark;
> So in the harbour horns I stand
> Till I forget the land.
>
> No passion stirs their depth, nor moves;
> No life disturbs their sweet dead loves;
> No being holds a crown or throne;
> They are, and I in them, alone:
> Only some lute player grown star
> Is heard like whispering flowers afar;
> And some divided, single tune,
> Sobs from sea and moon.

Like Keats in his sonnet 'Bright Star', he envies the painless perfection of two inviolate forms:

> Amid they mountains shall I rise
> O moon, and float about thy skies?
> Beneath thy waters shall I roam,
> O sea, and call thy valleys home,
> Or on daedalian oarage fare
> Forth in interlunar air?
> Imageless mirror-life! to be
> Sole between moon and sea.

Even in the context of such lulling mood-music, one stumbles over the syntax owing to Crowley's habit of blurring subject and object. What is the precise meaning of the second verse? The phrase "unfolds into" is difficult to visualise and what exactly are "the spark" and "sacred phantoms of the dark"? The moon? Other stars seen from the moon? The emotion is clear but the poem invites the reader to be swept along by vagueries of association rather than an exact impression of what is being said. There is a drowning of sense as the poet succumbs to the allure of alliteration, although the allusion to Orpheus – "some lute player grown star" – is effective and moving.

'The King-Ghost'

While exploring China on the back of a Burmese pony, Crowley wrote 'The King-Ghost' (1906) wherein he personifies accumulated forebodings about his mission. After an arduous magical experiment followed by the shock of his pony throwing him forty feet down a cliff, he was feeling disorientated and was further oppressed by an abominable draught of wind. Finally his gloom crystallised in the shape of a 'dark night of the soul' poem.

"I did not understand the essence of the doubt," he wrote in his *Confessions*, "and it is hard to explain it in prose, even now. It seems at first sight to be a reflection of the all-embracing doubt of the Abyss. It concentrated itself into the entirely practical question: is there an Augoeides [from the Greek for 'morning light' or 'dawn'] after all? Is there a Path of the Wise? Am I simply fooling myself? And in the 'King-Ghost' my only answer is to appeal to the very power whose existence is in dispute."

> The King-Ghost is abroad. His spectre legions
>   Sweep from their icy lakes and bleak ravines
> Unto those weary and untrodden regions
>   Where man lies penned amid his Might-have-beens.
>   Keep us in safety, Lord
>   What time the King-Ghost is abroad!
>
> The King-Ghost from his grey malefic slumbers
>   Awakes the malice of his bloodless brain.
> He marshals the innumerable numbers
>   Of shrieking shapes on the sepulchral plain.
>   Keep us, for Jesu's sake,
>   What time the King-Ghost is awake.
>
> The King-Ghost wears a crown of hopes forgotten;
>   Dead loves are woven in his ghastly robe;
> Bewildered wills and faiths grown old and rotten
>   And deeds undared his sceptre, sword and globe.
>   Keep us, O Mary maid,
>   What time the King-Ghost goes arrayed.
>
> The Hell-Wing whistles through his plumeless pinions;
>   Clanks all that melancholy host of bones;
> Fate's principalities and Death's dominions
>   Echo the drear discord, the tuneless tones.
>   Keep us, dear God, from ill,
>   What time the Hell-Wind whistles shrill.

> The King-Ghost hath no music but their rattling;
>   No scent but Death's grown faint and fugitive,
> No light but this their leprous pallor battling
>   Weakly with night. Lord, shall these dry bones live?
>   O keep us in the hour
>   Wherein the King-Ghost hath his power!
>
> The King-Ghost boasts eternal usurpature;
>   For in this pool of tears his fingers fret.
> I had imagined, by enduring nature,
>   The twin-gods 'Thus-will-I' and 'May-be-yet'.
>   God, keep us most from ill,
>   What time the King-Ghost grips the will!

The spiritual pilgrim lacks a constant point, a measuring rod, by which he can read his achievement. To gain the strength to carry on, he needs confirmation from the Secret Chiefs, but how can be sure that he is not merely puffing up his stature with blasts from his own ego? The 'King-Ghost' provides a partial answer by demonstrating how a mystical affirmation can conquer despair:

> Silver and gold, what flame resurges?
>   What living light pours forth in emerald waves?
>   What inmost Music drowns the clamorous dirges?
>   Shrieking they fly, the King-Ghost and his slaves.
>   Lord, let thy Ghost indwell,
>   And save us from the power of Hell.

In today's vocabulary, Crowley is writing about "the peak experience" or "eruption into consciousness", around which Colin Wilson (*pace* Abraham Maslow) has developed a philosophy, the vitalizing overflow of energy which recharges the seeker in his quest for a deeper sense of unity and purpose. Maslow, an atheist, tried to disassociate it from religious experience yet came perilously close in some of his definitions. "It's as if everything becomes simultaneous," he wrote, "and at the same time, there is some dimension of depths, or perhaps, better said, heights, in which one penetrates into a more central reality or essence." A sense of implicate meaning pierces the phenomenal screen, and the individual is empowered by the revelation that he is a distinct and central component in a world of freedom and choice.

The 'King-Ghost' shows the possibility of *becoming* dispersing past failures and defeats; the twin gods *Thus I Will* and *May Be Yet* subdue the forces of chaos and lethargy. (It is interesting to speculate to what degree Crowley was manic depressive, his moods varying between black despair and irrepressible enthusiasm, one of his stock phrases being "geyser-gush", used to imply a lift or elevation of mood.)

Although utilising some traditional vulgarisms of phraseology ("My dreams of old that never saw the sun"), the 'King-Ghost' personifies despair as a glamorous, Luciferian figure. The alliterative music recalls the Coleridge of *The Ancient Mariner*, and, while it does not achieve the numinous intensity of that great poem, it is a worthy second best and deserves to be better known. Its rhythms weave a web of appropriate echoes, and it was an inspired move to dovetail the quatrains with prayer-couplets – affecting to despise Christianity, the poet understood how it could be used to empower his poetry! Gothically gloomy to begin, then soaring into the empyrean of self-actualisation, 'The King-Ghost' is more profound and uplifting than Kipling's prosaically phrased 'If' and should be included in any future anthology of supernatural poetry.

But Crowley admitted that the answer he gave in 'The King-Ghost' was insufficient. The most difficult fact to realise is that we are "each one, eternal and individual", and there is no answer to such attacks save to boldly engage oneself upon tasks that re-affirm one's individual truth.

Sir Palamede

Both 'Aha!' and the 'King-Ghost' are spiritual quest poems, and their climax, almost inevitably, is the discovery of Crowley's own philosophy or a line of thought that was preoccupying him. Quest poems are interesting in the way *Pilgrim's Progress* is – for its stark personifications of a network of ideas and projections. Often they urge into existence a false reality by giving body to qualities that cannot exist alone: pride, avarice, vanity, sloth, lechery, courage and treachery. The poet sees life rather as if he is standing at the prow of a ship, cutting through the waters of society towards 'treasure island', where 'truth' lies buried in a silver casket – a conceit which Crowley, in his role of a guru, delighted in standing on its head. One of his lighter poems of this type is entitled 'The High History of the Good Sir Palemede and of his following the Questing Beast' (1905), a spectacular chronicle of effort and futility.

Sir Palemede is the Saracen knight who loved Isolde and was defeated by Tristram in a single combat, after which he became a Christian. But Crowley puts him to work in an entirely different way, opening with him riding on the shore of Syria. There he comes across the dead body of his father around which an albatross circles. Obtusely the lines hint a debt has been settled and the knight condones the deed:

> He knew his father. Still he sate,
> Nor quivered nerve, nor muscle stirred;
> While round them flapped insatiate
> The fell, abominable bird.
>
> The knight approves the justice done,
> And pays with that his rowel's debt;
> While yet the forehead of the son
> Stands beaded with an icy sweat.

The scene moves to the Arabian shore, where his mother is being embraced by a "loathly negro beneath blue pavilions", and he promptly murders her and sets fire to the encampment. This brash assault sets the tone for the rest of his adventures which, indeed, pile up thick and fast, drawing in Camelot, the wilds of Wales, the court of King Arthur, a mystic dwarf, a Druid at Stonehenge, a rationalist philosopher, the Cretan labyrinth, the jungles of India, the dunes of Brittany, the pit of Hell, barbaric sacrifice, orgasm and ecstasy, the rites of Ancient Egypt and other exotic sorceries. Sir Palemede pursues a certain Questing Beast who is the equivalent to Moby Dick in Melville's novel, good and evil, a shape-shifting, many-faceted, elusive truth containing all extensions and possibilities.

Towards the end, in a sunlit wood, he meets up with a hunchback who doubts the existence of the Beast or any quest and impertinently suggests the whole of Sir Palemede's life might be a vain illusion, for which impudence he is slain. (The knight's tendency to kill everyone, whether friend or foe, symbolises his renunciation of worldly attachments.) Finally Sir Palemede obtains a vision of Pan and regains the strength and vitality he had lost. But he is still denied any sacred or illuminating vision, for "upon the loftiest summit of a great mountain, he perceiveth Naught." So he returns to Camelot and announces his failure to King Arthur and his knights, upon which "the Beast cometh nestling to him" and Christ's voice congratulates him, saying that "each failure is a step in the Path".

Technically speaking, the quatrains are nimble and fleet of rhyme, and a certain enjoyment can be had following the knight's progress. The opening is confident and stately:

> Sir Palamede the Saracen
> Rode by the marge of many a sea:
> He had slain a thousand evil men
> And set a thousand ladies free.
>
> Armed to the teeth, the glittering knight
> Galloped along the sounding shore,
> His silver arms one lake of light,
> Their clash one symphony of war.
>
> How still the blue enamoured sea
> Lay in the blaze of Syria's noon!
> The eternal roll eternally
> Beat out its monotonic tune.

After that flying start, set-pieces and obstacles accumulate with an excess that is typical. Varied as they are, the encounters do not build on what has gone before but repeat themselves. Monotony sets in as one realises that this poem need not end anywhere. It is like listening to someone torrentially possessed. Steadily the reader becomes aware of the originality lying in the argument rather than the language. What the poem appears to be saying is that, only after the spiritual pilgrim has utterly ransacked his personal resources, does he obtain a sage-like indifference to the ripples of the phenomenal world. Hence energy is expended in order that an inner transaction takes place whereby that which has been used up is replaced by spiritual commission.

'The Ship'

Yet another spiritual excursion, recited at the funeral of Raoul Loveday, can be found in the mystery play 'The Ship' wherein Crowley articulates the values of Freemasonry. The stage consists of an azure veil through which can be seen a gold and ivory column, "on which are poised two intersecting disks, terrestrial and celestial, the cut-off part forming a true Vesica", and in front of the column is a candle beside which stands John, the high priest, dressed in robes of gold and scarlet embroidery, holding a sceptre and orb. The setting epitomises the 'higher pantheism' of Edwardian England – an over-draped pretentiousness that substitutes silks and soporific speeches for dramatic content.

Unexpectedly what follows is the violent sacrificial murder of the priest by a Chinaman, an Arab and a Zulu, who are themselves subsequently eviscerated. John's corpse, ceremoniously wrapped up, is launched on a sacred voyage from which it returns, still dead. The priestess and the virgin, Julia and Joanna, try to urge it into life by music and revel, but it does not respond. Only when they lift it and stand it against a tree do the wrappings fall away and the reborn John announces:

> I am that I am, the flame
> Hidden in the sacred ark.
> I am the unspoken name
> I the unbegotten spark.

Like Yeats, whose adaptation of the Noh plays drew critical approval, Crowley was trying to take drama back to its ritual roots. In this Frazerian skirmish of revenge and resurrection, he was aiming for plainness of character and design. However, if the actions and gestures are simple and violent, the language of 'The Ship' demurs to the decorative. Still, the play is vindicated by passages of lyrical vivacity and the added attraction of "a great beetle" who emerges from the pool of wisdom holding in its mandibles the sacred Vesica or bladder, symbolic of spirit and also of the 'Yoni'.

It seems likely that the central metaphor was borrowed from Longfellow whose *The Building of the Ship* was a patriotic celebration of the 'Union', praising the effort and dedication that goes into the making of "the ship of state" whereas Crowley's vessel has more in common with D.H. Lawrence's "ship of death", a vessel of renewal and immortality. The crowning speech, delivered by Young John, sums up the mystery of life and generation: the spark caught up in the endless flux, the gross merging into the fine, the fusion of sexual and spiritual. The paradox of personal development, the idea of Self as God, is lucidly formulated:

> I am He that ever goeth,
> Being in myself the Way;
> Known, that yet no mortal knoweth,
> Shewn, that yet no mortal showeth,
> I, the child of night and day.
> I am never-dying youth.
> I am Love, and I am Truth.

Note the deliberate pun in "Being in myself the Way", implying the ego blocking the path of personal development and also literally the 'Way' in the sense of each soul germinating the seed of a unique destiny:

> In the sea my father lieth,
> Wept by waters, lost for ever
> Where the waste of woe replieth:
> 'Naught and nowhere! Naught and Never!'
> I that served as once he served,
> I that shine as once he shone,
> I must swerve as he has swerved,
> I must go as he has gone.
>
> He begat me; in my season
> I must such a son beget,
> Suffer to the triple treason,
> Setting as my father set.
> These my witnesses and women –
> These shall dare the ark again,
> Find the sacred ark to swim in
> The remorseless realm of rain.

The wave-change of death is reconciled with the phallic flowering-rod and the solar and vegetation cycles. Echoes of 'The Tempest' ("In the sea my father lieth ...") invoke a desolation and beauty unmatched elsewhere. The alliteration is sad, grave and proper – all is nobly and musically fused. The result is one of the finest mystical poems in the language. Towards the end, the imagery takes on a quality of harvest richness in order to consecrate the ceremony, and the roles of priest and supplicant are Platonically idealised:

> Flowers and fruit I bring to bless you,
> Cakes or corn and wealth of wine;
> With my crown I will caress you,
> With my music make you mine.
> Though I perish, I preserve you;
> Through my fall, ye rise above;
> Ruling you, your priest, I serve you
> Being life, and being love.

In the climax to the drama – dedicated, significantly, to Theodore Reuss, the German Grand Master – Crowley was trying to provide a ritual centrepiece for his religion. It was the thelemic equivalent to the Catholic Mass, save the deity it addressed was not the Christian god, but the abiding presence behind all life-forms, "Who hast no nature, and no name."

> Thou who art I, beyond all I am,
> Who hast no nature, and no name.
> Who art, when all but Thou art gone.
> Thou, centre and secret of the Sun.
> Thou, hidden spring of all things known
> And unknown. Thou aloof, alone,
> Thou, the true fire within the reed
> Brooding and breeding, source and seed
> Of life, love, liberty and light,
> Thee I invoke, my faint fresh fire
> Kindling as my intents aspire.

By paying tribute to what is almost a divine vacuum, Crowley was seeking to preserve the dignity of religion while divesting it of the mythological clutter that affronted the scientific or rationally minded. Hence his Gnostic Mass – in fact, the concluding part of 'The Ship' – is a hymn to the generative and dissolutional processes of life. It has much in common with Dylan Thomas who also liked to celebrate time as a cyclic unity:

> The force that through the green fuse drives the flower
> Drives my green age; that blasts the roots of trees
> Is my destroyer.

Oddly enough, in view of his self-avowed non-intellectuality, Thomas borrowed his inspiration from a striking passage in Schopenhauer's *The World as Will and Idea*. The philosopher detects this will in "the force that shoots and vegetates in the plant, indeed the force by which the crystal is formed, the force that turns the magnet to the North Pole ... and finally even gravitation, which acts so powerfully in all matter, pulling the stone to the earth and the earth to the sun; all these he [the reader] will recognise as different only in the phenomenon, but the same according to their inner nature."

In Schopenhauer's view, one's duty was to thwart this overbearing will by renouncing the world and its sensual enticements. Instead of giving way, stand fast in a posture of ascetic detachment or escape into art or philosophy. But this was a long way from Crowley's approach – he was less negative. He believed that such a stance was a denial of the process by which life came into being. Although attracted to Buddhism, he saw love as the will finding its natural expression. Sexuality was the vehicle through which spirit manifested itself, and thus should feature prominently in religion. One mastered it by indulgence rather than self-denial.

'The World's Tragedy'

Like most poets, Crowley was attracted to drama, probably because it has a more 'essential' texture than straight prose. Poets seldom have the patience of novelists like Henry James who, by artfully drip-feeding description and psychological detail, build up a cast of characters bit by bit. If they desire to spread their talents across a larger canvas, they invariably opt for drama – seeing it as starker and closer to poetry. Unfortunately, although many poets borrow the form, few bother to master the technique and they produce dramas with entirely undifferentiated characters who pour out words in the mechanical, efficient fashion of a reservoir spillway. Crowley seemed to follow such models. His first effort *The Poem* (1898) is a naive little offering, while *The Fatal Force* (1899) has an Egyptian setting and is as unreal as *The Mother's Tragedy* (1899), a murky mélange of passion, bastardy and incest, culminating in a razor-slashing finale. In fact, every drama Crowley wrote, whether domestic or apocalyptic, is tinged with the antinomianism of an alienated psyche.

A fellow-mountaineer took him to task for erecting campsites in the most spectacular and impractical places. This habit spills over into his dramatic writing where the subject matter tends towards world-shaking incidents like the birth of a new Saviour or the coming of the Anti-Christ or the perpetration of some unspeakable act. Furthermore, instead of deepening and extending motifs and characters, he tries to maintain novelty by introducing new elements and personages, so the reader ends up bewildered by freewheeling invention and lack of focus. It is as if he is trying to stun by sheer excess rather than producing something ably crafted and psychologically penetrating.

While staying with his mother at Eastbourne in the spring of 1908, he wrote 'The World's Tragedy', a "Roman play" dedicated to Pan, featuring a varied cast including a company of rats, a company of toads, worms, monsters, a brass bottle containing a blue Mannikin, Alexander the Great, Govinda King of the Indies, and Chau, Son of Heaven. It sounds exciting, a farrago of excess and craziness but, like most of Crowley's 'plays', it is undiscussible in dramatic terms and prefaced by a satiric diatribe against the British establishment that is more strident than witty, attacking their sexual hypocrisy in a manner that sits awkwardly on the stasis of the page.

The list of characters is far more exciting than the drama itself which is a non-event. Each line of verse is smooth and inevitable as the shine on a slippery floor. One is instantly oppressed by the poet's mechanic verve, dropping a ton of pastoral clichés, treading monotonous measure after monotonous measure, presenting a sterile drawing-room Arcadia, "a glade of green moss" in which there is "a merry company languidly playing." While this improbable troupe are prancing, skipping and kissing, a vulture with a face like "a low-class Jew" looks down on them disgustedly and wonders how he might effectively poison their pleasure. Discussing this with a pigeon, he is beguiled by a gloomy notion:

> THE DOVE: Listen! I will find a woman ...
> And on her beget this lambkin
> In the image of a man ...

> Let the lamb grow up to manhood
> Then we'll have him whipped and tortured
> And eventually killed.
>
> VULTURE: That sounds lovely.
>
> THE LAMB: Do you think so?
> I record my vote against it.
>
> THE DOVE: Stupid! in a day or so
> We will have you rise again.

In order that the Golden Age will be supplanted by an aeon of disruption and spiritual repression, Jesus lets himself be sacrificed on the cross. But Christ's reign is destined to come to an end, and Alexander, the good magician, prophesies the arrival of none other than Crowley who will restore life and love to Arcady:

> ALEXANDER: I too have died to Pan, and he
> Hath begotten upon me
> A secret wonder that must wait
> For the hour of the falling of thy fate.
> Nineteen centuries shalt thou
> Plague earth with that agonizing brow,
> And then that age of sordid strife
> Give place to the aeon of love and life.
> A lion shall rise and swallow thee,
> Bringing back life into Arcady.

So what we have is a highly uninspired skit on Christianity as an anti-joy movement, a piece of arbitrarily devised folly to make life more painful and tortuous. But Crowley drops this line when the philosophers, Heraclitus and Chrysippus, enter. The latter styles existence as a placid mirror across which play a flickering succession of life-forms, legions of souls passing from being into non-being and back again, the perishable interpenetrating with the eternal, and both lit up by a quintessential radiance that fuses all phenomena. Brooding Heraclitus reflects that life renews itself amid the blood and spillage of its own striving. All noble things undergo dissolution and destruction in order that they shall be replenished and reborn in an altered guise, a tragic, unprogressive philosophy, moderated by a Hegelian hint of the world-spirit – in this instance Pan – aiming at some ultimate perfecting statement:

> Ah! but some evil things have brooded here
> Over the sleepers. May it be indeed
> The truth that some strange fate threatens the world?
> That Art and Love and Beauty, to renew
> Their glory, must be bathed in their own blood?
> But who shall understand the Soul of Pan?
> Involved in All and still apart from All!
> For steeped therein as I am all my life,
> I know but exquisite beatitude,
> Knowing the whole,
> Then who shall know or care
> What may befall the part?

Only the philosopher-mystic has the ability to be both observer and participant, to be part but also comprehend the whole. Crowley had travelled extensively in India and Ceylon and his outlook was deeply indebted to Buddhism, a religion that, in equating sorrow with worldly desire, urges men and women to turn their back on the world of appearances and seek the non-illusional realm.

The Angel of Venice

Slightly more disciplined – but still preposterous – is 'Mortadello' (1912), a fantastic, artificial drama, concerning power politics in Renaissance Venice – or perhaps that sounds too sophisticated for a play that it is as lurid as it is ludicrous. The mocking shadow of Machiavelli dominates the action; his cynical philosophy permeates the death-drenched scenario.

The play is written in Alexandrines, a verse form about which Pope wrote:

> A needless Alexandrine ends this song
> That, like a wounded snake, drags its slow length along.

In 'Mortadello', this scheme is further complicated by an irregular pattern of internal rhymes, rendering the crazy plot even more wilful, contrived and hard to follow.

> Oh for the blind kiss of the wind, the desert air
> Thrilling the blue and shrilling through my soul's despair.

By packing tight effects like these, Crowley thought he was giving good value – throwing in additional rhymes for no extra charge – but unfortunately he was only emasculating language by larding it with flummery and flim-flam.

At the centre of the action is Monica who wishes to become the autocrat of Venice. First she bids her Negro lover to murder the Doge's daughter. He flings the body in a canal but is later asked to retrieve it. Dragging it out and dressing it up, she tricks high-ranking Mortadello into marrying it. But scheming Monica has many enemies; her lover is murdered while she is praying passionately. Her enemies assail her but she stalls their vengeance by producing the stigmata. Finally she forces Mortadello (who finds marriage to a corpse unsatisfactory) to wed her, and later, disguised as a Saharan dancer, plies him with hashish whereupon he loses his wits and attempts to attack the papal legate. Monica kills him before he can harm the old man, thus presenting herself as 'The Angel of Venice'.

With its engaging props like poisoned crucifixes, 'Mortadello' might have played to a packed house during the Jacobean era, but reading it today one sees only a wasteful expenditure of literary stamina. As Gilbert Canaan, who reviewed it, remarked, "Mr Crowley ... refuses to be taken seriously. His bloodthirsty, lecherous play he calls a comedy. It is a riotous farce. Intoxication of blood, of words, of hysteria, of lust – takes the place of imagination. The play is exciting, but most amusing in its invective ... Mr Crowley has talents, scores of talents, but, seemingly, no power to use, discipline or develop them." Canaan's verdict is correct. 'Mortadello' is not 'imagined' in the strict sense of the word; it does not 'radiate' emotional connections but belongs to the world of cartoon cruelty, utterly removed from the sphere of psychological validity.

Yet another verse play was *The Argonauts* (1904). Unactable as drama, it makes better reading owing to several effective lyrics – notably the evocations of Hong Kong and Vera Cruz harbours – lifted from elsewhere and slotted into the design. Composing it, Crowley states that he was immersed in the Hindu religion "and Vedantist literature in general"; various footnotes explain Kundalini or "serpent power" and the significance of the "third eye" or the pineal gland.

The drama is lightened by patches of amiable buffoonery as in this speech by Hercules:

> The wise man thinks
> That nothing is but wisdom – and myself
> Think strongly that no other thing exists
> But strength: so with his subtleties of mind
> He baffles me; and I lift up my club
> And with one blow bespatter his wise brains.

And there is a sneer at Rudyard Kipling for employing his grasp of mechanical detail to vitalise his poetry and prose:

> JASON: Good Argus, thou are unsurpassed in art
> To curve the rougher timbers, to make smooth
> The joints and girders, and to plane and work
> The iron and the nailheads, and to lift
> Row after row the tiers of benches thrice
> In triple beauty, and to shape the oars,
> To raise the mast –
>
> ARGUS: Thy knowledge staggers me!
> How wast thou instructed?

Jason abashedly admits he knows nothing about ships; his knowledge is of the mind alone, and lest the reader be deficient in the finer points of appreciation, Crowley adds the footnote: "Argus is wittily characterised as a Scottish shipbuilder."

Strange Fits of Passion

John Symonds picked on the fact that Crowley was an accomplished writer of pornography. In most of his collections, there is an element of savage eroticism. Even the comparatively innocent and popular 'La Gitana', celebrating a brief love affair with a Spanish gypsy girl, is streaked with a kind of mad rapture; the roses and thorns of Spain are contrasted with the filth and fog of London. "I shall find you, I shall have you," the poet declares after the unabashed, starry-eyed opening:

> Your hair was full of roses in the dewfall as we danced,
> The sorceress enchanting and the paladin entranced,
> In the starlight as we wove us in a web of silk and steel
> Immemorial as the marble in the halls of Boabdil,
> In the pleasance of the roses with the fountains and the yews
> Where the snowy Sierra soothed us with the breezes and the dews!

As for 'The Return of Messalina' – yet another rampage of high-kicking couplets – that presents the voluptuous and corrupt wife of Claudius as a kind of sacred prostitute, determined to drain every perversion dry in order to achieve ultimate union. Although she pursues pleasure with a fanatic, missionary heroism, she can never be satisfied. Lust is not a personal craving so much as a cosmic urge, an eternal principle:

> Did Danaë win to slumber at the thrust of grievous gold?
> Did the bull bring Pasiphae to the palace of the cold?
> Could the sea avail to Sappho drifting dead upon the foam?
> What shall save me, Messalina, save the majesty of Rome?

Messalina is consumed by a longing that destroys her body yet nourishes her spirit. Each age mysteriously recreates her and finds in her the vessel of its pleasure:

> In the garden of Priapus, in the land of lost desire,
> I have made myself a monster and my soul a snake of fire.
> Ho! it stings me! Ho! it poisons! all the flesh is branded through,
> Branded with the steel of Vulcan, with the lava's deadly dew.
> All the kisses of the satyr, all the punishments of Pan,
> All that Eros hath given of arrows to the eyes of maid and man,
> At their lips and lives I suffered – I have borne me as a queen;
> Hear the roar of aeons that acclaim me Messaline!

The poem seems to hint that, at the point where lust becomes selfless, illumination takes place, so that it no longer stands for personal indulgence, but is more akin to the sacred signum of existence. Messalina reveres the vast abstract energy from which life draws impetus – sex as obsession is somehow holier than sex as recreation. Why that should be so, of course, is inexplicable. It is mere assertion relying upon the force of its rhetoric, rather like Graham Greene asserting that a Catholic murderer is far holier than a spiritually ignorant one because he knows the full implication of glory and damnation. In other words, such statements imply the backcloth of a belief-system or faith.

'White Stains'

The fact that so many of Crowley's poems are distinguished by an excess of "earthly passion" has added to their general collectability. Aside from the homosexual treatise, *Bagh-I-Muattar* (1910), he produced two significant works of pornography, 'White Stains' (1898), of which the majority of copies were destroyed by Her Majesty's Customs, and 'Snowdrops from a Curate's Garden', allegedly written to amuse his wife Rose while she was convalescing.

The earlier 'White Stains' was privately printed by Leonard Smithers in Amsterdam. The preface is a piece of elaborate, self-intoxicated prose, written by someone with not a little capacity for self-appreciation. Crowley has fair claim to be the Frank Richards of perverts – jolly japes revolving around the unmentionable, the forbidden and the gut-rippling. Issued pseudonymously, the poems are said to be the work of George Archibald Bishop, a young man who had a strict religious upbringing but who later fell into bad ways. He renounced the church he intended to enter, took rooms in the Quartier Latin and wrote and tasted new experiences. Later he was condemned to an asylum and chronicled his downfall in a sequence of poems whose subject matter ranges from pure religious enthusiasm down through to disillusion, gross sensualism, lesbianism, anal eroticism, bestiality, coprophilia and rabid insanity.

Despite the fact that it has been called "the most disgusting piece of erotica in the English Language", 'White Stains' is less than thrilling simply because it lacks the unity it makes a bid for in the preface. The latter appears to have been an afterthought, an attempt to force a design on some lewd parodies of Swinburne and various other 'daring' jottings. (Crowley was painfully aware of the muddled character of his early outpourings and tried to impose an artificial form; the same strategy is repeated in *Konx Om Pax* where bits of verse patch together a stilted dialogue on magic and paganism.) The range of references is erudite and certain practices are masked by recourse to Latinism and oblique allusion; other times he bluntly slaps down four-letter words like fish on a slab.

Traces of humour occur in pieces such as the 'Ballad of Passive Pederasty' where the poet hymns his enthusiasm for the physical charms of his own sex:

> Free women cast a lustful eye
>   On my gigantic charms, and seek
> By word and touch with me to lie,
>   And vainly proffer cunt and cheek;
>   Then, angry, they miscall me weak,
> Till one, divining me aright,
>   Points to her buttocks, whispers 'Greek!' –
> A strong man's love is my delight!

At the end his wife's voice breaks in:

> Husband, come early to my bed,
>   And stay beyond the dawn of light
> In mighty deeds of lustihead.
>   A strong man's love is my delight.

'Go Into the Highways and Compel Them to Come In' is a poem that hints at a brand of gourmandising only likely to appeal to the intrepid:

> Let my fond lips but drink thy golden wine,
>   My bright-eyed Arab, only let me eat
>   The rich brown globes of sacramental meat
> Steaming and firm, hot from their home divine,
> And let me linger with thy hands in mine,
>   And lick the sweat from dainty dirty feet
>   Fresh with the loose aroma of the street,
> And then anon I'll glue my mouth to thine.

Neither is he averse to sampling what women have to offer:

> The month of thirst is ended. From the lips
>   That hide their blushes in the golden wood
> A fervent fountain amorously slips,
>   The dainty rivers of thy luscious blood;
> Red streams of sweet nepenthe that eclipse

> The milder nectar that the gods hold good –
> How my dry throat, held hard between thy hips,
> Shall drain the moon-wrought flow of womanhood!
> ('Sleeping in Carthage')

The sequence ends unconvincingly in hell with the young man raving like a demented fiend.

> God! I am reeling brain and body! I swound!
> The floor heaves up! The worms devour my breast!
> Beasts and lewd fish and winged things infest
> Each vital part! Sceech, rats! more liquor! Come!
> Rumble, you rotting whore-skin of a drum!
> I care not! Scream, you rats! Snakes, bite and hiss!
> Hell's spawn, I mouth you with this putrid kiss!
> Satan! Damnation! This is the abyss!
> ('Abysmos')

Trying to express an appalling ordeal by a jerky itemisation of indignities rather than by understatement or indirect allusion is something that is bound to fail. Matthew Gregory Lewis (*The Monk* 1796) achieved it by the relentless piling-up of sadistic detail. George Archibald Bishop, Crowley's protagonist, cannot break through and communicate. Not only is he mad, he is mundanely mad and, despite the rats and serpents, an anonymous series of shrieks rather than a breathing being.

Snowdrops

As may be deduced from the title, 'Snowdrops from a Curate's Garden' is a piece of savage obscenity, reeking with buggery and ordure, yet funny for those who can stomach it. The first "snowdrop" is the autobiography of an archbishop as dictated to a *Daily Mail* reporter. "You shall take it down in that clever shorthand of yours," the extraordinary narrative begins, "the story of my life. I came back from the Bottomless Pit, and I have spent my life trying to get back. No sooner had I left my mother's breast than she put me on to her clitoris, and I was hardly laid in my father's arms before his doodle was between my baby legs and jerking its creamy essence into the sunny air of Rome, where, as you may be aware, I first drew breath."

Gleeful obscenities, interwined with genteelisms ("as you may be aware"), became the stock in trade of Joe Orton, the talented homosexual playwright, some fifty years later (although Crowley never strove to obtain that blend of high absurdism and epigrammatic polish). The knack is to stud the syntax of Latinate English with indecencies, maintaining a dignified appearance while subverting the contents, so that a ventriloquial effect is achieved: the form ratifies the grotesquely corrupted substance. The sacred and profane are mockingly united.

The technique is repeated in the Shakespearean parodies 'To Pe or Not to Pe' and 'All the World's a Brothel':

> All the world's a brothel,
> And all the men and women whores and buggers.
> They have their exits and their entrances,
> And one man in his time lets many farts,
> His arsehole being an octave. First the infant
> Violently rogered by an aged duke:
> And then the frigging schoolboy, with his scrotum
> And shining gland, his sperm mere slime of snail
> Unwilling from the tool. And the lover
> Fucking like a furnace, with woeful ballad
> Made to his mistress's bottom.

There is a certain verve, stemming from the need to besmirch traditional idols, yet it would be absurd to make literary claims for undergraduate spoofs of this kind. But one can isolate the attitude that produced it. A need to pull away the clamps of restraint – blast the lid off the psyche – let all the garbage spill out. Crowley thought such gestures essential; the very frenzy of rebuttal was bracing. Sacred cows like Shakespeare and archbishops were pilloried, not because of what they were, but in order to scandalize those who revered them. The heart of such scorn is a void – a void which doubles as a gymnasium where language and values are turned upside down and "stage" can be altered to "brothel" and "be" become "pee". Samuel Beckett entered this vista of meaninglessness when he mockingly upheld "sloth" as the greatest of "passions". It is a realm of nihilism which many minds of a rebellious cast explore briefly.

Such pornography is like lancing a boil, a purgative exhalation. It touches the nerve of insanity - one can almost hear manic cackles flying in its wake. Precedents include Rabelais and De Sade; antecedents are found in the freewheeling obscenities and blasphemies of Henry Miller, who reported – not altogether credibly – that he had borrowed money from Crowley in Paris and learned from him about Jung's theory of the 'anima' and 'animus'.

Paradoxically, both Crowley and Miller considered sex sacred. They were both mystics of the senses whose attitudes veered between reverence and detestation. The problem was that sex both exalted and humiliated them. One moment they were orgiastic gods, the next exhausted, clap-riddled failures. Possessed of a similar brand of spiritual anarchy, they tried to re-make the world after their own fashion, but the task left them isolated, as they were not concerned with the mechanics of social interaction, only in exploring inner space. But the psyche is infinite and insatiable. Whatever anger, revolt, reverence, prayer, protestation and blasphemy is channelled into it, the results will be dispersed and re-cycled ad infinitum.

The Scented Garden of Abdullah

Recent biographies emphasise the strength of Crowley's attraction to his own sex. Indeed, the relaxed happy tone of his homoerotic writings contrast with his ornate and high-pitched celebrations and denigrations of womanhood. A pseudonymous work, appearing around the same time as 'Clouds Without Water', was the *Bagh-I-Muttar* or *The Scented Garden of Abdullah the Satirist of Shiraz* (1910). If ever there was a piece of decorous obscenity, *The Scented Garden* qualifies. It is not hastily assembled like 'White Stains' from an assortment of pieces written on previous occasions but a work that has been integrally conceived. Purporting to be translations of the ghazals of a Sufi poet, Abdullah al Haji, who flourished around 1600 AD, by a certain Anglo-Indian Major Lutiy, the text follows the trail of his "amorous adventures" or chain of homosexual intrigues enacted by moonlight, under cherry trees, in sylvan and sordid settings.

Unlike some of Crowley's heterosexual writings, savagery and sadism is entirely absent, and the tone is playful and witty – in a sense this is an anal 'Song of Solomon'. The influence of Sir Richard Burton (whose translation of the Arabian *Perfumed Garden* was burned by his wife) is usually invoked as a model but as Crowley points out: "The two books have nothing in common but the name Garden is the almost universal glyph for a book of mystic lore, and Perfume for divine chrism. The Arab book is a treatise on the various methods of copulation, plus some obscene stories, and a collection of prescriptions against impotence, pregnancy, and the like."

In the (genuinely helpful) introduction we are told that "the kind of composition corresponds, upon the whole, with the Ode of the Greeks and Romans, or the Sonetta of the Italians. The most common subjects of which it treats are, the beauty of a mistress, and the sufferings of the despairing lover from her absence or indifference. Frequently it treats of other matters, such as the delights of the season of Spring, the beauties of the flowers of the garden, and the tuneful notes of the nightingales as they warble their melodies among the rose bushes; the joys resulting from wine and hilarity, are most particularly noticed at the same time; the whole interspersed with an occasional pithy allusion to the brevity of human life, and the vanity of sublunary matters in general."

The demure correctness of the themes alluded to hardly prepares the reader for the pungent, euphoniously packaged riot of the senses that follows. In its mingling of poetic sensuousness with ribald yarn and lewd learning, it recalls the Roman *Priapeia*, also translated by Sir Richard Burton. The pleasure the author takes in his creation is evident throughout. Each poem, prose pendant, essay and footnote seems to have been composed in a state of delighted concentration. Nowhere is Crowley's revelling in mock scholarship more apparent and the ironic, suggestive tone is set by the dedication: TO THOSE PERSONS WHOSE UNBENDING UPRIGHTNESS, PENE-TRATION, RETENTIVENESS, CAPACITY FOR HARD WORK, OVERFLOWING ABILITY, AND INSIDE KNOWLEDGE HAVE SO MUCH ENLARGED THE FUNDAMENTAL BASIS OF MY PHILOSOPHY, I DEDICATE THIS BOOK IN MEMORY OF THE MANY HAPPY HOURS THAT WE HAVE SPENT TOGETHER IN THE SCENTED GARDEN.

For anyone unacquainted with Persian literature, the notes are insightful if deliberately pedantic. Naturally, the subject matter being what it is, the imprint of the male buttocks impresses nearly every page and the obsessive anality – never has the word 'podex' been used more times – may offend those unacquainted with this class of literary diversion. But it must be admitted that Crowley has written a homoerotic landmark, a book that even today seems stunningly, startlingly frank. Quite literally, the sun does shine out of the 'arse' of this weird piece of Edwardian erotica. The homosexual encounters are framed by spiritual metaphors, so that it is essentially a piece of sacred salacity, as are other Crowley texts. For instance, the following is intended to demonstrate the "impotence of thought to perceive reality":

> Thy podex, like a rose, within
> Thy buttocks, sprays of jessamine,
>
> Buds to my kisses; then the wine
> Sets this old head of mine aspin,
>
> So that I push thee to thy knees –
> A worship, darling, not a sin.
> Deep as I plunge, I do not break
> Within the velvet of thy skin.
>
> Do what I will, thy Self is hid
> From me by envy of the Jinn.
>
> So, when I think, I cannot pierce
> The truth of things; I cannot win
>
> Unto the real; life's wheel is kept
> From turning by its axle-pin.
> ('The Curtain')

A note explains the "axle-pin" securing the wheel of being is 'desire', or the thrust of life itself, which hinders ascension to a higher plane. Such exegesis abounds, adding depth and texture to the accomplished if rather docile ghazals. However, a bawdy, facetious work of mock-scholarship, masquerading as a mystical Sufi text, backed up by a plethora of notes and false names that 'explode' the classic status it purports to embody, cannot be confidently classified. Basically it is the old joke of the professor who finds a lofty seriousness in the most basic of human functions, such an attitude also being typical of great naturalistic art. "Men and women are not free to love decently,"

Crowley maintained, "until they have analysed themselves completely and swept away every trace of mystery from sex; and this means the acquisition of a profound philosophical theory based on wide readings of anthropology and enlightened practice."

At that unbashful level, *The Scented Garden* achieves its aim. There is shameless, scabrous anthropology aplenty – but what does it offer those who do not share its predilections? A cry for tolerance, an erotic romp, an amusing show of learning, an essay in textual subversion? – Might it find a niche with Beckford's *Vathek* and works by Burton and Fitzgerald in a shadowy, jessamine-scented corridor of English Literature with a mock-shrine to Allah as its centrepiece? As robust as *Fanny Hill*, it cannot be historically assimilated in the same way, and thus, critically speaking, seems destined to linger on the perimeter like a rejected catamite.

Irony and Disenchantment

In view of his exuberant immersion in miry excesses, it seems hypocritical of Crowley to have felt "nauseated and ineffably contemptuous" after reading 'The Waste Land' in 1922 and go on to condemn the modern school of poetry for "sniffing sexual privies". After all, he had spent nearly fifty years composing obscene doggerel and should have been able to cope manfully with the fairly decorous innuendoes of a younger generation. Probably he would have defended the accusation by saying that at least his obscenities were frank and funny, but that would not have been true either, although several of Crowley's poems are amusing without being obscene, especially when he wields the ironic rapier instead of the abusive bludgeon. In a scornful mood, he wrote a sonnet 'Metempsychosis', setting in flight a romantic fancy and bumping it down to earth with an unexpected sideswipe against Catholicism:

> Dim goes the sun down there behind the tall
> And mighty crest of Orizaba's snow:
> Here, gathering at the nightfall, to and fro,
> Fat vultures, foul and carrion, flap, and call
> Their ghastly comrades to the domed wall
> That crowns the grey cathedral ...

> I think these birds were once the souls of priests.
> They haunt by ancient habit their old home
> Wherein they held high mass in days of old.
> But now they soar above it – for behold!
> God hath looked mercifully down on Rome
> Promoting thus her children to be beasts.

Other times the humour hardly rises above street or schoolboy-level; for instance 'The Moralist', taken from *Temperance*, versifies the old joke about drunkenness confronting the local bobby. The imbiber justifies each fresh bottle with a wise saw, a fragment of scripture or philosophy. The language degenerates as inebriation takes hold. Eventually he assaults the policeman and is arrested:

> On bread alone though a man can't thriv'
>   Saint Luke says nothing of brandy:
> It may be the thing to keep us alive,
>   And I see there's a bottle handy.
> Open it, Bill! That's only Five
> It may be the thing to keep us alive.
>
> The Road of Excess, said William Blake,
>   To the Palace of Wisdom leads one;
> Open a bottle for Wisdom's sake!
>   And I am the boy that needs one.
> It's a long, long way, but it's good to take –
> Open a bottle for Mishter Blake!

In similar vein, there is 'The Jolly Barber', composed in Naples and dedicated to Ginuccio, which is, as it purports, jolly and rollicking and might have been written to amuse commercial travellers. It is extraneous to add that a barber's shop is often a front for a broad range of transactions. As sea shanties do, it reveres the historic association between sexuality and nauticality:

> I met my love in a barber-shop.
>   Sing hey! Sing ho!
> He kissed me until I was ready to drop.
>   Sing hey! the ship's in harbour.
> He kissed me straight, and he kissed me oblique;
> He kissed me until I got so weak

> That I couldn't stand and I couldn't speak –
> > Sing ho! for the jolly barber!
>
> He couldn't shave and he couldn't shampoo.
> > Sing hey! Sing ho!
> But what he could do he could do.
> > Sing hey! the ship's in harbour.
> He kissed me hot, and he kissed me strong:
> And my mother said I should never go wrong
> If I always put things where they belong.
> > Sing ho! for the jolly barber!

Crowley's other attempts at wit tend to be lamentable. 'An Anthem to Anglo-Saxondom' merely repeats the word 'money' forty times and other 'funny' poems amount to little more than nursery-rhyme prattle. Considering himself wonderfully versatile, "might slumbering at his right hand", he attempted several epigrams but nearly all are half-baked and lacking pith:

> Kill of mankind
> > And give Earth a chance!
> Nature may find
> > In her inheritance
> The seedlings of a race
> > Less infinitely base.
> > > ('The Optimist')

For reasons best known to himself, he chose to reprint that in *Olla*, his last major collection of poetry, issued just before his death. Another of his epigrammatic verses – slightly better but still feeble – deals with Lord Alfred Douglas and Oscar Wilde:

> 'The purple pageant of my incommunicable woes'
> Was painted by the hand of gin-and-water on my nose.
> The mellow gold that filters through my rich autumnal style
> Is minted in me by a superfluity of bile.
> The feet of Christ I worship at appear so thin and pale
> Because of all the skilly that I ate in Reading Gaol.
> > ('The Spring of Dirce')

But Swinburne's brutal pun on the same subject – equally deficient in compassion – is far more devastating:

> When Oscar came to join his God,
> Not earth to earth, but sod to sod,
> It was for sinners such as this
> Hell was created bottomless.

The ability to nail home an epigram in verse, compactly and vividly, is lacking in Crowley. Like John Cowper Powys, he required space and elbow room, so that the reader could be eased into those outlandish structures devised by his mind with arbitrary, haphazard spontaneity. To understand him, you have to attune to his inmost rhythms – to become, in fact, a kind of convert. And the danger in taking such a step is that it precludes rational reservation or any sort of clear-eyed appraisal. You accept the total muddle and division of the man and become a disciple rather than a critic.

Patriotic Poems

Though, by the time he had entered the yellow leaf, Crowley had acquired a number of disciples, mainly in America. They sent him chocolates and brandy and helped finance his twilight publishing activities which included thelemic papers as well as patriotic verses like 'Thumbs Up' (1942). During this final decade, he made the acquaintance of a young naval intelligence officer called Ian Fleming who, it later transpired, shared his interest in flagellation and the more lurid areas of sexual pathology. Fleming made contact with Crowley, thinking he would be ideal bait to draw the superstitious Rudolf Hess into a disinformation plot centring around a fake horoscope and a body of traitorous Britons who sought to overthrow Churchill. But the plan was scotched when, on the eve of Germany's attack on Russia (May 1941), Hess flew to Scotland on a peace mission and was captured by the British, provoking Churchill's comment, "The maggot is in the apple."

Bizarrely the ghost of Aleister Crowley's wartime antics passed into occult lore and fuelled the later myth of Crowley and Churchill (after all, they both liked a good cigar!) magically conniving to frustrate Nazi world domination. Unfortunately, owing to poor health,

Crowley's battle against the Teutonic agents of Satan had to be conducted on a poetical rather than practical plane, as is evident in the war poems 'Anthem, England Stand Fast' and 'Toast'. In the latter, written to memorialise the Battle of the River Plate, he berates the Nazis and their sneaky strategies:

> Sinking merchant-men is fun;
> Chivalry is senseless,
> Prove your honour as a Hun,
> Murder the defenceless!
> (Chorus)
>
> *Horse and bridle, whip and spur!*
> *Give the Hun the Willies!*
> *Gentleman! Exeter,*
> *Ajax and Achilles!*
>
> Cruiser sighted – time to run!
> Well! there's one way surer;
> Scuttle quick and say we won,
> Trusting to the Führer.
> (Chorus)

Although the naming of the British cruisers is a touch that might have called forth a 'Bravo!' from Sir Henry Newbolt, they show Crowley's poetic flagship at its most utilitarian. Despite residual droplets of childish enthusiasm, the wizard sensed the waning of his earthly powers, the sinking of his vital energies. He had passed seventy and shortly he would have to put away his wands and robes and join Nuit in the atavistic darkness of non-being.

Death and Continuity of Consciousness

Earlier, in bitterly elegiac mode, he had penned some concentrated lines called 'The Poet' and slotted them in a lop-sided dialogue-interspersed-with-verse sequence in 'Konx om Pax'. More enterprisingly, he recorded them on an old wax cylinder in a London studio and it is now possible to download the original recording from the internet – a vehement sepulchral drone that sounds quite dark and alarming. They have little wit about them, only bitterness and swagger, but as John Symonds noted, they stand as a forceful epitaph:

> Bury me in a nameless grave!
> I came from God the world to save.
> I brought them wisdom from above,
> Worship and liberty and love.
> They slew me, for I did disparage
> Therefore religion, law and marriage.
> So be my grave without a name,
> The earth may swallow up my shame!

It sounds like an admission of failure, but such impassioned flourishes wallow in their negation. Failure – like Lucifer's fall from Heaven – can be as grand-sounding as success. It is free from smugness or complacency – a delicate gilding of despair actually enhances it. Besides, Crowley did not see those lines as a final verdict. In his view there was more to man than mortal existence. The body was a vehicle for the soul, and the soul held the seed of eternity. Crowley had Olympically elevated himself far above literary criticism by making himself 'a god' or Ipsissimus in 1921. He envisaged the souls of the dead fusing in a mysterious crucible of creation:

> As I near
> That gate of life that men call death, its cold
> Pale gleams begin to pulse, a throbbing sphere,
> Systole and diastole of eager gold,
> New life immortal, warmth of passion bleed
> Till night's black velvet burn to crimson.
>
> ('Logos')

In Volume XI, No. 12 of *The International* (1917), he wrote an epistle for an "Illustrious Damozel" called Anna Wright, so that she might be able to comfort "all them that are nigh death". It is a brief burst of poetic prose eulogising Nuit or the Goddess of Night – "Behold her bending down above thee, a flame of blue, touching, all penetrant, her lovely hands upon the black earth and her lithe body arched for love as a dewdrop into the kisses of the sunrise." Mortal pain is based on a life separate from Nuit, and that fades as her soul absorbs the departing ones: "Time that eateth his children hath now no power on them that would not be children of time."

Using disconcertingly erotic imagery, for Nuit is the mother of dreams, sleep and sexual pleasure, the Mage attempts to prime the sick and weary for the "great adventure" which is presented as a maternal re-union rather than a shedding of the senses.[4] Crowley does not imply by Nuit a mere absence of sunlight, but the deep, germinal darkness of the womb. Nuit is synonymous with the Greek Nyx, the goddess clad in a black star-studded robe, who dwells in a cave far off in the west, until the time comes for her to mount her chariot drawn by black horses. The moon was styled by Aeschylus as "the eye of Nuit", who keeps vigil over her slumbering earth-born progeny, and that accounts for the tenderness of Crowley's evocation.

But he also voiced uncertainty about these matters and the nature of the soul. In 'Hymn to Astarte'[5] he stated that "the soul itself is division" and was forged "at the evil beginning of things" when "the All broke its peace with the thought of itself" – in other words, consciousness created a schism resulting in the birth of "the crazy catastrophe man." (This is not far from Thomas Hardy who believed that the tragedy of existence sprang from non-conscious life giving birth to self-conscious life, ever since when man has been staring in the mirror, morbidly transfixed by the spectacle of his own guilt and suffering.) After expressing such malingering doubts, he proceeds to the affirmative:

> The soul is no ghost to conjure with the spell of: "Illusion begone!"
> It is true, and hath might to endure, unassailable, travelling on,
> None hinders, commands or deflects; none alters its course by a jot;
> Space cannot contain it, and time the waster erodeth it not.
> ('Hymn to Astarte')

Though he claimed to have enjoyed past lives as, among others, Pope Alexandar VI, Cagliostro and Eliphas Levi, he is not adamant about reincarnation and continuity of the consciousness.

In 'Happy Dust', he open-mindedly anticipates self-annihilation:

> I have rolled myself up, and revolved the wheel of my being to Naught.

> Is there even the memory left? That I was, that I am? It is lost.
> As I utter the Word, I am cleft by the last swift spear of the frost.
> Snow! I am nothing at last; I sit, and am utterly still;
> They are perished, the phantoms, and past; they were born of my weariness-will
> When I craved, craved being and form, when the consciousness cloud as a mist
> Precursor of stupor and storm, when I and my shadow had kissed,
> And brought into life all the shapes that confused the clear space with their marks,
> Vain spectres whose vapour escapes, a whirlwind of ruinous sparks.
>
> ('Happy Dust')

For once, the Beast is not talking as a god but as an ordinary mortal stoically confronting the Void. The sentiment lacks the bracing boastfulness one has come to expect. There is evidence of a struggle between the Buddhist who yields to the perfection of Nirvana and the 'self-centred' Magus who craved "new life immortal" and rebirth.

In the following lines, written at Netherwood in 1946, the imagery has changed, from sacred fire and humble dust to life-giving water. His power has leaked out and he looks forward to immersion in the immortal ocean:

> The serpent dips his head beneath the sea
> His mother, source of all his energy
> Eternal, thence to draw the strength he needs
> On earth to do indomitable deeds
> Once more; and they, who saw but understood
> Naught of his nature of beatitude
> Were awed; they murmured with abated breath;
> Alas the Master; so he sinks in death.
> But whoso knows the mystery of this man
> Sees life and death as curves of one same plan.
>
> ('Thanatos Basileos')

In other words, Crowley toyed with the idea of death as both a shedding of the self as well as a cycle of transmutation. As prophet of a New Aeon, he had predicted the demise of God as the supreme point-of-view to which every person is subordinate. In future, men and women will discover what is divine within themselves by means of spiritual self-discipline. Immortality lies in understanding that consciousness does not belong to them; they are merely expressions of it. As Kenneth Grant observed, "It is not an individual possession; rather it possesses the individual."

Curiously the poems of this last phase are emphatically Late Victorian in style and flavour, looking back, significantly, to the verses of G.K. Chesterton (e.g. 'The Pessimist') who also dextrously wielded the long rolling line in the service of his religious convictions. No contact had taken place between the two men since Chesterton had written those early reviews of *The Soul of Osiris* and 'The Sword of Song' and, as Crowley's reputation cast a pall of scandal over the pages of the cheaper dailies, Chesterton must have thought that he had a near brush with the Devil. For Crowley's subsequent adventures outshone any villainy Father Brown had encountered.

Because of Chesterton's immense reputation, Crowley administered sly digs here and there, as in his banned lecture on Gilles de Rais (1930), where he berated Chesterton's rosy view of the Middle Ages. Yet, as always, with stark contrasts, they seem to put each other in perspective, the fat Catholic Apologist and the stout Diabolic Apologist. One peddled a jovial Jesus; the other a smiling Pan. One held up the image of demure, sacred womanhood; the other ravished such an illusion at every opportunity. Chesterton's most famous poem 'The Rolling English Road', after affecting a show of merry, mazy inebriation, abruptly turns holy in the last line, indicating "Paradise by way of Kensal Green." Likewise Crowley's writings are always turning 'holy'. He invoked the 'sublime' as a cure for social ills and could never rest long in an ordinary life situation without some deity with a crazy name popping up whom one was supposed to worship, imitate or revere. Both he and Chesterton had got religion deep in their souls. They loved paradox, crazy thinking and all things mystical and magical. The Catholic died revered; the Gnostic died reviled.

Whereas Chesterton upheld Christianity, Crowley believed in a supreme but impersonal force that, on achieving material form, becomes personal-erotic and creative-destructive: hence by sex one can 'work back' to the divine source. Gods and goddesses, like Ra,

Horus, Astarte and the many Hindu deities, are the masks this principle assumes in the material world. They can be utilised by the adroit priest or magician to bring about certain ends. But there is a soft centre to this harsh, intermittently morbid gospel. For consistently Crowley – again like Chesterton – promoted the sanctity of the soul. The latter, always elusive, has been defined by Robert Musil as "what curls up and hides when there is any mention of an algebraic series", but Crowley stubbornly held on to it as a lifeline to immortality, a redemptive possibility. He did not see it in the Catholic sense, as something that can be tainted by sins and disavowals, but as a steady source of consolation. A bedrock of Platonism supported his meditations and inspired him to pen lyrics, some of which achieve a surprising metaphysical delicacy, such as 'Cradle Song':

> Slumber my soul, a little while,
> The butterfly may fold its wings.
> Soften thy silence with a smile,
> But brood not on the truth of things.
>
> "A little while." What words to thee?
> Thou ended never nor begun.
> To thee, to sleep is not to be.
> To be and not to be are one.

The poet addresses his soul as if it were a baby in whom states of sleeping and waking merge seamlessly. But he pulls up against this assumption. If the soul sleeps, then it must die as anything that moves through time. Mind alone conjures the strange dreams that destroy inner repose. The soul is a restorative that spreads ripples of content and human life a "tear" that it weeps or a brief physical incarnation that must one day dissolve. Hence the truly blessed attitude is of innocent acceptance:

> Thou art in all, no soul apart,
> And all in thee eternal springs;
> Nothing can be save that thou art,
> Naught can move save light-waves of thy wings.
>
> Thou sleep. 'Tis mind that sleeps or dies.
> I? But a tear thou hast loved to weep.

> It wearies me to be so wise –
> Watch thou. I turn my face to sleep.

Traditionally Pan was considered the youngest of the gods, and throughout his life Crowley combined a childlike wisdom with a childish selfishness and impetuosity. In making a cradle the axis of the cosmos, he colludes with George Herbert, Henry Vaughan, Thomas Traherne and that forsaken friend of his youth, Jesus Christ. The image is hardly original but it is fundamental. As this book makes plain, he was a man of contradictions whose religious attitude unites him with many who might have shunned his company. Always convinced of man's inherent divinity, he was a genuine mystic who harnessed passion to his spiritual chariot.

Footnotes

[1] The Russian philosopher Nikolai Berdyaev (1874 – 1948), thought the Decadents' rejection of normal sex showed active revolt against the thrall of nature and was thus more commendable than ordinary reproduction.

[2] 'Lola' was the nickname of one of Aleister Crowley's mistresses, Vera Snepp.

[3] *Aleister Crowley 1898 – 1911: An Introductory Essay* by Major-General J.F.C. Fuller (1966).

[4] Where most see death as a time when the kissing has to stop, Crowley's writings are replete with postmortal orgies.

[5] Dedicated to 'Deirdre' or Patricia Doherty, grand-daughter of the painter Gotch, who created a sun-child, Aleister Ataturk Crowley, with Crowley after he had lost his court case against Constable in 1934.

4

Fictional Diversions

> One man to whom I spoke lauded Crowley as a poet of rare delicacy, the author of 'Hail Mary', a garland of verses in honour of the Mother of God. Another alluded to him as an unsparing critic of American literature. Another knew him as the holder of some world records for mountain-climbing. Still another warned me against him as a thoroughly bad man, a Satanist or devil-worshipper steeped in black magic, the high priest of Beelzebub. An actor knew of him only as a theatrical producer and as the designer of extraordinary stage costumes. A publisher told me that Crowley was an essayist and philosopher whose books, nearly all privately printed, were masterpieces of modern printing ... Some said that he was a man of real attainments, others that he was a faker. All agreed he was extraordinary ...
> (*New York World*, December 1914)

Poetry is traditionally the medium of religious or erotic rapture. By contrast, prose is the medium of thought and ideas, and in the latter Crowley was prolific and persuasive. Where he failed was when his vanity intruded, and that is hinted at in the epigraph, which shows him as he liked to promote himself, inscrutable, Mephistopholean and multi-talented. For the conscious legend-making *did* interfere with his style. At times he is like a man who loves his image too much to get down to the simple business of communicating. There is a melodramatic 'laying it on' and 'writing up' (or down) to his reputation. Hence, as a stylist, he is not invariably accessible, but there is a concise pressure behind works like the *Confessions* where, instead of flaunting his leaves in the sun, the magician sets down the record plainly and forcibly. Literary exhaustion has taken hold, impelled him to trim his metaphorical excesses – at last the voice is brisk, urgent, authoritarian. The result is one of the strangest, most eloquent autobiographies of the period – a jarring, paradoxical work, crammed with gossip, abuse and vitriolic asides, yet also being the record of a man obsessed with personal evolution or 'magical' advancement.

The flaws and merits of his autobiographical prose are self-evident, but what of the fiction? While the novels *Diary of a Drug Fiend* (1922), in which substance abusers find thelemic salvation, and *Moonchild* (1929), in which the spirit of the moon is invoked into the being of an expectant mother in order to foil the machinations of a Black Lodge of rival magicians[1], have been commercially published and analysed at some length, other longer works such as the intermittently funny *Not the Life* and *Adventures of Sir Roger Bloxham* (written in New Orleans in 1916) are incomplete or less than satisfactory.

In the *Confessions* he tells us that he wrote the latter "from the depths of my spiritual misery", but apart from the conceit of using vital parts of his anatomy as characters (the character Porphyria Poppoea stands for Crowley's anus and Hippolytus for his first love, Herbert Pollitt), *Sir Roger Bloxham* has no form or plot in which the message can be demonstrated, breaking down into a series of epigrams, affectations and mildly outrageous statements interspersed with 'forced' spiritual exhortation. What could be said in defence of such a work was that Crowley was attempting to write a 'metafiction' – an undertaking which has tried the resources of many first rate writers. The late B.S. Johnson, for instance, found it irksome inventing characters, situations and plots when he desperately wanted to write about his own personal misery and dissatisfaction with literature. Crowley, similarly, wanted to set down all his disjointed thoughts, erotic whims, opinions, flashes of poetry and description so that it read as excitingly as a thriller. The struggle of discovering the right form for so arbitrary a structure, possibly beginning with *Tristram Shandy*, goes on through De Quincey, Proust, Doris Lessing, writers of the Beat generation and endless other creators who are drawn to the notion, making out of the bric-à-brac of their circumstances a permanent literary artefact.

Truncated experiments like *Sir Roger Bloxham*, aside, Crowley wrote pornography, the recently published *Simon Iff* detective stories, tales of mystery and moral satires together with a sequence of eight myths, *Golden Twigs,* based upon themes from Sir James Frazer's *The Golden Bough.* His best-known short story *The Stratagem* has been issued by the Temple Press in a volume identical in content with the Mandrake Press edition of 1929, save for the addition of an extra story and a foreword by Keith Rhys.

Of the four yarns published, *The Stratagem* dates from January 1914 and has been reprinted several times. However, the casual reader might question Keith Rhys's assertion that it is "commonly found in school libraries." It first appeared in *The English Review* and was praised by Joseph Conrad and later by Cyril Connolly who called it "truly occult and sinister". This is misleading – there is nothing occult in it. It came to Crowley in a dream and he was delighted with it. "It was a story," he wrote in his *Confessions,* "a subtle exposure of English stupidity set in the frame of the craziest and most fantastically gorgeous workmanship."

On a deserted railway station, a Frenchman starts talking to a hidebound and unappealing Englishman, confessing that he is an ex-convict. After he found his wife in the act of adultery, he promptly killed her, their three children, their servants and set the castle where they lived alight – apparently his blood was "more fiery" in those days. He describes his incarceration on Devil's Island in language that is grotesquely heightened and exaggerated. Tormented by the brutal conditions, he makes the acquaintance of a fellow-prisoner, who happens to be a scientific genius, and together they devise a stratagem by which they will escape. Although the plan of escape is idiotically simple, the two prisoners communicate by means of impenetrable codes, ciphers and blinds. The obscurities become so stupendously complicated that they resemble insanity itself – which, in fact, is what they turn out to be. In the end, no one is who he purports – all attempts to clarify result in further obfuscation. Crowley's intention seems to have been to produce a story that is bottomless in the same way that life is bottomless. *The Stratagem* is exasperating in the way that a maze can be when, after attempting every avenue of escape, one finds oneself back in the centre.

Though marred by a ponderous jocosity (it is set in "Muckshire south of the Tream"), the tale does break new ground. Like certain anecdotes of Borges or the impenetrable fables Zen masters inflict upon their pupils, it is designed to frustrate, bewilder and finally instil an awareness of what Keats would call the "negative capability" or the benefit derived from accepting that purpose and meaning cannot be 'worried' out of each event. At the point of giving up altogether, a sense of deeper meaning will seep in, and that will concern itself with listening and absorbing rather than endless pattern-making.

The Testament of Magdalen Blair dates from 1912 and is an attempt to take forward the work of writers like Poe and Sheridan Le Fanu. An idea of his friend Allan Bennett prompted Crowley to write it. "Since thoughts are the accompaniments of modifications of the cerebral tissues," as he put it, "what thoughts must be the concomitants of its putrefaction?" In other words, the story explores the theme of physical degeneration brought about by Bright's Disease and its relation to consciousness. It uses the device of a hypersensitive woman who registers every single thought and tremor of her dying husband, from slow decline down through physical death, bodily decay, cremation and dispersal into the Absolute. The terminal stages are depicted with a kind of lip-smacking relish – the author is not detached enough – but it is an advance on the average horror story and describes processes which have seldom been put into words:

> The minute bacterial corruption now assumed a gross chemistry. The gases of putrefaction forming in the brain and interpenetrating it were represented in his consciousness by the denizens of the pustules becoming formless and impersonal – Arthur had not yet fathomed the abyss.
>
> Creeping, winding, embracing, the Universe enfolded him, violated him with a nameless and intimate contamination, involved his being in a more suffocating terror.

The third story 'His Secret Sin' was admired by Maurice Richardson who thought it "extremely funny." Unfortunately it is not as rib-tickling as all that, though its opening paragraphs have a Saki-like scathingness. It is a moral satire about a rich grocer from the Midlands, Theodore Bugg, who visits Paris in search of pornography but only manages to secure a photograph of the Venus de Milo. Ignorant of artistic matters, he projects his fantasies into the postcard but simulates shock and horror when he finds that his liberated daughter, an art student, keeps the same image in her portfolio. Believing that she has discovered his postcard or "secret sin", he loses all control and berates her for her lax morals. Furious, she leaves home and becomes an artist's model in Paris. In despair, he contemplates killing himself but decides against it, throwing down his gun. It goes off, however, shooting away half of his face, and he becomes known by the local boys as 'Old Venus'. The story shows an unpredictable cast of mind, a talent for odd connections, but is flawed by that intrusive authorial tone which no doubt Crowley believed was ironic.

The final story *Which Things Are – An Allegory* reflects the influence of Wilde's parables but lacks the strict cadential control and narrational skill. It is about hypocrisy, drunkenness and double-standards but, owing either to the author not taking sufficient pains over the finished product or the fact that the manuscript was patched together from two versions, the story at one point seems to vanish altogether. If it is an allegory, then it is an allegory on the banks of the Nile, muddy and aesthetically displeasing!

Crowley published other stories, mainly occult fables and macabre vignettes, most of them appearing in the *Equinox*, a favourite of his being *The Woodcutter*, which he seems to have regarded as deliriously funny. It is about a woodcutter called Placide Gervez who dwells in the forest of Fontainbleau. He cannot read or write but lives only to chop down trees until he has an encounter with the artist-philosopher Theophraste Goulet and his ladyfriend who make him tragically conscious of the limitations of his existence. Goulet stops and lectures Placide on fame, art, posterity and usefulness while his ladyfriend erotically enflames him by a series of pouting, tongue-teasing gestures. They then go off together, leaving Placide in a distressed state, mind abuzz with difficult, confusing ideas.

How can he raise his calling to the level of art, of craftsmanship? He goes back to his hut to find a titled young English lady inside, lost and sheltering from the storm, and it becomes clear that she will have to stay the night. When she does not return in the morning, a search party is sent out, and they find her severed limbs neatly stacked in a pile outside Placide's hut. Deep inside the forest they hear the cheerful ring of his axe.

There is no great merit in this Rousseauesque farce of sophistication corrupting simplicity. Reducing character to automata – to cartoon-like representations of single obsessions – can be amusing if the edges of the confrontation are softened and concessions made to realistic portrayal, but Crowley's technique like Placide's is all chop, chop, chop. It might be termed a crude demonstration of the thelemic philosophy in that Gervez had found his own 'true will' in chopping logs until the bohemian interlopers muddied up the pure spring of his satisfaction with ideas of fame, philosophy and art, as a result of which he is transformed into a kind of Kurtz, a perpetrator of mindless violence.

Simon Iff

As for the *Simon Iff* stories, they are best understood as puzzles to be deciphered rather than narratives to thrill. Hale, buoyant, fêted by the powerful and famous, Simon Iff, a mystic Sherlock Holmes, is exactly the figure Crowley would have comfortably settled into during his advancing years, had his reputation not preceded him. Iff's manner is genial; his disposition generous; his philosophy garnished with paradox and witty inscrutabilities.

The prose of the *Iff* stories has a parodic quality; the psychological quirks of the suspected criminals often take an extreme form – blood sacrifice, false confession, obsessive indifference – and the plots teeter on absurdism. They have more in common with G.K. Chesterton's *Father Brown* yarns than those of Conan Doyle or Wilkie Collins. Apparently they were assembled on mechanical principles, "to think of a situation as inexplicable as possible, then to stop up all chinks with putty, and having satisfied myself that no explanation was possible, to make a further effort and find one."

Such a method guaranteed an improbable narrative followed by an even more improbable explanation; readers with a low concentration threshold, or the habit of forgetting names and details, may have to keep checking back. The setting is usually clubland London, and the stories take the form of dialogues between Simon Iff, the mystic detective, and someone involved, either directly or tangentially, with the murder, robbery or mystery. The best invention is the Hemlock Club, the epicentre of all the Thelemic analysis, whose forfeits, fines and heretical customs are amusingly described in *Outside the Bank's Routine*:

> [The] Head Porter was always dressed in mole-skin in honour of the mole whose hill tripped the horse of William the Third; the members whose Christian name happened to be George

had to pay double the usual subscription, in memory of the Club's long hatred of the Four Georges; and at the annual banquet a bowl of hemlock was passed round in the great hall, decorated for the occasion as a funeral chamber; for it was always claimed that Socrates was the real founder of the Club. There was a solemn pretence, every year, of a search for the 'missing archives of the Club'. On November the fifth there was a feast in honour of Guy Fawkes; and on the eleventh of the same month the Lord Mayor of London of the year was burnt in effigy.

The opening story, *Big Game,* sprinkles a false trail across London and Paris, weaving in a carving knife murder, chess, drugs and legal shenanigans. *The Conduct of John Briggs* shows an elderly scientist – of manically inflexible disposition – being accused of the murder of his nephew. *Not Good Enough* is an adroit diversion, dealing (rather 'racistly' from a contemporary perspective) with a Eurasian falsely accused of murder, and combines jewel thieving and an adulterous liaison with a lofty analysis of Buddhism, "a religion of the most dauntless courage ..."

Silliest of all is *The Artistic Temperament*, a tale of a biscuit-manufacturer of Armenian ancestry who goes against the grain of his own 'true will' by driving himself to become a successful artist. The upshot of this unnatural suppression is material success – he becomes president of the Royal Academy – yoked to waxing insanity. In a grim mansion, perched on a remote Scottish islet, he ends up gruesomely sacrificing his only son, believing it might make him a better painter. Crowley's brother-in-law, Gerald Kelly, was himself President of the Royal Academy, and it is not difficult to read aspects of him in the titled villain, Joseph Cudlipp.

Far better is 'Ineligible', set during the period of the Napoleonic wars. It is the story of a brave sergeant of the marines named Glass who forfeits an arm while thwarting and decoying the enemy. Promoted for his valour to the rank of lieutenant, he returns home to Scotland where he marries the mean-spirited daughter of a minister. The marriage is ill-matched and unhappy – nevertheless a son is born to the couple, a morose, withdrawn boy.

Despite his natural talent and application, Glass' hoped-for promotion to colonelcy does not manifest in an army that values aristocratic connections above aptitude. The situation is made worse when he suffers further injury while under siege in Belgium. A sabre-stroke severs his remaining arm; he is carried to the ruins of a farm to have his wound bandaged, but then a cannon-ball shatters the rafters and brings down the remains of the roof, crushing both his legs.

Now reduced to a living torso, Glass is invalided out of the army. He returns to Scotland and the ministrations of his wife, who bitterly resents her lot, and becomes vindictive and vengeful after he makes out a will preventing her from profiting in the event of his sudden death. Together with Joseph, Glass' son and heir, she connives to make her husband's last days a misery – here the developments become genuinely horrifying, and the subsequent coda, when Iff dovetails the Hemlock Club into the story, is satisfying and ingenious.

Effective, too, in its way, is the (unpublished) *Desert Justice*, in which Simon Iff, on magical retirement in the Sahara, solves the riddle of how a dancing girl was nearly murdered. It opens with some genial mystic banter between master and pupil, followed by a contrived dialogue with an American Baptist missionary. Then later that day, after they have smoked hashish, Simon Iff and his apprentice make their way at twilight to the dancing-hall of the village. Darkness, being the sphere of Nuit, is evoked with reverence: "The moon lit the world with incorruptible phantasy. All was white, even the sand, save only for the soft blue shadows, and the gold stars in the impenetrable indigo of Heaven. Only the low monotonous clang of cymbals stirred the night. Only the flitting forms of men, like ghosts, disturbed the shrine-like sanctity of the square."

Simon Iff enters the dancing-hall, takes his seat and through a veil of hashish watches Fatima perform. Under the effect of the drug, his perceptions expand and shatter until the object of his focus is altered into some startling cosmic principle:

> The music seemed to hush itself to low, muttering intensity as she danced. The night was stifling hot; in that airless barn, with its heavy candles, the smoke of oil, it seemed to Simon Iff as though Time were abrogated, as though the fantastic movements of the brooch on the girl's belly were the geometry of some insane and sensual god. With one side-twitch he swooped down slippery wave-summits of glaucous air until he came nigh swooning; a circular heave, and he saw a billion

> universes set awhirl by lust; she shook her shoulders, and he thought of God with his winnowing-fan, driving the light souls as chaff into annihilation.

In the midst of her undulations, Fatima collapses and it is discovered that she has been poisoned. In the course of solving the crime, there is much bowing and scraping and rhetorical deferentiality – "O Father of Justice and Perspecuity, O Chief of Warriors, O Protector of thy People" – mixed in with thelemic exhortations on the 'true will'. At one point the reader is privy to a disquisition on hashish or "dawamesk", as it is called, that has the authority of an addict or at least a wholehearted convert. The unfortunate suspect (who turns out to be the dancer's mother) ends up by being dragged along by a length of cord that runs from a camel's leg to a ring soldered through her nose: "Behind her, a carefree boy was trying his skill with a long lash of hippopotamus hide ..."

Such retribution, though it might be approved by Bulldog Drummond, creates a jarring effect on the reader who prefers a more even-tempered approach to justice. On a purely technical level, the tale would be improved by greater briskness in the telling and subtler orchestration of character, but one can see that, with a little ferocious editing and skilful promotion, Crowley might have entertained a select audience with these literary puzzles.

To conclude, despite intermittent felicities and a rudimentary grasp of the form, Crowley was never a creator of character in the short story, but a dramatiser of ideas and concepts. Although able to use his insights into subjects like magic, physiology and religion to enrich his plots, he was essentially a puppet-master, a manipulator of strings rather than a writer who endowed his characters with the breath of natural life. Artistically he was inclined to be heavy-handed – a defect lightened by an original cast of mind, a wayward imagination and a pervasive use of irony.

* * * *

Not only did Crowley write fiction, he also provided a handy model of nefarious villainy for various fiction writers. They were quick to appreciate the potential of one whose life and habits seemed so outré and remote from the common run. In *Things Near and Far* (1923),

Arthur Machen alluded to "a fiend in human form, a man who was well known to be an expert in Black Magic, a man who hung up naked women in cupboards by hooks which pierced the flesh of their arms" – but not explaining how the latter was mechanically feasible.

There was also a concomitant problem in portraying Crowley. His presence tended to drain energy from the printed page, particularly when the fiction ran close to life. The very fact of such a character existing tended to set up diversionary echoes, breaking down the hermetic pact between text and reader. In a sense, Crowley's presence has so far proven too loud and fantastic for a story to digest, and he has not yet found a novelist skilful enough to resolve the contradictions. The same could be said, incidentally, of Adolf Hitler, although Richard Hughes in the *The Fox in the Attic* achieves a creditable piece of Freudian illusionism.

It was Somerset Maugham who opened the batting by portraying Crowley as the Faustian villain, Oliver Haddo, in his sensational tale *The Magician*. Haddo was a stout braggart of a man with a ponderous way of addressing waitresses: "Marie, disembarrass me of this coat of frieze. Hang my sombrero upon a convenient peg." The story becomes darker when Haddo involves a young woman in his efforts to devise homunculi. Crowley reviewed the novel in the magazine *Vanity Fair* and feigned amazement at all the plagiarism, but essentially he found the portrait flattering in that it brought his genius before a wider public.

Anthony Powell encountered Crowley on several occasions during the twenties and thirties. He found The Beast lantern-jawed, dusty-suited and sinister, intent on whitewashing his heavily besmirched reputation. As an editor at Duckworth's, he had received from Crowley the manuscript of *The Butterfly Net* or *Moonchild*, a novel which he considered irredeemably bad. Although he wrote of the magician dismissively, one senses an underlying fascination with a man so apart from the common run, and eventually he packaged Crowley as Dr Trelawney, the lapsed guru of his novel sequence *A Dance to the Music of Time*.

Trelawney is first portrayed as an athletic, luxuriantly bearded sage whose disturbing personal magnetism caused at least one young woman to commit suicide by casting herself off a Welsh mountain. His formal greeting is: "The Essence of the All is the Godhead of the

True" which invites the corollary "The Vision of Visions heals the Blindness of Sight."

In *The Kindly Ones* (1962), we see Trelawney in decline; he is thin and stooped with dry, blotchy skin and a nicotine-stained goatee. Weakened by asthma, he emits a strange sickly smell; his collapsing visage recalls lines from *Marmion*:

> Dire dealings with the fiendish race
> Had mark'd strange lines upon his face;
> Vigil and fast had worn him grim,
> His eyesight dazzled seem'd and dim ...

Powell's portrait has little authority beyond the dispiritingly factual and his dialogue, studiously founded upon Crowley's maxims, lacks incisiveness or spontaneity. Trelawney does little more than woodenly pontificate, using esoteric words – lupanar, Osiris and Godhead – in order to express views that are controversial but absurdly reductionist. War, for instance, is a man's revenge on his personal handicaps:

> The Four Horsemen are at the gate. The Kaiser went to war
> for shame of his withered arm. Hitler will go to war because
> at official receptions the tails of his evening cloak sweep the
> floor like a clown's.

Parenthetically it might be noted the above argument is Freudian. Trelawney implies that political leaders avenge their shames and humiliations in their policies. If allowed a free rein, they may articulate whatever damage they have suffered in their childhood in the wars they wage, the treaties they forge, as did Hitler against the Jews and Stalin against the Soviet intelligentsia. The state is none other than psychosis writ large. This ego-centred reasoning tends to blame the Unconscious for chipping away at Cartesian rationality. It excludes the pantheon of 'occult' forces – active agents of good and evil – that wage their battles through the intermediary of the human soul. Also it overlooks the 'objective' element in the formation of a state that draws its boundaries from some degree of consensus. Laws transcend the purely personal. But it must be admitted that Crowley was steeped in Freud and Jung, and it would not be unlike him to sport such opinions.

There were other attempts to portray Crowley, by Ian Fleming, whose first major villain Le Chiffre was based upon him; by M.R. James who depicted him as Karswell, a cynical and malevolent dabbler in the black arts, in *The Casting of the Runes,* and by H.R. Wakefield in the short story *He Cometh and he Passeth By* (1928).

In the latter, Crowley appears in the guise of Oscar Clinton, a ponderous relic of the 1890s, with an incisive but evil intellect. Well over six feet tall, he has a white mottled face and the torso of a champion wrestler. One of his eyes appears to be soaking wet because of excessive humidity caused by injections of heroin.

Clinton's philosophy is 'Do What Thou Wilt' without the Platonic implications. Despite his alleged genius, Clinton expresses himself in stock villainese: "All my life I have been a law unto myself," he explains, "and that is probably why the Law has shown so much interest in me. I know myself to be a being apart, one to whom the codes and conventions of the herd can never be applied. I have sampled every so-called 'vice', including every known drug. Always, however, with an object in view. Mere purposeless debauchery is not in my character. My art, to which you have so kindly referred, must always come first. Sometimes it demands that I sleep with a Negress, that I take opium or hashish, sometimes it dictates rigid asceticism ... In other words, I have gained absolute control over my senses after the most exhaustive experiments with them ..."

It is curious that a host of villains from Carl Petersen to Dr No have justified their moral delinquency in similarly uninspiring argot – dispensing Nietszchean stridencies like tired Civil Servants. And Clinton demonstrates his malevolent apartness by sending a talisman to Phillip Franton and causing him to die horribly. It was an outline cut out with scissors with a figure painted over it:

> It appeared to be a crouching figure in the posture of pursuit. The robes it wore seemed to rise and billow above its head. Its arms were long – too long – scraping the ground with curved and spiked nails. Its head was not quite human, its expression devilish and venomous. A horrid, hunting thing, its eyes encarnadined and infinitely evil, glowing animal eyes in the foul dark face.

To avenge his friend's death, the lawyer Edward Bellamy contacts a beneficent occultist called Solan, who advises him on the best strategy. Then Bellamy worms his way into the parlour of the sinister Clinton, quoting his poetry aloud, flattering him to excess, and while the magician is drunk, persuading him to replicate the talisman. Clinton blearily obeys but Bellamy pushes him further:

> 'Wake up,' he said. 'I want to know what would make that piece of paper actually deadly.'
> Clinton looked up blearily and then rallied slightly.
> 'You'd like me to tell you, wouldn't you?'
> 'Yes,' said Bellamy. 'Tell me.'
> 'Just repeating six words,' said Clinton, 'but I shall not repeat them.'
> Bellamy rushes at Clinton and proceeds to throttle him.
> 'Now Clinton,' he cries, 'say those words!'
> And then Clinton rose to his feet, and his face was working hideously. His eyes seemed bursting from his head, their pupils stretched and curved, foam streamed from his lips.
> He flung his hands above his head and cried in a voice of agony: 'He cometh and he passeth by!'

The story ends with the appearance of the strange talismanic figure striking the black magician dead. Lacking plausible psychological motive or deeper layers of meaning, *He Cometh and He Passeth By* is more melodramatic than believable, but the coloured crayons and the straw paper are sinisterly innocent touches that redeem the overall predictability. A superficial knowledge of occult technique is displayed in the working out of a karmic equation. Clinton's evil is visited back upon him and that is the appropriate retribution, classically speaking. By making a talisman intended to curse or damage another, he disobeyed a major magical injunction stated in 'The Greater Key of King Solomon':

> I command thee, my Son, to carefully engrave in thy memory all that I say unto thee, in order that it may never leave thee. If thou dost not intend to use for a good purpose the secrets which I here teach thee, I command thee rather to cast this Testament into the fire, than to abuse the power thou wilt have of constraining the Spirits, for I warn thee that the beneficent

> Angels, wearied and fatigued by thine illicit demands, would to thy sorrow execute the commands of God ...

In other words, a talisman should be made to improve the spiritual welfare of mankind or not at all. A causal abnormality will be counterbalanced. Evil will boomerang back upon those who pursue it. Despite its moral fervour, Wakefield's story doesn't finally convince because his characters are so obviously cut-outs who have been manipulated into living so that they can die horribly. The figure scribbled on the piece of paper is not explored or explained, although its ancestry is traceable to that blind ghoul with the swirling draperies emanating from the whistle-call in M.R. James' *O Whistle and I'll Come to You*.

The steady trickle of Beast-based fiction did not peter out. In *Man Without A Shadow* (1963), Colin Wilson presented a full-length portrait of Caradoc Cunningham, a magician so closely based on Crowley that the references to him in the text seem erroneous. The author does not take the occult as seriously here as he does in later works, and the diary format plays down the plot, opting for discussion and reflection on such issues as sexual magic – prolonging the orgasm to induce visionary states – and other techniques of turning up the pressure of consciousness. There is a comic element in the author's cautionary scepticism. Aware that magic carries a whiff of pantomime, Wilson eschews trafficking with denizens of the other world, using the occult as a vehicle by which one may study the psychology of perception. Cunningham's magical operation, requiring the consumption of cantharides and cocaine, calls up sickness and nausea rather than spirits, and there is the de rigueur scandal at the end, forcing the magician to leave the country. In his introduction to a reprinted version, Timothy Leary commented confusingly:

> Cunningham evokes and exploits the spiritual potentials which all of us contain within. But, as a dutiful product of a factory society, he does it for power. And spiritual efficiency. This is what "magic" meant in smokestack Victorian England. Power and control. Gung-ho spiritual engineering to exploit supernatural resources. Cunningham is like a madcap Monty Python industrial manager, a frenzied John Cleese frantically organising assembly-lines of sex workers in the satanic mills.

This was in keeping with an earlier spaced-out assessment of Leary's who, in 1979, stated that Crowley stood for "human intelligence at its transition point". He was comparable to a "rapturous body, floating detached from terrestrial life-lines, all wired up and nowhere to go". But despite his satanic pranks and childishness, he "understood the interstellar goal of human evolution and was bitterly aware of his imprisonment on this planet."

Another contemporary writer, much drawn to Cornwall and the supernatural, Mary Williams, portrayed Crowley in a story called *Benighted*, first appearing in the *Cornish Review* (Summer 1973). The narrator of the story is a decent chap, Richard Lane, who wishes to retrieve his friend's wife, Eleanor, from the clutches of Gregory Whale, a sculptor and poet who dabbles in black magic and exerts an unhealthy influence on anyone with whom he comes in contact.

Richard Lane drives to Cornwall and stays at a place called Porth Carn. The following morning he sets off for Whale's house which, we are told, the locals superstitiously avoid. After crossing a wet, windy moor (reminiscent of the uplands above Zennor where Crowley is rumoured to have stayed) on which humped stones crouch in beast-like postures, he arrives at the cottage, the door of which is inscribed with a circle and a triangle.

Whale greets him amiably, offering whisky and cigarettes, but Eleanor's manner is cold and distant. Richard questions her; she tells him that her old life means nothing. He notices bruises on her shoulder; she seems far from happy, yet any attempt at reconciliation is rebuked. Abandoning his pleading, Richard succumbs to Whale as a conversationalist. He is beguiled by the latter's ready flow of words, his capacity to persuade and suck one into his hedonistic imperative, but the atmosphere of the room brings on an attack of claustrophobic nausea followed by a Bosch-like vision of horned shapes leering at him. Eventually it is time for Richard to leave. Manfully he decides to tell Whale of his intention to take back Eleanor to her husband:

> 'Of course ... of course.' His voice had softened into sly silkiness. 'A fine fellow, I believe. The girl's a fool, don't you think? I've told her so many times. "I stared at him, and he went on, 'I'm not keeping her here you know. She's quite free to leave. That's so, isn't it, my dear?'

I looked at her, and her eyes stared back accusingly.

'You shouldn't have come,' she said. 'I told you ... I told you.'

With a flurry of skirts, she turned and left the room, ghost-like in her grey dress, with her pale hair loose on her shoulders. Whale shrugged. 'Women,' he said. 'There's no understanding them.'

But he understood all right; I thought as I made my way down the hill a minute later. Such dark power did not spring from ignorance or chance, but had its roots in a positive malignant force ...

Benighted has more atmosphere than development, more description than drama. It is so overloaded with baneful phrases that beads of rhetorical perspiration run down the paragraphs, and any powerful clash of wills is pre-empted by Whale's mocking approval of Richard's attempt to draw Eleanor back to her salubrious husband. But it is precisely this attitude of sophisticated acquiescence that makes *Benighted* more subtly memorable than Wheatleyesque antics featuring love potions and sacrificial victims. It hints at a subversive truth: some women may prefer corruption and sly sensuality to dogged decency.

In an occultural publication called *Rapid Eye* (1989), a phantasmagoric short story appeared, set in pre-war Berlin, in which the Beast has a discussion with his friend, Aldous Huxley, whom he was supposed to have introduced to mescaline during the 1920s. In the story – no more than a conversation piece – each comments upon the other's outlook; the novelist finds the magician flagrantly indulgent while the other, using such models as Baudelaire and De Quincey, argues that hedonism and indulgence in drugs is validated by the self-knowledge it confers. In parenthesis, it may be added that the friendship between Crowley and Huxley never amounted to much. On several occasions the Beast tried to contact Huxley in London but was turned down owing to illness or disinclination.

Less ambitious – but more assured – is the effort of the Sicilian novelist Leonard Sciascia, who devised an apocryphal correspondence over Crowley between the Chief of Police and Benito Mussolini, in his short story collection *The Wine-Dark Sea* (1973). The local commissioner investigates the abbey at Cefalu, founded by Crowley in the early 1920s as the prototype of a new religious community. He converses with the magician who expounds a philosophy combining Epicureanism with a "savage pessimism". Chains and instruments of flagellation are on display; pain is validated by a creed of sun, blood and pleasure, whose rituals combine Freemasonry with elements borrowed from the Catholic Church. As for the frescoes painted on the walls, "the paintings depict, not unskilfully, strange positions for intercourse and also scenes of depravity including sodomy; and everywhere are displayed, like recurring ornamental motifs, those parts of the human anatomy which common decency requires should be concealed and never mentioned. Crowley attempted to convince the undersigned that the entire content and meaning of life consists solely in that which is practised and portrayed by himself..." The episode ends, as it did in history, with the expulsion of Crowley from Italy.

One can see that Sciascia was intrigued by the odd Englishman and his bisexual persona. This preoccupied several other notable minds: John Cowper Powys, a champion of androgynous passion, invented a new word for the Beast's curious sexual make-up. He saw Crowley as akin to a woman in a man's body petrified in a state of ecstasy. "I think," he wrote to Louis Wilkinson, "that he suffered from a mental disease for which I here & now invent the name gynaesclerosis, from 'gynae' – having to do with the nature of women and 'sclerosis' – the hardening of the tissues, by which I mean that he gradually assumed the physical & mental & emotional qualities of women, but in the process of his taking them on they hardened themselves so they ceased to resemble the qualities of women ...The emotions and all the feelings of the sexual act differ in women completely from those which men experience, and Crowley was by inheritance and environment and by the fiat of pure chance an embodiment of all the feelings women have in the sexual act hardened into a permanent attitude of body and mind ..."

To Powys – a painfully inhibited man at the best of times – Crowley's shameless fervour and enthusiasm appeared like a clinical condition, a sickness, whereas John Symonds saw it as an essential part of the Beast's Dionysian philosophy. An able novelist and short story writer, the greater part of Symonds' life seems to have been taken up with exploring the literary remains of Crowley and his most recent effort – a novel called *The Medusa's Head* – may be seen as a kind of swan-song. Expanding the uncorroborated hint that one of Crowley's followers – Martha Küntzel – sent Hitler a copy of *Book of the Law*, it records a succession of apocryphal meetings between Crowley and the Führer.

Apart from sharing a sinister aura, it is not obvious what the duo have in common, save for self-admiration coupled with a contempt for the brainless masses. Naturally both place a high emphasis on the power of the will. Crowley greets his friends and disciples with the proclamation "Do What Thou Wilt Shall Be the Whole of the Law" to which the travel writer and novelist Norman Douglas (no novice debauchee himself) responded, 'To hell with all laws.'

The Medusa's Head is a plainly written but not unamusing series of exchanges between two egomaniacs. Virtually plotless, it hardly stands as a masterpiece of dramatic progression, yet is enlivened by a chill, droll humour and an awareness of the bizarre mix of influences that shaped the period. Given the bulwark of amazing facts and anecdotes surrounding Adolf and Aleister, it could hardly suffer from a lack of sensational raw material.

Between platefuls of cream cakes, Hitler outlines his plans for world domination, and Crowley in turn impresses Hitler with his supernatural abilities – foretelling the death of the Führer's niece, Geli. Together they discuss the doctrine of the will, neo-paganism, the Antichrist, Houston Stewart Chamberlain and political expediency. Their differences are highlighted. Crowley, a bohemian monster, dominates small groups of disciples and mistresses – his power fantasies are small beer compared with Hitler's. Unlike the other, he does not sublimate his sexual urge but indulges it freely – allegedly to pursue the higher magic, but also to gratify his several perversions. In an amusing passage, Hitler berates him for the disgusting things he gets up to – after all, the Führer may be capable of killing millions of men and women but at least he observes certain bourgeois decencies. "A pig is a pig," he says, "whether it is practising magical rituals or saying its prayers backwards."

What both have in common, however, is a reverence for the symbol of the swastika:

> The swastika! Our sign. You are in tune with our magical or current or, I should say, the magical current. Just as the universe of time and space is symbolised by the tail-biting serpent, the

> Uroborus, emblem of eternal cyclical recurrence – all things return! – so the whirling swastika, which you in your wisdom chose as your emblem, is the symbol of the Demiurge or divine power ...

It is amusing to see Symonds laying blame for the Second World War at the feet of the unknown examiner of the School of Painting at the Vienna Academy who turned down Adolf Hitler in 1907 because his landscapes and portraits were not up to scratch. In rejecting a harmless 18-year old artist, they nurtured a raging megalomaniac. Small wonder it is the present policy of art colleges to admit most students nowadays – obviously they don't want a Third World War on their consciences!

Since Symonds' exploration of the Occult Reich, Snoo Wilson and Watkins Jones have added their contributions to the ensemble, the first *I, Crowley*, a highly amusing, sexually frank farrago, and the second *The Case of the Scarlet Woman*, a pastiche investigation conducted by Sherlock Holmes into the world of ritual magic and murder. From such treatments, one appreciates how the reputation of Aleister Crowley has swelled since his death in 1947. His most notorious portrait, by Hector Murchison, in which his shaven-headed countenance challenges the world with malevolent directness, is now branded into the Unconscious of millions. Sardonic and mocking, poised somewhere between bliss and Apocalypse, it has certainly worked its unsympathetic magic on posterity.

Footnotes

[1] 'Presumably more interesting than it sounds', was the comment in a bookseller's catalogue.

5

Conclusion

> Our little lives are kept in equipoise
> By opposite attractions and desires;
> The struggle of the instinct that enjoys,
> And the more noble instinct that aspires.
> (Longfellow – 'Haunted Houses')

Today, over half a century after his death, websites are neon-lit with Crowleyana and nearly all of his works have been reprinted. If one takes exception to his career, his central creed that people should harness their efforts into discovering their own unique and harmonious destiny is neither startling nor offensive. Plato would have approved and perhaps Nietzsche, Heidegger and Sartre, too.

Despite these laudable strictures, Crowley's status as a Utopian – or Platonian – thinker has never been high. The complex disarray of his personality – his broad range of interests, his savage epicureanism, his startling, often shocking life – attracted the attention of the scandal sheets, and he died much as he had lived, amid the flames of gossip and ignominy. But with the advent of the 1960s and a renewed interest in ecstatic, drug-induced states, his rebellious, anarchic nature found new readers and sympathisers, and bookshops reported that Crowley titles were often taken without payment – a case of customers doing what they wilt!

That today his name holds a stronger taint of notoriety than distinction is ironic, for Crowley had sought finer things. All his life he was preoccupied with 'greatness' as though it were a hard, absolutely definable quality. Conceivably, as a Victorian schoolboy, he may have had a whiff of early impregnation by perusing books with titles like 'Hours with Great Writers' or 'Great Men in History.' He chose to be a magician because he did not want to be forgotten and, as a young man, adopted the *nom de guerre* 'Aleister' – he was christened 'Alexander' – because he hated the idea of being called 'Sandy' and had read somewhere that a dactyl followed by a spondee was a propitious combination for anyone desirous of making their mark. "I can't say that I feel sure it facilitated the process of becoming famous," he wrote in the *Confessions*. "I should doubtless have done so, whatever name I adopted."

From a contemporary standpoint, this seems a highly inflated view for a young man to take of himself. But in the narrow world of Victorian Britain, Crowley was starting out with spectacular advantages in terms of education and inheritance. Of course, most men or women 'grow' into greatness as they develop their skills or faculties in some important area. Few focus on it as an abstract 'goal' at the outset of their careers. Furthermore 'greatness' – in the sense of achieving international excellence in a discipline like astronomy – is played down today. Emphasis is more on celebrity, and celebrities need not do a great deal to secure attention. You can become a celebrity by being good-looking or failing your driving test 40 times.

Crowley sustained the instinctive assumption that he was far above the common herd, and his essays, poems and magical writings are larded with references to figures he admired. In the arena of war or politics, he might have assented to Tolstoy's view (as set out in *War and Peace*) that men like Napoleon are mere froth tossed up by the tide of history, but outstanding scientists and artists he saw as pioneers, vital to the psychic health of nations. In his occult 'thriller' *Moonchild*, after the 'butterfly net' or spell has been cast, the atmosphere changes and there appears a whirling incandescent cone, a crucible of soul-imprints, in which various 'immortal' manifestations simultaneously appear, including Joseph Smith, Chopin, Byron, Keats, Blake, Kipling, Tolstoy and Thomas Henry Huxley, nearly all of whom are presented as severe, unbending archetypes. For instance, here is Byron:

> And first came one with 'branded and ensanguined brow', a mighty figure, although suffering from a deformity of one foot, virile, Herculean, intense, but with a fierce sadness upon him. He came with a rush and roar as of many waters, and about him were a great company of men and women, almost as real as he was himself. And the waves (which Iliel

recognised as music) surged about him, a stormy sea, and there were lightnings, and thunders, and desolations.

There is little of Byron's geniality or humour, only zeal and melancholy, and that applies to the others. Whatever greatness is, it is here presented as a grimly serious, soberly statuesque state. Although Crowley occasionally showed generosity and good humour, it was frequently drowned by an overweening desire to make men stand aghast and admiring, and it was, ironically, the pantomime diabolist who won through to the larger public and not the urbane authority on magic and mysticism.

He was born in 1875, the year when Rainer Maria Rilke was born and Carl Gustav Jung, two contemporaries with whom he had much in common. In the former's poems, particularly the 'Duino Elegies', the enigma of 'being here' is wrestled with and resolved. Difficult questions are asked: How does one meaningfully use one's life? How does one praise – express gratitude – in the face of the terrible suffering in the world? How does one open out to existence rather than be obsessed with human love? In verses of supple incandescence, Rilke managed to frame replies:

> For this is wrong, if anything is wrong:
> not to enlarge the freedom of love
> with all the inner freedom one can summon.
> We need, in love, to practice only this:
> letting each other go. For holding on
> comes easily; we do not need to learn it.
> (Rilke – 'Requiem')

This insight – pure Rilke – enshrines the mysticism at the heart of Crowley's thinking, save the latter tended to 'ram' his perceptions into rhyme rather than cultivate them like plants. But in his finer, meditative moments, such as when he yielded to a desert or mountain landscape, he managed to 'switch off' the thinking side and enter a realm of broader sympathies.

Similarly Jung spent a lifetime throwing a beam into the caves of the unconscious. He charted labyrinthine tunnels of dream and vision and managed to synthesise new insights and traditional wisdom. While he took up with Freud and patiently evolved a social structure around his thought, Crowley, impulsively, sought to startle the world.

Despite Jung's vastly inflated status alongside the misfit magician, it is not preposterous to compare them. In some ways Crowley was ahead, for while the young German professor was studying clinical psychology in Europe, the Englishman had already plunged himself in a maelstrom of madness and reverie. He had already analysed states of mind, travelled widely and immersed himself in symbol, myth, magic and meditation. Like Jung, Crowley was prepared to undertake a disquieting 'night journey' in order that the experience should be recorded. It was not so much his lack of insight but his unbalanced character and the strangeness and coarseness of his presentation that consigned his more serious contributions to the fringe.

Thus his posthumous celebrity is based, not on the substantial body of work he left behind, so much as the fact that his life was shot through with sensation, rage and ecstasy, and people are instinctively drawn to those who externalise the shames and dreads of their secret selves. Crowley *did* what others hide in their heads. There are few people who, if all their thoughts, reveries and secret vices were set down as Crowley's were, would not seem at least moderately depraved. He was a clown of the Abyss[1] who capered on a tightrope between the cliffs of Order and Apocalypse. He sucked energy out of dark grandiosities and high-sounding titles. In his bisexuality, blasphemy and excess, one can find precedents in men like Kit Marlowe and the Earl of Rochester, but he cannot be confidently slotted into the 19th century context out of which he arose, save as a rebel or *fin de siècle* occultist.

Nevertheless he was by no means all rampage and revolt. While shocking conventional proprieties, he displayed enough humour, erudition and culture to interest that portion of the educated who were themselves possessed of an anarchic or subversive streak. And in a rather vulgar sense – not in the way he intended – Crowley's example has become pervasive, for this is an age when negative publicity can be made into an asset. At times the Beast twisted his precept 'Do What Thou Wilt' into acts of tenacious self-assertion, so that he should stand out and be heard above all others.

Such an attitude strikes a contemporary chord, for more than in any previous age, we regard it as important to be seen as individuals rather than part of a collective. We like to read our names in newspapers, minutes of meetings and letterheads. The solipsistic 'I' is constantly cultivated and nurtured by psychologists and counsellors. "What do *you* want?" is the oft-repeated question. "How do *you* feel?" And yet, ironically, simultaneous with this inflation of the ego, runs a parallel denial that any such entity as the 'self' exists. There are philosophers who delight in styling personal identity as no more than a side-effect of mental circuitry, an illusion of wholeness to which we cling. In reality, they tell us, we are no more than transmitters caught in a crossfire of verbal signals. We are 'constructs' of a language that dictates and imprisons us in its paradigms and concepts.

But such disclaimers touch no one at a personal level. People continue to promote themselves as freestanding personalities with the right to be acknowledged and gratified. Andy Warhol thought everyone was entitled to 15 of minutes fame, and in such a climate the contemporary artist feels duty-bound to brand his signature on the none-too-responsive hide of the public. In order to do so, his symbiology may run to excrement, intestines, underwear and the contents of dustbins. Well, Crowley explored self-promotion by shocking, astounding and making the gorge rise long before surrealists like Dali and conceptual artists like Tracey Emin. Proclaiming "Love is Law, Love Under Will", he craved to be loved for himself alone and it was appropriate that his bald glaring face should appear pressed up against other celebrities on the Sergeant Pepper LP cover, for he was as much a posturing icon as Oscar Wilde. Reviled in newspapers, immortalised in stories and novels, and diabolically glamorised in Rex Ingram's masterpiece of the silent screen *The Magician* (1927), by the time of his death, his legendary status had eclipsed the dwindling wreck of his body.

"My own life," he once wrote, "has been indescribably ecstatic, because even when I thought there was a reward and rest at the end, my imagination pictured them as so remote that I was in no danger of getting what I wanted. I am now wise enough to understand that every beat of my pulse marks a moment of exquisite rapture in the consciousness that the curve of my career is infinite, that with every breath I climb closer and closer to the limit, yet can never reach it. I am always aspiring, always attaining; nothing can stop me, not even success."

The passage not only undermines Crowley's determination but also his restlessness. Utterly headstrong, he always had to be leader

– he seemed quite unable to adapt to any rhythm or pace set by another. Perpetually bursting with ideas and initiatives, the core of his character combined creativity with collapsibility. He was able to handle failure and success with equal aplomb. He was initially drawn to Buddhism but eventually turned against the idea that sorrow was "inherent in everything". Hinduism at least allowed for the dimension of joy while admitting it was almost impossible to stabilise or fix it. In fact, the Beast 666 did not mind things falling apart – loss, pain, suffering and ecstasy were all part of the web and woof of existence. He did not mind if the centre did not hold. He did not mind possessions and loved ones being torn from his grasp. A hardline Dionsyian, he swooped from riches to ruination and welcomed the rebirth the latter (hopefully) brought. As Jean Baudrillard has observed, "The sadistic irony of catastrophe is that it secretly awaits for things, even ruins, to regain their beauty and meaning only to destroy them again. It is intent on destroying the illusion of eternity, but also plays with that illusion since it fixates in an alternative reality."

And it is this attitude of dancing defiance (so easily degenerating into a petrified callousness, a mannered coldness, a destructive indifference) that is responsible for both the appeal and repulsion his character provokes. Set on exploring the every self, Crowley did not value one mental state above another; always he stressed interrelation, holding that "ecstatic affirmation and sceptical negation are neither of them valid in themselves but are alternate terms in an infinite series, a progression which is in itself a sublime and delightful path to pursue. Disappointment arises from the fact that every joy is transient. If we accept it as such and delight to destroy our own ideas in the faith that the very act of destruction will encourage us to rebuild a nobler and loftier temple from the debris of the old, each phase of our progress will be increasingly pleasant."

Noble words. His own career, however, hardly stands as a calm record of spiritual ascendancy, more a frantic assault, a determined and thorough ransacking of every variety of experience, from the brutal to the subtle, from the sensual to the ascetic. And naturally accounts of his scandal-studded life attract enduring sales, the most renowned being John Symonds' *King of the Shadow Realm* (1989), replete with buffoonesque set-pieces and withering ironies, an update of *The Great Beast* (1952) and a travesty of an "official" biography, in that it teems with eccentric and appalling details. But more moderate, better-informed chroniclers have added their contribution: Israel Regardie, Martin Booth and Laurence Sutin have produced solid, thoughtful life-histories while Kenneth Grant has supplied detailed exegeses of the 'magickal' theory and method. Of the biographers, Regardie is the most insightful as regards Crowley's mysticism, but Booth and Sutin had access to a broader range of sources and are far more assured in their handling of the social milieu through which Crowley operated.

Curiously enough, none of these adroit biographers have yet managed to plausibly account for the man. Crowley is undoubtedly 'weird' and slips through the net of conventional Freudian analysis. What was wrong – or right – with him? Why did he make out of his life a Faustian pantomime? "Explain to me the riddle of this man," echoed his Old Etonian friend, Charles Richard Cammell. One small clue, that we can gather from his personal observations, is that he did not 'connect' but lived one step removed from ordinary people. A measure of icy narcissism enabled him to see mankind as just "a pack of cards". That was why his prose tended to be remote, sardonic, lacking the facility for character drawing. He preferred to distort things or make them grotesque rather than report them plainly. This profound sense of apartness both flattered and 'froze' his ego:

> Exiled from humankind! The snow's fresh flakes
> Are warmer than men's hearts. My mind is wrought
> Into dark shapes of solitary thought
> That loves and sympathises but awakes
> No answering lover or pity.
>
> ('Perdurabo')

To 'earth' or hold down this rather lofty mental apparatus, a strong and frequent sexual charge was required; above all, this seemed to awaken and anchor his emotional side. Furthermore indirect communication – through books, oracles, and visions – was the same to him as direct experience. What people stood for was more important to him than their individual characters. He 'abstracted' friends and mistresses as emblems and archetypes: the Ape of Thoth, the Scarlet Woman, the Whore of Babylon. Just as the word of God – logos – impressed the medieval saints, symbols and signs created realities for him. He did not *see* things so much as *conceive* things, forcing his life into the mould of an ecstatic reverie, a Messianic delirium.

In his essay *On Running After One's Hat* (1908), an equally 'magical' thinker, G.K. Chesterton, says that the way to transform menial tasks is to pretend they're heroic encounters. Imagine, say, if you're forcing open a stubborn chest of drawers, you're St George battling with the dragon. Imagine, when struggling to untie your shoelace, you're Alexander severing the Gordian knot. Crowley had this Chestertonian knack. He 'translated' phenomena 'magically' – thinking that the truly rational approach – and, what's more, spent a fortune chasing his readings through to their culmination. His life was fantastic in the same way that William Beckford's was, in that it was lived out in terms of a series of exotic, costly inspirations, and from this special angle on reality arose a taxing and paradoxical body of work.

In his passion for large words and philosophical reflection, Crowley has something in common with De Quincey who also believed that the musing, solitary side of man was under attack from technology and science. Living in the palace of Kubla Khan was not practical when vehicles were jamming the streets and creditors demanding payment, but throughout his tortuous career Crowley maintained his pact with the non-visible. A secondary aspect of their spiritual alliance was opium-eating and the mapping out of dream and fantasia. De Quincey was a crazy humorist, drawn to the occult, the macabre and the playful justification of violent and shocking acts – exemplifed in *On Murder considered as One of the Fine Arts* – as well as being a connoisseur of strange theologies. From a contemporary standpoint, the arrant non-modernity of much of Crowley's writing sets him apart, but if one explores the set-pieces of Romantic literature, it is possible to place his essays and reveries alongside those of similar inclination.

Deciding a writer's place in literature or their historical significance is always questionable and presumptive, for no judgement is likely to prove definitive. Time ushers in shifts of perspective that bring hitherto ignored qualities or themes to the fore, while others are consigned to the shadows, and this is certainly true of Crowley. His writings on yoga, sex and mysticism have found a new context and relevance today. Like Hermann Hesse, yet over thirty years earlier, he started looking to the East to find an added depth and resonance in the concept of individual destiny and purpose. Despite the valiant efforts of the Deconstructionists to dissolve the very concept of 'personality' or 'presence', the notion of finding one's 'true will' or 'true self' holds as firm as ever. We like to think that, underneath all the wrappings of civilisation, a more essential 'I' is there who can be gainfully contacted. Psychologists peddle this and so do counsellors and social workers. Like Narcissus, you must plunge into your reflection until you drown or learn to swim in an exciting new direction. Hence Crowley's writings which explore this whole notion of individuation and fulfilment continue to be discussed and disseminated.

A work like *Magick in Theory and Practice*, for instance, will prove of permanent interest to those interested in emulating or learning about the path of development it traces. It is a work of philosophy as well as instruction. Upholding the cognitive authority of the imagination, it articulates an outlook, a way of translating phenomena and the causal realm, that scientists may mock yet cannot, as Crowley knew, absolutely refute, allowing that we are all predestined to inhabit Bishop Berkeley's non-solid realm of ideas, signs and sensations. We cannot state with total authority that things are *this* rather than *that*, and *Magick* nestles happily within this irrefutable absurdism. Scientists like Schrödinger and Heisenburg have further complicated matters by replacing the solid, reliable atom for a ghostlier, more elusive structure, melting the landscape around us into a mysterious continuum of pulses and waves of possibility. Yet even so, the greatest scientist of the century, Albert Einstein, shared common ground with mystics like Crowley when he wrote:

> A human being is part of a whole, called by us the 'Universe', a part limited in time and space. He experiences himself, his thoughts and feelings, as something separated from the rest – a kind of optical delusion of his consciousness. This delusion is a kind of prison for us, restricting us to our personal desires and to affection for a few persons nearest us. Our task must be to free ourselves from this prison by widening our circles of compassion to embrace all living creatures and the whole of nature in its beauty.

Thus, on the subject of his 'Great Work', or his occultism, it is rash to pass judgment, without having tried it out. The 'death of God' has brought with it an atavistic hunger. People still seek mystical ratification for their emotions. Hence they take up magic and regard it in a similar light to travelling or enlarging the mind. The invisible world, they claim, is every bit as packed and busy as the phenomenal one, with its own cartography and characters. By following the correct procedure, you can summon astral-equivalents of priests, wise men, virgins and juvenile delinquents. You may also gainfully – or banefully – contact ghouls, freaks and vampires. Anything that's in the head has its spirit counterpart, so the theory goes. Some have gone gibbering mad exploring this terrain. Others feel happy in no other. And for professional explorers, Crowley is regarded highly as a courier and ambassador, although some claim his techniques spring surprises and shocks. It seems even beyond the grave he is able to stir agitation and disarray.

An ancillary approach *Magick* is to see it as a supporting arch of his literary edifice. Often the rituals, spells, semi-stories and accounts of visions are cast in biblical language and infused with poetry and rhetoric. Some are like recordings of trance states strained through the imagination and, beneath the sonorous surface, artistic ambition prowls. Whatever their practical efficacy, they stand as potent supplements to the myth of the Beast, extending the reach of his pen, sacred texts, direct transcripts from demons, wraiths and angels, documents of such power that (allegedly) the reading of them can corrupt the innocent page-turner, promoting scholarly enquiry to the level of risk. Like the charts in *Treasure Island* that strengthen the fictive illusion, they lay claim to a larger reality: hence *Magick* is raised to the 'Godgame', as it was in *The Magus* by John Fowles.

If *Magick* is primarily an instructional work, an autobiography like the *Confessions* should attempt to show the whole man. As there were skeletons enough in Crowley's cupboard to make up a cemetery, it holds back from doing that, but strong self-analysis is there and the prose has an authoritarian force. It rescues from the flux a series of unique, extraordinary adventures, viewed from a single, stubborn, emphatic viewpoint. It has already outlived those more ephemeral autobiographies by important men that refuse to question or probe the workings of the phenomenal world.

The novels *Moonchild* and *Diary of a Drug Fiend*, while far from riveting, may moulder on as literary curiosities, replete with satires and social observations relevant to their period and arcane knowledge attractively simplified by way of dialogue and analogy. Although admired by select scholars as gripping occult narratives, they are not on par with the best stories by, say, H.P. Lovecraft, Arthur Machen or Algernon Blackwood. And while many of Crowley's shorter fictions have a Dadaist or Absurdist flavour, they endure as little more than literary ornaments or addendum; they are not artfully fashioned enough to stand alone as do, say, the great short stories of Chekov, Guy de Maupassant, Franz Kafka or Prosper Mérimé.

Having said that, coincidentally or by quirk of temperament, Crowley did anticipate devices commonly found in postmodern texts. For instance, we find him employing mocking, mad pseudonyms, as if to undermine or render absurd the concept of identity and authorship. He devises names and past histories with all the delighted attention of his friend and fellow-poet, Fernando Pessoa. Often he breaks through the printed page to berate himself on some trifling technical point like a lunatic bursting out of an asylum. He designs stories and plays that destroy all trace of the fictive illusion by dint of their overstatement and riot of fantastical happenings. Like Nabokov, he likes to incorporate authorial criticism in the body of the text, as if to emphasise he has already been there and thought that. But because of their confusingly heterogeneous nature, mixing verse, mysticism, essay and personal tirade, one cannot single out a specific text and confidently slot Crowley in the avant garde mainstream like one can, say, Eliot, Pound or Wyndham Lewis. Though his preoccupations and outlook are often aggressively contemporary, the shape and impulse of his language hark back to the 19th century.

As an apostle of sexual liberation, the likeness of his outlook to that of D.H. Lawrence has been emphasised. "We are wed, we are wild, we are one!" goes a line in one of his poems, hinting at a secure unity of body and spirit that was the theoretical goal of both men. But it has to be acknowledged that Lawrence was the confident, instinctive artist, while Crowley was an adapter, an imitator of pre-established forms who never quite succeeded in 'opening out' his vision. His inspiration was drawn too much from dream, phantasmagoria, morbid obsession. He made verse-pantomimes and loud rhymes out of his inner life and the result – though often vigorous – does not compare with the subtlety and suppleness of the miner's son. But his philosophical and esoteric range was far wider than that of Lawrence and it is curious that, while the latter's ideas are discussed with the utmost seriousness, Crowley's often identical views are consigned to the lunatic fringe.

Probably more resilient than some of his creative ventures will prove, Crowley's reviews and essays on subjects like drug-taking, ontology, literature, magic, science and Buddhism. The majority have been reprinted and have established themselves as groundbreaking and percipient and, in the same way that one can produce a compact volume of Wilde, it would be possible to gather some of these, together with a selection of poems, stories and autobiographical fragments, and make a volume that is varied, piquant and intellectually stimulating.

But the editing would have to be rigorous, for many people became interested in Crowley through John Symonds' pioneer biography *The Great Beast* (1952). The latter used quotation to such clever effect that it somehow made Crowley's work seem vastly intriguing. Larded with verse extracts, tart vignettes and witty sallies, it gave one the impression that a trove of fascinating texts awaited study and investigation. But when one laid one's hands on these, they often turned out stodgy, prolix tomes. The events they attempted to satirise were dead on the page, the verse tiresome to read and the learning drowned under thick drapes of symbolism and allusion. Although quality stuff was there, it took a good deal of sifting and heavy extraction.

As for the poems, which Crowley considered his most enduring contribution to posterity, they remain a weird mix of doggerel, decadence and mystic elation. How does one sum up the poetic legacy of Edward Alexander Crowley? A Victorian Mystic? A Minor Decadent? A Late Romantic Pantheist? A Gnostic Prankster? This is not so easy to answer, for Crowley is all of these and several other things, but if a judiciously edited anthology of his work were put before the public, how would he compare with his peers?

Crowley wrote a vast quantity of disposable material. He is definitely not a great poet – for he poured his self-expression into a pre-cast mould rather than developed new shapes to contain his insights. When all the crass satire and rhyming rubble have been cleared away, we are left with several highly successful – if derivative – poems, putting forth a genuinely Gnostic gospel; a handful of sonnets notable for their sexual frankness; a few pleasant – if lightweight – love lyrics and some individual pieces like 'Hymn to Pan' or 'The King Ghost' which could reasonably claim inclusion in any Victorian or Edwardian anthology. And there are also the erotic works, notably *The Scented Garden*, which will find a place among the upper shelves of connoisseurs of the outré and exotic.

His work is undoubtedly deserving of greater recognition than it has so far received, in that Crowley voiced loudly and frankly many contemporary concerns at a time when he could have been prosecuted for merely airing them. He showed a sexual boldness in poetry and prose that had to wait half a century to find its equal. His voice is frequently affected – he never quite managed to switch over to the more relaxed vocabulary of the Georgians – yet he succeeded in breaking away from the sentimentality of the Victorians and developing an individual voice, blending Dionysian passion with his own brand of mysticism. As a poet, he stands pinned between two centuries, an exotic hybrid, stippled and barred with satanic stripes, but showing moments of daring and originality.

Yet even this may be too specific a judgement, for Crowley demands a different approach to that of the average literary figure. So far as this present century is concerned, as with Wilde, the shadow of his outrageous career and Dadaist antics somehow become an extension of his work. He is a composite personality, and to reach a full assessment, it is perhaps necessary not to separate or compartmentalise the poetry and drama, but to swallow whole the myth of the man, to consider his poetry, his work on the Tarot and I Ching, his plays and demonic visions, his essays in personal autobiography, his finished and half-finished novels, his holy books and obscene limericks, his writings on hashish, heroin and cocaine, his speculations on psychology and sex, his pseudonymous offerings, false trails and gloating diabolic art and see them as a total œuvre, a bejewelled, grotesque, literary folly, with jagged cracks running across the foundations, but often carved out in strong lines and crowned by gargoyles who conceal a measure of wit and wisdom beneath their leering, bulbous countenances.

Footnotes

[1] Nietzsche said, "Gaze long into the abyss, and the abyss gazes into you."

Bibliography

Over thirty years ago, in a review of Aleister Crowley's *Confessions*, poet and critic D.J. Enright noted that Crowleyana had declined in value. He had managed to pick up cheaply in Leamington a novel of Conrad's with Crowley's signature on the flyleaf. "The declining market-value of Crowley's autograph, he wrote, "indicates the low esteem into which he had fallen before his death in 1947. This 'autohagiography' is unlikely to establish him as anything more than another English Eccentric, *fin de siècle* variety, graded unsuitable for promotion by the British Council."

The situation is dramatically different today. The *Confessions* are regularly reprinted and the Beast is a highly collectable creature whose signature is much sought after. Listed below are the more important works of Aleister Crowley (1875-1947), including a selection of reprints. Many single occasional poems, which first came out as broadsheets or diversions, are not listed – nor are the individual poems or clusters of poems that appeared in the *Equinox* and did not find their way into the collections. But Crowley's writings are now obtainable through the OTO archives and collections at the University of Texas, the Warburg Institute and elsewhere. At one time his work was extremely rare, but today the bulk of it is freely obtainable. Rare manuscripts like the unfinished novel *The Fish* have been published for the first time and a massive amount of minor Crowleyana such as *The Tango Song* (music by Bernard F. Page). Furthermore – for those who wish to browse economically – there is the astral realm of cyberspace.

Poetry and Drama
Aceldama (1898)
The Tale of Archais (1898)
White Stains (1898)
Songs of the Spirit (1988)

The Poem (1898)
Jepthah (1898)
Jezebel (1898)
The Honourable Adulterers (1899)
Jepthah and Other Mysteries (1899)
An Appeal to the American Republic (1899)
The Mother's Tragedy and Other Poems (1901)
The Soul of Osiris (1901)
Carmen Saeculare (1901)
Tanhäuser (1902)
Ahab (1903)
Alice: An Adultery (1903)
Snowdrops from a Curate's Garden (1903)
The Star & the Garter (1903)
The God-Eater (1903)
The Sword of Song (1904)
The Argonauts (1904)
Why Jesus Wept (1904)
In Residence (1904)
Oracles (1905)
Orpheus (1905)
The Works of Aleister Crowley: Volume 1 (1905)
Rosa Mundi (1905)
Gargoyles (1906)
The Works of Aleister Crowley: Volume 2 (1906)
Rosa Inferni (1907)
Rodin in Rime (1907)
Konx Om Pax (1907)
The Works of Aleister Crowley: Volume 3 (1907)
Amphora (1908)
Clouds Without Water (1909)
Rosa Decidua (1910)
The Winged Beetle (1910)
Ambergris (1910)
The Scented Garden of Abdullah the Satirist of Shiraz (1910)
The World's Tragedy (1910)
Alexandra (1911)
Mortadello (1912)

Hail Mary (1912)
The Ship (1913)
Little Poems in Prose (1913)
Chicago May (1914)
The Giant's Thumb (1915)
Songs for Italy (1923)
Temperance (1939)
La Gauloise (1942)
The Fun of the Fair (1942)
The City of God (1943)
Olla (1946)

Novels, Autobiography and Short Stories
Diary of a Drug Fiend (1922)
Moonchild (1929)
The Spirit of Solitude (1929)
The Confessions of Aleister Crowley (1929-30, 2 vols.)
The Stratagem and Other Stories (1930)
The Confessions of Aleister Crowley (1969, revised 1979)
The Aleister Crowley Scrapbook (1988)
Golden Twigs (1988)
The Scrutinies of Simon Iff (1987)
The Fish (1992)

Magical & Thelemic
Berashith: An Essay in Ontology (1903)
The Book of the Goetia (1904)
The Soldier and the Hunchback (1909)
The Rites of Eleusis (1910)
The Book of Lies (1913)
Magick in Theory and Practice (1929)
The Banned Lecture (1930)
The Equinox of the Gods (1937)
The Book of the Law (1938)
The Book of Thoth (1945)
The Vision and the Voice (1972)
The Magical Record of the Beast 666 (1972)

The Heart of the Master (1973)
Khing Kang King (1973)
Magick Without Tears (1973)
Magick (1973)
The Soul of the Desert (1974)
Crowley on Christ [Crowley's commentary on Bernard Shaw] (1974)
The Complete Astrological Writings (1974)
Gems From the Equinox (1974)
The Equinox of the Gods (1974)
Magical and Philosophical Commentaries on the Book of the Law (1974)
The Law is For All (1975)
The Method of Science – The Aim of Religion (1980)
777 and Other Qabbalistic Writings (1982)
Magick and Mysticism (1982)
Eight Lectures on Yoga (1985)
Aegypt (1987)
Portable Darkness (1989)
Amrita (1990)

Index

Abbey of Thelema ix, 21, 57
'Aceldama' 63, 74
Adventures of Sir Roger Bloxham 153
'Aha!' 115
Ajax by Sophocles 107
'Alexandra' 64
'Alice – An Adultery' 63, 96
'Ambergris' 63
'Amphora' 64
Amsterdam 134
'Angel of Venice', The 130
Anger, Kenneth 22
Anhelonium 18
Anton, cartoonist 42
Apocalypse by D.H. Lawrence 28
Apollo 39
Arcadian shepherds 41
Arcady, withering of 40
Argonauts, The 131
Aschenbach, Gustave 44
Astrology 5
Auden, W.H. 65
Aurelius, Marcus 61

Babalon 27
Baudelaire, Charles 75, 77
Bax, Clifford vii
Beardsley, Aubrey 42
    cover for *The Great God Pan* designed by 50
Beast 666 as sunlight 27
Beerbohm, Max 43
Benighted by Mary Williams 166
Berkeley, Bishop, *Three Dialogues* by xi
Berlin, Crowley's reaction to chess tournament in 4
    exhibition of Crowley paintings at Porza Galleries in 34

Bibliography 184
Birch, Lamorna 1
Blackwood, Algernon 41
   The Touch of Pan by 43
Blake, William 45, 80
Blavatsky, Madame 32
Blyton, Enid 2
Boleskine, Crowley's lodge in Scotland 9
Book of the Law, The viii, 26, 56, 57
   dictated to Crowley by Aiwass, the minister of Horns 10
Book of Thoth, The paintings by Lady Frieda Harris for 2
Booth, Martin 63, 177
Brooke, Rupert, compared with Crowley 102
Browning, Elizabeth Barrett 38
Browning, Robert 65
Bruce, Kathleen 98
Buddha 92
Buddhism 10, 127
Butts, Mary ix
Byron, George Gordon, Lord 38

Cabala 5
Cairo, experiences of the Crowleys in 9
Cambridge University, the Pan Society of 36
Cammell, Charles Richard 1, 177
   Aleister Crowley: The Man, Mage, and Poet by 35
   on Crowley's poetry 66
Canaan, Gilbert 131
Cassanova, Jacques 51
Cause-and-effect, Crowley on 23
Caxton Hall, performance of 'Rites of Eleusis' at 16
Cefalu, Sicily ix, 22, 57, 61, 167
Celan, Paul 41
Celtic Revival, the Golden Dawn and the 5
Chapman, George, translator of Homer 38
Chess, Crowley and 3
Chesterton, G.K. 149, 157
   on Crowley's verse 10
   The Wrong Shape by 13, 52

Christ, death of Pan and 37
'Chicago May' 110
Chronozon 105
Churchill, Winston 144
'City of God, The' 91
'Clouds Without Water' 64, 98
Cobbett, William 40
Cocaine, Crowley on the use of 19
Coleridge, Samuel Taylor 121
Collins, Wilkie 157
Confessions 21, 33, 57, 116, 119, 152, 180
Connolly, Cyril 154
Conrad, Joseph 46, 154
   Heart of Darkness by, 46
   Karain by, 48
   Cornish Review, 166
Cornwall 1
   Mousehole 2
Crabbe, George 40
Crowley, Aleister, and the schism of the Golden Dawn 7
   as culmination of Western philosophy and Eastern mysticism 14
   as German propagandist in America 64
   attitude toward labour of 16
   benefited from a stay in America 21
   character of 177
   death of in Hastings 34
   dedicates *Golden Twigs* to D.H. Lawrence 57
   diary entry of on Greta Sequeira 2
   division of history by 58
   divorce from Rose 15
   dramas by 127
   exhibition of paintings by 34
   ideal community of 57
   identification with numerals 666 9
   initiation of into the Golden Dawn 6
   meaning of the word 'love' for 26
   name of 172
   on cause-and-effect 23
   on the literature of the Decadents 74

on marriage 17
on Mexico 59
on sex and magick 29
on Sigmund Freud 48
on the use of cocaine 19
on the use of ethyl oxide 19
personal mythology based on the teachings of Mathers 7
plays by 127
poetry defined by 64
poetry of, opinions on 65
pornography by 136
prose style of 25
seen as "a fiend in human form" by Machen 50
suspected suicide of in Portugal 34
use of narcotics by 18
works by:
    'Aceldama' 63, 74
    Adventures of Sir Roger Bloxham 153
    'Aha!' 115
    'Alice – An Adultery' 63, 96
    'Alexandra' 64
    'Ambergris' 63
    Amphora 33, 64
    Argonauts, The 131
    Book of Law, The 56
    Book of Lies, The 64
    Book of Thoth, The 64
    'Chicago May' 110
    'City of God, The' 88, 91
    Clouds Without Water 33, 64, 98
    Confessions 33, 57, 116, 152, 180
    Diary of a Drug Fiend 22, 64, 153
    Dramas 127
    Fiction 152
    'Fun of the Fair, The' 99
    'Gargoyles' 63
    Gospel According to St Bernard Shaw, The 71
    'Hail Mary' 33
    Heart of Holy Russia, The 88

'Hermit's Hymn', The 68
'His Secret Sin' 155
'Hong Kong Harbour' 117
'Hymn to Pan' 32, 39, 64, 106
'Ineligible' 158
'In My Harem' 110
'Jezebel' 112
'Kali' 116
'King-Ghost, The 118
'La Gitana' 133
'Leah Sublime' 113
Little Essays Towards Truth 30, 64
Magick in Theory and Practice 28, 64, 179
Moonchild 57, 64, 153
'Mortadello' 130
'Mother's Tragedy, The' 67
Not The Life 153
Old Absinthe House, The 64
'Olla' 64
'Orpheus' 77, 117
Outside the Bank's Routine 157
'Pan to Artemis' 108
'Penelope' 112
Plays 127
Pornography 134
'Priestess of Panormita' 69
Psychology of Hashish, The 65
'Return of Messalina, The' 133
Rodin sonnets 73
'Rosa Coeli' 64, 82
'Rosa Decidua' 64, 85
'Rosa Inferni' 81
'Rosa Mundi' 64, 79
'Scented Garden of Abdullah, The' 33, 64, 138
'Ship, The' 64, 124
Simon Iff 153, 157
Sir Palamede 121
'Snowdrops from a Curate's Garden' 136
'Songs of the Spirit' 63

    Soul of the Desert, The 25
    Soul of Osiris, The 63
    Stratagem, The 57, 154
    'Tale of Archais, The' 63
    'Tanhäuser' 63
    Testament of Magdalen Blair, The 155
    'Thumbs Up' 144
    'To Any Unborn Child' 88
    Vision and the Voice, The 105
    Which Things Are –An Allegory 156
    'White Stains' 75, 134
    'Why Jesus Wept' 117
    Woodcutter, The 156
    World's Tragedy, The 127
    Zen and 117
Crowley, Edward Alexander or 'Aleister' 3
Crowley, Nuit, death of 15
Crowley, Rose 9
Crowley versus Constable trial ix

Death in Venice by Thomas Mann 44, 49
Decadents, and Crowley 74
    French, Crowley on 75
Dee, Dr John 105
Diary of a Drug Fiend 22, 153
Dionysus 39
    attributes of borrowed by Pan 37
Disturber of Traffic, The, by Rudyard Kipling 49
Divination 5
Doors of Perception, The, by Aldous Huxley 24
Dorian Gray by Oscar Wilde 29
Dostoyevsky, Fyodor 89
Douglas, Lord Alfred 143
Doyle, Arthur Conan 157
Dramas by Aleister Crowley 127
Dreiser, Theodore 18

Eckenstein, Oscar 79
Einstein, Albert 179

Elgin Marbles 38
Eliot, T.S. 65
   'Waste Land, The' by 89
Ellis, Havelock 41
Emin, Tracey 175
English Review The 66, 88, 154
Equinox, The 64, 156
Ethyl oxide 18

Fads, 20th century 58
Fascism, Lawrence's central idea and 55
Fatherland 64
   edited by Crowley in US 17
Father Brown stories by Chesterton 157
Fauns, no lack of in literature 43
Fiction by Aleister Crowley 152
Fin de siecle 52, 63
First World War, D.H. Lawrence on 54
   effects of on society 21
Fitzgibbon, Constantine 65
Fleming, Alexander 2
Fleming, Ian 144, 163
Ford, Ford Maddox 66
Forster, E.M., *The Story of a Panic* by 41
Fowles, John *The Magus* by, 180
Fox in the Attic, The, by Richard Hughes 161
Freemasonry 26
   and Crowley's 'The Ship' 124
French Decadents, Crowley on 75
Freud, Sigmund 22
   Crowley on 48
Fuller, Captain J.F.C., on Crowley's poems and plays 13
   on Crowley's view of marriage 13
   on Crowley's view of religion 14
Star in the West, The, by 65
'Fun of the Fair, The' 94
'Gargoyles' 63
Gissing, George 88
Golden Dawn, Hermetic Order of the 4, 50

   prominent members of 5
   schism in, roles of Crowley and Yeats in 7
Golden Twigs 21
   dedicated to D.H. Lawrence 57
Golding, William, *The Hot Gates* by 50
   Lord of the Flies by 50
Gospel According to St Bernard Shaw, The 71
Gosse, Philip Henry 3
Grahame, Kenneth, *The Wind in the Willows* by 43
Grant, Kenneth 149, 177
Great Beast 27
Great Beast, The, by John Symonds vii
Great God Pan, The, by Arthur Machen 35, 50, 52

Hadit 27
Hargraves, John 41
Harris, Frank 85
Harris, Lady Frieda 2
Harrison, Austin 66, 88
Harrison, Frederick 88
Heart of Darkness by Joseph Conrad 46, 49
Heart of Holy Russia, The 88
Heidegger, Martin 41
Heidrick, Bill 26
Hemlock Club 157
Hermes, as father of Pan 42
'Hermit's Hymn to Solitude, The' 68
Hess, Rudolph 144
Hesse, Hermann 89, 179
Hirsig, Leah, 113
His Secret Sin 155
Hitler, Adolph viii, 41
Holmes, Sherlock 157, 170
Homer, George Chapman as translator of 38
Homosexuality, Crowley and 3
Homosexual pornography, Crowley's 138
Hong Kong 131
'Hong Kong Harbour' 117

Horus 16, 27
   age of 58
   role of in vision of Rose Crowley in Cairo 9
Hot Gates, The, by William Golding 50
'Hugh Selwyn Mauberley' by Ezra Pound 21
Hughes, Richard, *The Fox in the Attic* by 161
Hume, David 4, 9
   Essays of xi
Husserl, Edmund 19
Huxley, Aldous 24
   Thomas Henry 4
   'Hymn to Pan' 32, 39, 106
   translated into the Portuguese by Pessoa 32

Ideal community, Crowley's 57
'If' by Rudyard Kipling 121
Imakita, Kosen 117
Immortality, Crowley and 4
India, influence of on thought in Britain 10
Industrial revolution 38
'Ineligible' 158
Ingram, Rex, *The Magician* by 175
'In My Harem' 110
International, The, edited by Crowley 17, 64
Isis, age of 58

Jaeger, Hann 34
James, M.R. 163, 165
James, William, *Varieties of Religious Experience* by xi
'Jezebel' 63, 112
John Bull, review of Crowley's poems in 67
Johnson, B.S. 153
Jones, George Cecil 4
Jones, Watkins 170
Jung, Carl 173

'Kali' 116
Kant, Immanuel, *Prolegomena* by xi
Karain by Joseph Conrad 48

Keats, John 38
Kelly, Gerald 9, 158
Kelly, Rose, wife of Crowley 79
Kindly Ones, The, by Anthony Powell 162
Kindred of the Kibbo Kiff 41
'King-Ghost, The' 118
Kinsey, Dr Alfred C., sexologist 22
Kipling, Rudyard 132
   Disturber of Traffic, The, by 49
   'If' by 121
   'Pan' stories by 49
   stories by 10
Kremlin 90
Kuntzel, Martha viii, 168
Kurtz in *Heart of Darkness* 46

Lady Chatterley trial vii
'La Gitana' 132
Law of Thelema 10
Lawrence, D.H. 39, 41, 181
   and fascism 55
   Apocalypse by 28
   on the First World War 54
   on Mexico 59
   opinion of Crowley 57
   Pan In America by 58
   Plumed Serpent, The, by 59
   Woman Who Rode Away, The by 60
   Women In Love by 55
Lawrence, Frieda 61
Leadbetter, C.W. 32, 92
'Leah Sublime' 113
Leamington Spa, Crowley's birthplace 3
Leary, Timothy 165
Leighton, Frederick 38
Leverson, Ada 98
Levi, Eliphas 4
Libido, analysis of 44

Little Essays Towards Truth 30
Longfellow, Henry Wadsworth 65
Lord of the Flies by William Golding 50
Love, Crowley's definition of 26
Loveday, Raoul 124
    death of 22

Machen, Arthur 35, 41, 50
    Great God Pan, The by 50, 52
    Pan defined by 52
    Things Near and Far by, 160
    Three Impostors, The by 51
Magician, The by Somerset Maugham 161
Magick in Theory and Practice 179
Man Without A Shadow by Colin Wilson 165
Mandrake Press 56
Mann, Thomas, *Death in Venice* by 44
Marlow in *Heart of Darkness* 46
Marriage, Crowley on 17
Martin, Stoddard 63
Maslow, Abraham 120
Mathers, Samuel Liddell 4, 7
Maugham, Somerset 65
    fictional portrayal of Crowley by 161
    Magician, The by 161
Mexico, Crowley and Lawrence on 59
Miller, Henry 39
    and Crowley 138
Miller, Henry Valentine vii
Missolonghi, Byron's death at 38
Monro, Harold, *Overheard in a Saltmarsh* by 41
Moonchild 21, 57, 153
'Mortadello' 130
Moscow 88
'Mother's Tragedy, The' 67
Mousehole, Cornwall 2
Murchison, Hector 170
Murry, John Middleton 60

Nabokov, Vladmir 98
Nazis, affiliation of Heidegger with 41
Neuberg, Victor 16, 40, 105
    founder of Pan Society at Cambridge 36
    Triumph of Pan, The by 61
Newman, Bertram ix
Newman, Caspar viii
Nietzsche, Frederick, *The Birth of Tragedy* by 39
Noh plays 124
Not The Life 153
Nuit 27

Old Absinthe House, The 17
'Olla' 64
Oracles 5
Order and orgy 38
'Orpheus' 77, 117
Orthodox Heresy 63
Osiris, age of 58
Outside the Bank's Routine 157

Paintings of D.H. Lawrence, The 56
Pan 16, 39
    ancestry of 42
    as goat-god of Arcadian shepherds 41
    association of 37
    Christian legend and 37
    Conrad's view of 47
    cult of 36
    death of 36
    derivation of the name 42
    Edwardian literature and 43
    equivalent of in other cultures 37
    Machen's definition of 52
    Sir Palamede's vision of 122
Pan in America by D.H. Lawrence 58
Pan Society at Cambridge University 36
'Pan to Artemis' 108
Paxi, island of 37

Penelope, nymph who was Pan's mother 42
'Penelope' 112
Perennial Philosophy, The by Aldous Huxley 24
Pessoa, Fernando 31, 181
Phallus hatred, D.H. Lawrence on 54
Pipe, Pan's 37
Plumed Serpent, The by D.H. Lawrence 59
Plutarch 36
Plymouth Brothers, and Crowley's upbringing 3
Poetry, Crowley's definition of 64
Poetry Review, The 65
Pollitt, Herbert Charles Jerome 74, 153
Pornography by Crowley 134, 136
    homosexual 138
Postmodernism, traits of in Crowley's work 181
Pound, Ezra 65
    'Hugh Selwyn Mauberley' by 21
Powell, Anthony 161
Powys, John Cowper 144
    on Crowley's sexuality 168
Powys brothers 66
'Priestess of Panormita' 69
Priestley, J.B. 18
Prose style, Crowley's 25
Psychology of Hashish, The 9, 65
Pythagoreans 61

Queen Victoria 48
    death of 7
Quetzalcoatl 59

Rabelais, Francois 138
Ragged Rag-time Girls 88
Rais, Gilles de 149
Regardie, Israel 177
Reuss, Theodor 16, 126
Richardson, Maurice 155
Rilke, Rainer Marie 80, 173
Rimbaud, Arthur 17

'Rites of Eleusis' 16
Rodin 98
Rodin sonnets by Crowley 73
Rogers, Alice 96
Rom, Leon 47
Romantic movement in literature 38
'Rosa Coeli' 82
'Rosa Decidua' 85
'Rosa Inferni' 81
'Rosa Mundi' 79
Rose Quartet, The 79
Rosicrucian imagery, Crowley's use of 79
Rousseau, Jacques 40
Royal Academy 158
Russell, Bertrand 46
Russell, George, or 'AE' 5

Saint Basil's Cathedral, Moscow 90
Said (H.H. Munro) 41
Scarlet woman 27
Scented Garden of Abdullah, The 138
Schiller, Friedrich von 39
Schism in the Golden Dawn 7
Schopenhauer, Arthur, *The World as Will and Idea* by 127
Sciascia, Leonard, *The Wine-Dark Sea* by 167
Science and Buddhism 8
Scott, Captain Robert Falcon 98
Secret Sanctuary of the Saints 4
Sequeira, Greta 1
   Crowley's diary entry on 2
Shakespeare, William 17
   Tempest, The by 125
Shelley, Percy, 'Alastor, the Spirit of Solitude' by 3
'Ship, The' 64, 124
Sicily ix, 57, 167
Silver Star 15
Simon Iff 21, 153, 157
'Sir Palamede' 121
Sitwell, Dame Edith 13

Smithers, Leonard 134
'Snowdrops from a Curate's Garden' 136
Socrates 45
'Soldier and the Hunchback, The' 8
'Songs of the Spirit' 63
Sonnets, Rodin, by Crowley 73
Sophocles 107
Soul of the Desert, The 25
Soul of Osiris, The 10, 63
Spiritual experience, Crowley's, in Stockholm 3
Spiritualism, rise of interest in 5
Star in the West, The by Captain J.F.C. Fuller 13, 35
Steiner, Rudolph 2
Stephens, James, *The Crock of Gold* by 41
Stephensen, P.R. 56
Stockholm 3
Stratagem, The 57, 154
Sutin, Laurence 177
Swastika, as a symbol 169
Swinburne, Algernon 36, 63, 65
Symonds, John vii, 65, 91, 103, 132, 168
    Great Beast, The by 176, 182
    King of the Shadow Realm by 176
    Medusa's Head, The by 169
Syrinx, nymph changed to reed 42
    the pipe Pan plays 37

Tagore, Rabindranath 41
'Tale of Archais, The' 63
'Tanhäuser' 63
Tarot 2
Tertullian 90
Tennyson, Alfred, Lord 65
Testament of Magdalen Blair, The 155
Texts and Pretexts by Aldous Huxley 24
Thamus 37
Thelema 61
    Abbey of 21
    Law of 10

Thelemic philosophy in Crowley's fiction 157
Theosophical Society 5
Things Near and Far by Arthur Machen 161
Thomas, Dylan 126
Three Impostors, The by Arthur Machen 51
'Thumbs Up' 144
Tiberius, death of Pan announced during reign of 36
'To Any Unborn Child' 88
Touch of Pan, The, by Algernon Blackwood 43
Trinity College, Cambridge 3
Tristram Shandy 153
Twentieth century fads 58

United States of America, effects of on Crowley 21

Valentine, Ranald 1
Vaugham, Helen, in *The Great God Pan* 51
Venice 130
Venus de Milo 155
Vera Cruz 131
Verlaine, Paul 17
Vesica 124
Victoria, Queen 48
    reign of 38
Victorian morality, Arthur Machen and 51
Vision, A, by W.B. Yeats 28
Vision and the Voice, The 105

Waddell, Leila 16, 89
Wakefield, H.R. 163
Warhol, Andy 175
'Waste Land, The', by T.S. Eliot 89
Waters, Alec viii
Watson-Watt, Sir Robert 2
Westcott, Dr William Wynn 5
Wells, H.G. 41
Which Things Are – An Allegory 156
'White Stains' 75, 134
'Why Jesus Wept' 117

Wilde, Oscar 45, 98, 143, 175
   Dorian Gray by 29
Williams, Mary 166
Wilkinson, Louis 66, 168
Wilson, Colin 65, 120
   fictional portrayal of Crowley by 165
Wilson, Snoo 170
Wittgenstein, Ludwig 31
Woman Who Rode Away, The by D.H. Lawrence 60
Women in Love by D.H. Lawrence 55
Wood Demon, The 40
Woodcutter, The, 156
'World's Tragedy, The' 127
Wormleighton, Austin 2
Wrong Shape, The, by G.K. Chesterton 13, 52

Yeats, W.B. 5, 65, 80, 124
   A Vision, by 28
   on Crowley's personality and poetry 6
   schism in the Golden Dawn and 7

Zen, Crowley and 117

GREENWICH EXCHANGE BOOKS

Greenwich Exchange Student Guides are critical studies of major or contemporary serious writers in English and selected European languages. The series is for the student, the teacher and 'common readers' and is an ideal resource for libraries. The *Times Educational Supplement* praised these books, saying, "The style of these guides has a pressure of meaning behind it. Students should learn from that ... If art is about selection, perception and taste, then this is it."

(ISBN prefix 1-871551- applies)
The series includes:
W.H. Auden by Stephen Wade (36-6)
Honoré de Balzac by Wendy Mercer (48-X)
William Blake by Peter Davies (27-7)
The Brontës by Peter Davies (24-2)
Robert Browning by John Lucas (59-5)
Samuel Taylor Coleridge by Andrew Keanie (64-1)
Joseph Conrad by Martin Seymour-Smith (18-8)
William Cowper by Michael Thorn (25-0)
Charles Dickens by Robert Giddings (26-9)
Emily Dickinson by Marnie Pomeroy (68-4)
John Donne by Sean Haldane (23-4)
Ford Madox Ford by Anthony Fowles (63-3)
The Stagecraft of Brian Friel by David Grant (74-9)
Robert Frost by Warren Hope (70-6)
Thomas Hardy by Sean Haldane (33-1)
Seamus Heaney by Warren Hope (37-4)
James Joyce by Michael Murphy (73-0)
Philip Larkin by Warren Hope (35-8)
Laughter in the Dark – The Plays of Joe Orton by Arthur Burke (56-0)
Philip Roth by Paul McDonald (72-2)
Shakespeare's *Macbeth* by Matt Simpson (69-2)
Shakespeare's *Othello* by Matt Simpson (71-4)
Shakespeare's *The Tempest* by Matt Simpson (75-7)
Shakespeare's Non-Dramatic Poetry by Martin Seymour-Smith (22-6)
Shakespeare's Sonnets by Martin Seymour-Smith (38-2)
Tobias Smollett by Robert Giddings (21-8)
Alfred, Lord Tennyson by Michael Thorn (20-X)
William Wordsworth by Andrew Keanie (57-9)

OTHER GREENWICH EXCHANGE BOOKS
Paperback unless otherwise stated.

Shakespeare's Sonnets
Martin Seymour-Smith
Martin Seymour-Smith's outstanding achievement lies in the field of literary biography and criticism. In 1963 he produced his comprehensive edition, in the old spelling, of *Shakespeare's Sonnets* (here revised and corrected by himself and Peter Davies in 1998). With its landmark introduction and its brilliant critical commentary on each sonnet, it was praised by William Empson and John Dover Wilson. Stephen Spender said of him "I greatly admire Martin Seymour-Smith for the independence of his views and the great interest of his mind"; and both Robert Graves and Anthony Burgess described him as the leading critic of his time. His exegesis of the *Sonnets* remains unsurpassed.
2001 • 194 pages • ISBN 1-871551-38-2

English Language Skills
Vera Hughes
If you want to be sure, (as a student, or in your business or personal life), that your written English is correct, this book is for you. Vera Hughes' aim is to help you remember the basic rules of spelling, grammar and punctuation. 'Noun', 'verb', 'subject', 'object' and 'adjective' are the only technical terms used. The book teaches the clear, accurate English required by the business and office world. It coaches acceptable current usage and makes the rules easier to remember.
Vera Hughes was a civil servant and is a trainer and author of training manuals.
2002 • 142 pages • ISBN 1-871551-60-9

LITERARY CRITICISM

The Author, the Book and the Reader
Robert Giddings
This collection of essays analyses the effects of changing technology and the attendant commercial pressures on literary styles and subject matter. Authors covered include Charles Dickens, Tobias George Smollett, Mark Twain, Dr Johnson and John le Carré.
1991 • 220 pages • illustrated • ISBN 1-871551-01-3

John Dryden
Anthony Fowles
Of all the poets of the Augustan age, John Dryden was the most worldly. Anthony Fowles traces Dryden's evolution from 'wordsmith' to major poet. This critical study shows a poet of vigour and technical panache whose art was forged in the heat and battle of a turbulent polemical and pamphleteering age. Although Dryden's status as a literary critic has long been established, Fowles draws attention to Dryden's neglected achievements as a translator of poetry. He deals also with the less well-known aspects of Dryden's work – his plays and occasional pieces.
Born in London and educated at the Universities of Oxford and Southern California, Anthony Fowles began his career in filmmaking before becoming an author of film and television scripts and more than twenty books. Readers will welcome the many contemporary references to novels and film with which Fowles illuminates the life and work of this decisively influential English poetic voice.
2003 • 292 pages • ISBN 1-871551-58-7

Liar! Liar!: Jack Kerouac – Novelist
R.J. Ellis
The fullest study of Jack Kerouac's fiction to date. It is the first book to devote an individual chapter to every one of his novels. *On the Road*, *Visions of Cody* and *The Subterraneans* are reread in-depth, in a new and exciting way. *Visions of Gerard* and *Doctor Sax* are also strikingly reinterpreted, as are other daringly innovative writings, like 'The Railroad Earth' and his "try at a spontaneous *Finnegans Wake*" – *Old Angel Midnight*. Neglected writings, such as *Tristessa* and *Big Sur*, are also analysed, alongside better-known novels such as *Dharma Bums* and *Desolation Angels*.
R.J. Ellis is Senior Lecturer in English at Nottingham Trent University.
1999 • 295 pages • ISBN 1-871551-53-6

BIOGRAPHY

The Good That We Do
John Lucas
John Lucas' book blends fiction, biography and social history in order to tell the story of his grandfather, Horace Kelly. Headteacher of a succession of elementary schools in impoverished areas of London, 'Hod' Kelly was also a keen cricketer, a devotee of the music hall, and included among his friends the great Trade Union leader, Ernest Bevin. In telling the story of his life, Lucas has provided a fascinating range of insights into the lives of ordinary Londoners from the First World War until the outbreak of the

Second World War. Threaded throughout is an account of such people's hunger for education, and of the different ways government, church and educational officialdom ministered to that hunger. *The Good That We Do* is both a study of one man and of a period when England changed, drastically and forever.

John Lucas is Professor of English at Nottingham Trent University and is a poet and critic.

2001 • 214 pages • ISBN 1-871551-54-4

In Pursuit of Lewis Carroll
Raphael Shaberman

Sherlock Holmes and the author uncover new evidence in their investigations into the mysterious life and writing of Lewis Carroll. They examine published works by Carroll that have been overlooked by previous commentators. A newly discovered poem, almost certainly by Carroll, is published here.

Amongst many aspects of Carroll's highly complex personality, this book explores his relationship with his parents, numerous child friends, and the formidable Mrs Liddell, mother of the immortal Alice. Raphael Shaberman was a founder member of the Lewis Carroll Society and a teacher of autistic children.

1994 • 118 pages • illustrated • ISBN 1-871551-13-7

Musical Offering
Yolanthe Leigh

In a series of vivid sketches, anecdotes and reflections, Yolanthe Leigh tells the story of her growing up in the Poland of the 1930s and the Second World War. These are poignant episodes of a child's first encounters with both the enchantments and the cruelties of the world; and from a later time, stark memories of the brutality of the Nazi invasion, and the hardships of student life in Warsaw under the Occupation. But most of all this is a record of inward development; passages of remarkable intensity and simplicity describe the girl's response to religion, to music, and to her discovery of philosophy.

Yolanthe Leigh was formerly a Lecturer in Philosophy at Reading University.

2000 • 57 pages • ISBN: 1-871551-46-3

Norman Cameron
Warren Hope

Norman Cameron's poetry was admired by W.H. Auden, celebrated by Dylan Thomas and valued by Robert Graves. He was described by Martin

Seymour-Smith as, "one of ... the most rewarding and pure poets of his generation ..." and is at last given a full length biography. This eminently sociable man, who had periods of darkness and despair, wrote little poetry by comparison with others of his time, but always of a consistently high quality – imaginative and profound.
2000 • 221 pages • illustrated • ISBN 1-871551-05-6

POETRY

Adam's Thoughts in Winter
Warren Hope
Warren Hope's poems have appeared from time to time in a number of literary periodicals, pamphlets and anthologies on both sides of the Atlantic. They appeal to lovers of poetry everywhere. His poems are brief, clear, frequently lyrical, characterised by wit, but often distinguished by tenderness. The poems gathered in this first book-length collection counter the brutalising ethos of contemporary life, speaking of and for the virtues of modesty, honesty and gentleness in an individual, memorable way.
2000 • 47 pages • ISBN 1-871551-40-4

Baudelaire: Les Fleurs du Mal
Translated by F.W. Leakey
Selected poems from *Les Fleurs du Mal* are translated with parallel French texts and are designed to be read with pleasure by readers who have no French as well as those who are practised in the French language.
F.W. Leakey was Professor of French in the University of London. As a scholar, critic and teacher he specialised in the work of Baudelaire for 50 years and published a number of books on the poet.
2001 • 153 pages • ISBN 1-871551-10-2

Lines from the Stone Age
Sean Haldane
Reviewing Sean Haldane's 1992 volume *Desire in Belfast*, Robert Nye wrote in *The Times* that "Haldane can be sure of his place among the English poets." This place is not yet a conspicuous one, mainly because his early volumes appeared in Canada and because he has earned his living by other means than literature. Despite this, his poems have always had their circle of readers. The 60 previously unpublished poems of *Lines from the Stone Age* – "lines of longing, terror, pride, lust and pain" – may widen this circle.
2000 • 53 pages • ISBN 1-871551-39-0

Wilderness
Martin Seymour-Smith
This is Martin Seymour-Smith's first publication of his poetry for more than twenty years. This collection of 36 poems is a fearless account of an inner life of love, frustration, guilt, laughter and the celebration of others. He is best known to the general public as the author of the controversial and bestselling *Hardy* (1994).
1994 • 52 pages • ISBN 1-871551-08-0